Crisis at the Crossroads:
The First Day at Gettysburg

D1510054

CRISIS AT THE CROSSROADS

The First Day at Gettysburg

Warren W. Hassler, Jr.

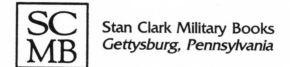

Stan Clark Military Books
Gettysburg, Pennsylvania

Reprinted 1991 with permission of
University of Alabama Press by:

STAN CLARK MILITARY BOOKS
915 Fairview Avenue
Gettysburg, PA 17325
(717) 337-1728

ISBN: 1-879664-05-4 (Hardbound)
ISBN: 1-879644-06-2 (Softbound)

Cover Illustration: "THE FIGHT
FOR THE COLORS" by Don Troiani,
courtesy Historical Art Prints,
Southbury, CT.

Photograph credits:
Battles and Leaders (B & L)
Gettysburg National Military Park (GNMP)
Military Order of the Loyal Legion of the United States (MOLLUS)
Massachusetts Commandery (MASS)
United States Army Military History Institute (USAMHI)

COPYRIGHT © 1970
UNIVERSITY OF ALABAMA PRESS
Standard Book Number: 8173-5103-5
Library of Congress Catalog Card Number: 72-104930
Manufactured in the United States of America

for Chris

"The world will little note, nor long remember what we say here, but it can never forget what they did here."

Lincoln at Gettysburg,
19 November 1863.

Foreword

IT HAS IN GENERAL BEEN CONCEDED THAT THE BATTLE OF GET-
tysburg, July 1–3, 1863, was one of the most decisive—indeed pivotal—combats waged during the American Civil War. Certainly it was
the greatest clash of arms that has ever occurred in the Western
Hemisphere. So vast and so momentous were the consequences hing-
ing on this terrible battle that Gettysburg is justly termed one of the
mountain peaks of the American historical past.

This book presents, for the first time in such detail, a fully comprehensive account of the first day at Gettysburg. Chroniclers of this
campaign have often seen fit to emphasize the second and third days'
battles, while largely minimizing the fighting on the first day. "Thus
far, indeed," declares Jesse Bowman Young, "no historian has done
justice to the devotion, steadfastness, and superior service rendered by
the officers and men . . . in this part of the Battle of Gettysburg." [1]
Glenn Tucker, more recently, terms the contest on July 1, 1863,
"one of the best day's fighting in the whole history of the Army of the
Potomac"—"one of the great fights in American history." [2] It is the
present writer's contention that the first day's battle at Gettysburg
was quite as important and significant as the succeeding two days' combat, which were of greater proportions though of less duration than
the opening day's struggle. The casualties on the first day, in percentage of numbers engaged, were staggering in both armies.

On July 1, 1863, two Federal army corps were pitted against four
Confederate divisions. The two Union corps totaled approximately

one-fifth of Major General George G. Meade's Army of the Potomac, while the four Southern divisions comprised almost one-half of General Robert E. Lee's Army of Northern Virginia. It will be seen that, by holding back an enemy—that eventually became almost twice their number—for over eight hours, the Federal First and Eleventh Corps prevented the better-concentrated Confederate army from occupying the vital and strategic Cemetery heights south of the town of Gettysburg until the scattered Union corps could arrive and concentrate on those elevations and thereby render the position impregnable to the ensuing Southern assaults on the following two days of battle. It will be noted that many of the Confederate brigades and regiments were so shattered by the fearful fighting on the first day that their resulting crippled condition seriously weakened their effectiveness when Lee called on them for renewed combat on July 2 and 3.

On one point, however, let there be no misunderstanding. As Cecil Battine has so aptly said, "To criticize the work of the great masters of military art . . . with the best maps on the table in the quiet of the library and with information available which in many instances was wanting to the commanders in the field, is not to assert that one could have done better oneself." [3] In this present study, troop position maps showing roads and the battlefield terrain are included wherever it is felt they would prove helpful. The work is based on diverse primary sources and on recognized secondary monographs.

Finally, the author would like to acknowledge the invaluable assistance of a host of scholars and friends, chief among whom are Mr. George T. Ness, Jr., of Baltimore, Maryland, and Dr. Frederick Tilberg, of the Gettysburg and Antietam National Military Parks. I would be remiss if I failed to mention the financial grants extended to me by the Central Fund for Research of The Pennsylvania State University; they proved most helpful. My special personal thanks go to my wife, Elizabeth Vaughn Hassler, who read the entire manuscript and offered a number of useful suggestions for its improvement.

WARREN W. HASSLER, JR.

The Pennsylvania State University
University Park, Pa.
September, 1969

Table of Contents

Crisis at the Crossroads:
The First Day at Gettysburg

CHAPTER 1

The
Convergence on Gettysburg

THE CIVIL WAR WAS INTO ITS THIRD YEAR IN JUNE 1863, BUT IT had hardly touched the sleepy little market town of Gettysburg, Pennsylvania. Founded in 1780 by James Gettys, an early settler, and situated amidst the magnificent rolling farmlands of the Keystone State, the village numbered little more than 2,000 inhabitants, and was known chiefly as the county seat of Adams County, and for its Lutheran Theological Seminary and Pennsylvania College. Leather and carriage manufacture flourished, and Thaddeus Stevens had owned some property in the area, but the town was little known to the outside world.[1]

In the summer of 1863, upon learning of the approach of the invading Confederate Army of Northern Virginia, Gettysburg promptly raised a company of emergency militiamen, composed largely of students from the college and seminary. Designated as Company A, it was mustered into temporary service at Harrisburg, and attached to the 26th Pennsylvania Emergency Volunteer Militia Regiment, under the command of Colonel W.W. Jennings.[2]

On June 23, 1863, this regiment left Harrisburg for Gettysburg in order to report the advance of the Confederate units marching eastward from Chambersburg, which is twenty-five miles west of Gettysburg. The regiment moved out the Chambersburg pike from Gettysburg to a distance of about three and one-half miles, where it encountered the advance elements of Major General Jubal A. Early's First Division of Lieutenant General Richard S. Ewell's Second Corps,

3

swinging down the Chambersburg pike from the west. Skirmishing commenced between the entire 26th Pennsylvania Emergency Regiment and Early's leading brigade, the Fourth, commanded by Brigadier General John B. Gordon. Aiding Gordon was a small battalion of cavalry. It was hardly a contest. The local militiamen were easily brushed aside, and attempted to make their way back to Harrisburg. The rear guard of the 26th, however, was caught and brought into action by the pursuing gray legions at the Witmer farm house, approximately four and one-half miles north from Gettysburg on the Carlisle road. Again the Pennsylvanians were no match for the bronzed Southern veterans, and suffered some 200 casualties before reaching the friendly environs of the state capital. After this almost insignificant resistance, the invading Confederate force pushed on.[3]

By the evening of June 26, the various units of General Robert E. Lee's Army of Northern Virginia were located as follows: on the road between Chambersburg and Carlisle were Major General Edward Johnson's Second Division and Major General Robert E. Rodes' Third Division, both of Ewell's Second Corps, and Brigadier General A.G. Jenkins' cavalry brigade of Major General J.E.B. Stuart's cavalry division; Early's division was at Mummasburg, after its brief joust with the Pennsylvania militia regiment; one of Early's brigades, Gordon's, occupied Gettysburg for a few hours before pushing eastward toward York; Major General Lafayette McLaws' First Division of Lieutenant General James Longstreet's First Corps was encamped near Williamsport, after crossing the Potomac River; Major General George E. Pickett's Second Division and Major General John B. Hood's Third Division of the same corps were at Greencastle; Major General Henry Heth's Second Division and Major General Dorsey Pender's Third Division of Lieutenant General A.P. Hill's Third Corps were bivouacked near Fayetteville; and three brigades of Stuart's cavalry, departing from the spirit of Lee's orders, and making another daring raid around the Federal army, moved from Buckland through Brentsville to a point near Wolf Run Shoals.[4]

On the same evening—June 26—the various units of Major General Joseph Hooker's Union Army of the Potomac were situated as follows: Army Headquarters were at Poolesville, Maryland; Major General John F. Reynolds' First Corps was stretched out between Barnesville and Jefferson; Major General Winfield S. Hancock's Second Corps was at Edward's Ferry, on the north bank of the Potomac;

Major General Daniel E. Sickles' Third Corps was encamped at Point of Rocks; Major General George G. Meade's Fifth Corps was about four miles from the mouth of the Monocacy River; Major General John Sedgwick's Sixth Corps was bivouacked at Dranesville, Virginia; Major General Oliver O. Howard's Eleventh Corps was at Middletown; Major General Henry W. Slocum's Twelfth Corps was at the mouth of the Monocacy; Brigadier General John Buford's First Cavalry Division and Brigadier General David M. Gregg's Second Cavalry Division, both of Major General Alfred Pleasonton's Cavalry Corps, were at Leesburg, Virginia.[5]

Lee's immediate object was the occupation of Harrisburg. After that, he could threaten the great port of Philadelphia—distant 139 miles from his present headquarters near Chambersburg—or menace Baltimore and Washington. Good roads leading to these key cities would expedite the rapid marches of his soldiers. Ewell's corps was well advanced in two columns: Rodes' division as far as Carlisle on the road to Harrisburg, and Early's division within six miles of the important industrial city of York.[6] Ewell was ordered to take Harrisburg, if possible, and Early was instructed to cut the Northern Central Railroad[7] between Harrisburg and Baltimore and to destroy the vital Columbia-Wrightsville bridge spanning the Susquehanna River east of York so as to prevent its use by the enemy.[8]

In Stuart's absence, Lee still believed that the National army was still south of the Potomac.[9] This absence of the bulk of his cavalry from the main army was to greatly hamper Lee's campaign, and is certainly one reason why the Southern chieftain was to fail in his bid for a decisive victory on Northern soil. Lee was somewhat annoyed by Stuart's truancy, and at his headquarters outside Chambersburg closely questioned a number of officers as to where they thought the dashing cavalryman might be.[10]

While on Northern soil, Lee was determined that his army should conduct itself in an exemplary manner. He issued a notable order to his troops on June 27, exhorting them to behave well in enemy territory—especially as to private property—and warning those who had not done so that they would be brought "to summary punishment." The General referred to "barbarous outrages," "atrocities," and "wanton destruction of private property" wrought by the Federals in Virginia, and indicated clearly that he would have none of this on the part of his own troops while in the Keystone State.[11]

As to Lee's plans for defeating the Army of the Potomac whenever he should meet it, Major General Isaac Trimble quotes the Confederate commander as saying, "I shall throw an overwhelming force on their advance, crush it, follow up the success, drive one corps back on another, and by successive repulses and surprises, *before they can concentrate*, create a panic and virtually destroy the army." [12] In other words, Lee designed to defeat his opponent in detail, and thereby remove from serious contention the only large and effective Union field army in the Eastern theater of operations. This would open the way to Philadelphia, Baltimore, or Washington.[13] Thus, perhaps, a peace based on the recognition of Southern independence could be won on Pennsylvania soil. The chances of doing this had seldom looked brighter for the Dixie cause. Following their two spectacular victories at Fredericksburg and Chancellorsville, the grayclad soldiers were possessed of the highest morale.[14] Lee himself apparently felt that he could defeat the Army of the Potomac under any circumstances.

The reception given the Southerners north of the Mason and Dixon Line was far from encouraging. As Longstreet's troops passed through Chambersburg, there could be little doubt among the Confederate generals that the townsfolk were anything but friendly to the invaders. Many of the houses were closed up and locked. The citizens who gazed at the marching Southerners, either from upper windows or along the streets, generally had scowls on their faces.[15] Sentries were placed at the doors of all the larger homes. Merchandise procured by Southerners in the town stores was paid for in Confederate scrip, redeemable in specie when the Confederacy should be finally victorious.[16]

The welcome accorded the Federal soldiers by the inhabitants of Maryland and Pennsylvania was in striking contrast to the surly stares which greeted Lee's men. Even at sunrise, the entire population of a town, old and young alike, would line the streets, wave miniature flags, and pass out bread, cake, fruit, milk, water, and coffee to the marching bluecoats. Each regiment, as it passed the cheering civilians, would rend the air with chants and songs in happy acknowledgment of the warm accolades. The only place in one town which kept its doors closed to the Union soldiery was a local convent, where the Mother Superior bolted the doors and turned out all the lights in the place! [17]

Up to June 27, in the march northward from Falmouth, Virginia,

Fighting Joe Hooker had handled the Army of the Potomac skillfully. But when he demanded the untrammeled use of the garrison of some 10,000 men at Harper's Ferry, his unfriendly superior, Major General Henry W. Halleck, General-in-Chief of all the Union armies, refused the request. At 1:00 p.m. on the 27th, Hooker dispatched to Washington this telegram: "My original instructions require me to cover Harper's Ferry and Washington. I have now imposed upon me, in addition, an enemy in my front of more than my number. I beg to be understood, respectfully, but firmly, that I am unable to comply with this condition with the means at my disposal, and earnestly request that I may at once be relieved from the position I occupy." [18] Halleck and Lincoln accepted almost immediately this resignation, and selected as Hooker's successor the commander of the Fifth Corps, Major General George G. Meade, a favorite with "Old Brains." [19] Major General George Sykes assumed command of the Fifth Corps.

The forty-seven-year-old Meade had a splendid fighting record during the first two years of civil war. Starting out as an officer in the celebrated Pennsylvania Reserves, he had worked his way up as brigade, division and corps commander. He had conducted himself admirably on the Peninsula (where he had been severely wounded at Glendale), at Second Manassas, Antietam, Fredericksburg, and Chancellorsville. Meade was honest, steady, sound, and reliable, though scarcely brilliant. Yet he was destined to win for the hard-pressed Union cause such a pivotal victory that Gettysburg would be inscribed on the same scroll of honor with Saratoga, Lundy's Lane, Buena Vista, San Juan Hill, Chateau-Thierry, Guadalcanal, and Inchon.

Upon receiving the command, Meade was granted two favors that had been withheld from Hooker; namely, the use of the Harper's Ferry garrison, and the placing under his orders of Major General Darius N. Couch, then commanding the Department of the Susquehanna, with headquarters at Harrisburg.[20] Meade received also the following liberal directive from Halleck, late on June 27: "You will not be hampered by any minute instructions from these headquarters. Your army is free to act as you may deem proper under the circumstances as they arise." The General-in-Chief instructed Meade, however, that he was always to cover Baltimore and Washington against any possible enemy thrust. "All forces within the sphere of your operations," declared Halleck, "will be held subject to your orders. Harper's Ferry and its garrison are under your direct orders." [21]

Early on June 28, shortly after having assumed the command, Meade issued this cautiously worded order to his army:

> As a soldier, in obeying this order—an order totally unexpected and unsolicited—I have no promises or pledges to make.
>
> The country looks to this army to relieve it from the devastation and disgrace of a hostile invasion. Whatever fatigues and sacrifices we may be called upon to undergo, let us have in view constantly the magnitude of the interests involved, and let each man determine to do his duty, leaving to an all-controlling Providence the decision of the contest.
>
> It is with just diffidence that I relieve in the command of this army an eminent and accomplished soldier, whose name must ever appear conspicuous in the history of its achievements; but I rely upon the hearty support of my companions in arms to assist me in the discharge of the duties of the important trust which has been confided in me.[22]

Handicapped in that a topographical map of Pennsylvania did not reach his headquarters until the morning of July 1,[23] Meade replied to Halleck from Frederick, Maryland, at 7:00 a.m. on June 28 to the order placing him in command: "Totally unexpected as it has been, and in ignorance of the exact condition of the troops and position of the enemy, I can only now say that it appears to me I must move toward the Susquehanna, keeping Washington and Baltimore well covered, and if the enemy is checked in his attempt to cross the Susquehanna, or if he turns toward Baltimore, to give him battle."[24] Believing that his own army and Lee's each numbered "a little over 100,000" men,[25] Meade asked Halleck for reinforcements.[26]

The new Federal commander posted up on the myriad problems confronting a general who has been suddenly thrust into a trying position of great responsibility. "June 28," said Meade in his official report, "was spent in ascertaining the position and strength of the different corps of the army, but principally in bringing up the cavalry, which had been covering the rear of the army in its passage over the Potomac . . . ."[27] He conferred at length with Reynolds, his most trusted lieutenant and long-time associate. In later testimony before the Committee on the Conduct of the War, Meade stated that, when he assumed command, he desired a "rapid concentration" of the various corps of his army, but he seems actually to have been in little hurry to achieve this.[28] In fact, in his first several days in command, Meade further scattered his various units instead of concentrating

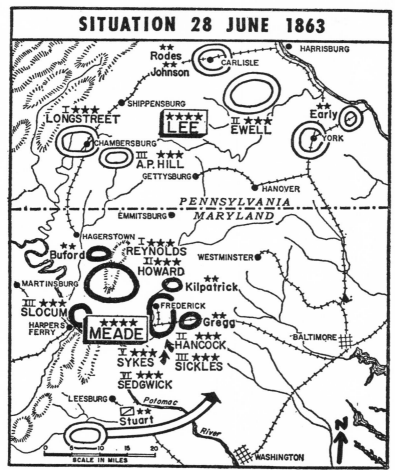

SITUATION 28 JUNE 1863

them. Hooker had been operating against Lee's line of communications; but Meade showed that he was diverging from his predecessor's plans by ordering Slocum's Twelfth Corps, then in western Maryland, to move eastward and rejoin the main body of the army.[29] At the same time, the Union engineers were directed to survey a defensive battle line, which could be used if needed, along Parr's Ridge behind Pipe Creek, covering the new Federal advanced base at Westminster, Maryland. Thus, the initiative in the days immediately after the change in the Union command still remained with Meade's opponent.

On the evening of June 28, at his headquarters outside of Chambersburg, Lee was preparing to issue orders for the crossing of the Susquehanna River and the seizure of Harrisburg, when a strange man was ushered into his tent.[30] This individual was dressed in civilian garb of a dark shade, and his clothes and boots showed signs of hard travel. He was about five feet eight inches tall, slender and wiry, with stooped shoulders. His brown beard and dark hair and complexion were set off by a pair of keen, penetrating, hazel eyes. This man was Longstreet's favorite scout or spy, a man known as Harrison.[31]

Harrison had been traveling with the Union army and drinking with its officers. He knew his business thoroughly. The information which he brought astounded the Confederate leader. Lee thought the Army of the Potomac still in Virginia; but the scout informed him that the Federals were in Maryland, in a position to threaten Lee's line of communications if the Union commander so desired. In order to live off the country, as he had been doing so far, Lee had to keep his units well dispersed. However, this was now very dangerous to do in the presence of the Army of the Potomac. Lee correctly saw the threat that his opponent would try to attack him before he could concentrate his widely separated divisions.[32]

When the scout informed Lee that Meade had replaced Hooker in command of the National Army, the Confederate general voiced the opinion that Meade was an abler soldier than Hooker, but that this would be somewhat counterbalanced by the difficulties he would experience in taking over the command in the midst of an onerous campaign.[33] Lee stated further that Meade would commit no blunders in his presence, and that he would be quick to take advantage of any mistakes which Lee should make.[34] But with the exception of Stuart's cavalry, the Army of Northern Virginia was somewhat better concentrated than the Federal army.[35] However, Lee was restless and worried about the absence of his valuable mounted arm.[36] He asked of Heth, "Harry, where is my cavalry? Where is Stuart? I hope nothing has happened to him." [37] Other officers were similarly interrogated by Lee as to their guess of Stuart's location.[38]

Meade was kept informed of Lee's whereabouts by the loyal citizens of Maryland and Pennsylvania. But the Confederate commander could expect little such assistance while operating on Northern soil.[39] Had Lee known a few days earlier that the Federal army was north of the Potomac, he would most likely have kept his army in hand on the Chambersburg-Gettysburg pike at Cashtown, which point is located at the eastern foot of the South Mountain range.[40] Lee perceived that he would have to concentrate his army immediately in order to guard against the threat to his line of communications west of the mountains. To ensure drawing the Army of the Potomac away from his rear, Lee determined to concentrate *east* of the South Mountains as rapidly as possible.[41]

Nightfall of the 28th found the various units of the Army of Northern Virginia situated as follows: at Carlisle were Rodes' and Johnson's divisions of Ewell's corps; Early's division of the same corps was at York, with one of its brigades—Gordon's—halted at the Susquehanna River by the burning of the vital Wrightsville-Columbia bridge—to keep the graycoats east of the river—by local militiamen;[42] the three divisions of Hill's corps were at or near Fayetteville; Longstreet's three divisions were about Chambersburg; and, probably unknown to Lee, the raiding cavalry of Stuart was at Brookeville.[43]

Orders, therefore, were issued by Lee on the evening of June 28, immediately after he received the disturbing information from the scout.[44] Ewell's corps was recalled from York, Carlisle, and its move on Harrisburg.[45] Messengers were sent to pull back the cavalry brigades of Brigadier Generals Beverly Robertson and William E. Jones from the gaps they were guarding in the Blue Ridge Mountains in Virginia.[46] Pickett's division was to remain behind on the western side of the South Mountain at Chambersburg until relieved by the expected arrival of Brigadier General John D. Imboden's brigade of cavalry.[47] As at Magenta and Solferino, both armies were being drawn by the road network towards the battlefield, as if by a magnet.[48]

Lee's decision to concentrate east of South Mountain was made without knowledge of the movement of Buford's Federal cavalry division towards the road-hub of Gettysburg.[49] Lee made probably the best possible decision and plans to meet any likely contingency. His intended point of concentration—Cashtown—eight miles west of Gettysburg, was an excellent defensive place, with a good highway at his rear in the event of a forced withdrawal, and with the frowning heights of the South Mountain affording positions for his infantry and artillery.

On the Union side, after the first full day of Meade's command, the movements of the Army of the Potomac had yielded the following dispositions by the evening of June 28th: Army Headquarters were at Frederick, where also the First, Eleventh, and Twelfth Corps were encamped; the Second Corps was at Monocacy Junction; the Third

Corps was bivouacked near Woodsborough; the Fifth Corps was at Ballinger's Creek; the Sixth Corps was halted at Hyattstown; and, of the cavalry divisions, Buford's was at Middletown, Gregg's at New Market and Ridgeville, and Brigadier General Judson Kilpatrick's at Frederick.[50]

June 29th was a hot day, with scattered showers prevalent.[51] Early in the forenoon, Ewell received Lee's orders recalling him from his siege of Harrisburg and instructing him to concentrate with the rest of the Confederate army "at Cashtown or Gettysburg, as circumstances might require." [52] By the afternoon, Ewell's three divisions were well on their way toward the rendezvous area east of the South Mountains. Rodes marched through Petersburg to Mummasburg, Johnson from Carlisle through Scotland to Greenwood, and Early to Heidlersburg.[53] On the 29th also, Hill received orders to move to Cashtown, with Longstreet to follow on the 30th.[54] So Heth's division of Hill's corps on the 29th marched the ten miles over the South Mountain from Fayetteville to Cashtown.[55] Lee's vexation on that day over Stuart's absence was concealed to the extent that he could say, jestingly, to Hood, "Ah, General, the enemy is a long time in finding us; if he does not succeed soon, we must go in search of him." [56] Actually, the advantages were still somewhat in Lee's favor. His army was better concentrated than that of Meade, and he had seven roads at his disposal for concentration as against three for his opponent.[57]

Meade continued on the 29th to feel his way cautiously. At 11:00 a.m., he wired Halleck, saying that he intended to move toward Westminster and Emmitsburg, Maryland. "My endeavor," he asserted, "will be in my movements to hold my force well together, with the hope of falling upon some portion of Lee's army in detail . . . . My main point being to find and fight the enemy, I shall have to submit to the cavalry raid around me in some measure . . . ." [58] This dispatch was found on the body of a Federal soldier, killed on June 30, four and one-half miles from Glen Rock, Pennsylvania.[59] However, Meade did *not* keep his army units well concentrated, but allowed them to scatter a bit. By the next day, they were well spread out, with Sedgwick's Sixth Corps at Manchester, Maryland, some thirty miles south of Gettysburg. As it turned out, it was Lee's better concentrated army that "fell upon a portion" of Meade's army at Gettysburg on July 1st! Nonetheless, Meade's determination, as of late on June 29, was indicated in a letter written at that time to his wife, in which he stated that the Confederates "have a cavalry force in our rear, destroying railroads, etc., with the view of getting me to turn back, but I shall not do it. I am going straight at them and will settle this thing one way or the other." [60]

The movements of John Buford's Federal cavalry division now become significant. One of Buford's brigades, that of Brigadier General Wesley Merritt, was in reserve at Mechanicstown. [61] With his two other brigades—Colonel William Gamble's First and Colonel Thomas C. Devin's Second—Buford made a long, circuitous tour of observation from Middletown to Hagerstown, Maryland. From there, he pushed on through Monterey Gap in the South Mountain range to Fountaindale, near Fairfield, Pennsylvania. At this place, about eight miles south of Cashtown, he bivouacked on the night of the 29th. Between Buford and Cashtown were two Confederate regiments of Brigadier General Joseph R. Davis' brigade of Heth's division. [62] On the evening of June 29, Meade's Army of the Potomac was encamped on a line extending roughly from Westminster to Emmitsburg. [63]

The consequential day of June 30 was still another in which warm sunshine was mingled with intermittent and scattered showers. [64] Meade remained still somewhat hesitant as to a specific course of action. He issued a general circular to his corps commanders on the 30th, saying: "The commanding general has received information that the enemy are advancing, probably in strong force, on Gettysburg. . . . It is the intention to hold this army pretty nearly in the position it now occupies until the plans of the enemy shall have been more fully developed." [65] General-in-Chief Halleck, in Washington, telegraphed his approval of Meade's plans. [66] Thus, the initiative remained with Lee and his army. Meade's wait-and-see policy gave the Confederate leader time to advance his forces eastward through the South Mountain gap on the Chambersburg pike, westward from York, and southward from Carlisle and Harrisburg, and to assemble them in one body at Cashtown or Gettysburg.

In order to cover his contemplated occupation of the Pipe Creek position, just south of the Mason and Dixon Line, Meade ordered Buford's two cavalry brigades to Gettysburg on June 30, with the First and Eleventh Corps to follow there a day later. [67] The Third Corps was ordered to Emmitsburg. [68] At 11:30 on the morning of the 30th, Meade wrote Reynolds as follows:

We are as concentrated as my present information of the position of the enemy justifies. I have pushed out the cavalry in all directions to feel for them, and so soon as I can make up any positive opinion as to their position, I will move again. In the meantime, if they advance against me, I must concentrate at that point where they show the strongest force. . . . Your present position [at Marsh Creek] was given more with a view to an advance on Gettysburg, than a defensive point.[69]

Reynolds was placed in command of the Left Wing of the Army of the Potomac, comprising his own First Corps, now commanded by Major General Abner Doubleday, of baseball fame, Sickles' Third Corps, and Howard's Eleventh Corps. To his trusted Reynolds, Meade gave wide discretion, saying that the former "will make such dispositions and give such orders as circumstances may require . . . ."[70] Slocum was appointed to the command of the Right Wing of the army, composed of his own Twelfth Corps, now to be commanded by Brigadier General Alpheus S. Williams, and Sykes' Fifth Corps.[71] This policy of consolidating several corps under the command of a superior was in some degree a reversion to the grand division concept of Major General Ambrose E. Burnside, who had used it at Fredericksburg in December 1862.

The decisions made by Meade on June 30 were strategically sound. While issuing orders to prepare the line of Pipe Creek for defense, he ordered also an offensive in force in the event that movements by the Confederates would justify it.[72] But the Federal commander is open to some criticism for his failure to support adequately the First and Eleventh Corps. According to his own dispatch to Halleck, it is apparent that Meade knew the enemy was concentrating at or near Gettysburg. He must have realized that ordering the aggressive and offensive-minded Reynolds to Gettysburg would likely bring on a major battle near that place.

On the Confederate side on June 30, Lee increased the tempo of his concentration. Hill pushed on with Pender's division to Cashtown, thereby placing that unit directly behind Heth's division on the Chambersburg pike leading toward Gettysburg. Hood's and McLaws' divisions of Longstreet's First Corps followed Pender at some distance. Pickett's division of the First Corps remained behind at Chambersburg, waiting to be relieved by Imboden's cavalry.[73] The brigade of Brigadier General Evander Law, of Hood's division, was left on duty at New Guilford with the wagon trains.[74] Major General Richard H.

Anderson's division of Hill's corps, encamped at Fayetteville to the east of Chambersburg on the pike to Gettysburg, was directed to move eastward on that road on the 1st of July.[75]

As subsequent events seem to indicate, Hill apparently misconstrued Lee's orders, or else was confused by the sudden change in the directives following the scout's information that the Union army was north of the Potomac. Apparently he believed that Lee wanted him to march to York, cross the Susquehanna, and move on Harrisburg or Philadelphia.[76]

Meanwhile, the dashing Confederate cavalryman, "Jeb" Stuart, was being kept out in limbo. Although he was able, by riding along crossroads to Hanover, to elude a trap set for him on the morning of June 30 at Littlestown by Kilpatrick, Stuart was nonetheless kept from reaching Heidlersburg. Kilpatrick's decision to keep the Southern *beau sabreur* away from Heidlersburg was of inestimable service to the Army of the Potomac. Had Stuart been permitted to move to Heidlersburg, he would have joined Early's command there on July 1, and been present for service by Lee at the opening of the battle at Gettysburg.[77]

No sooner had Stuart reached Hanover, however, than he ran into formidable opponents. First, some Federal cavalrymen had to be driven out of town. Then, Jeb was confronted by Kilpatrick's pursuing blue horsemen. The two main cavalry bodies clashed in a fierce encounter in the square and through the streets of the town. Stuart was finally impelled to pull out after the Nationals had received reinforcements in the form of Brigadier General George A. Custer's brigade of Michigan cavalry. This combat prevented Stuart once again from moving further west. Now, he was compelled to move northward in search of Ewell.[78]

Stuart and his weary troopers finally arrived outside Carlisle, expecting to find the Second Corps there. But Ewell had departed, and the place was occupied by Federal militia units under the command of staunch Major General William F. Smith. Stuart attempted to bluff Smith on July 1 into surrendering the town upon the threat of bombardment; but "Baldy" refused to capitulate, and Jeb had no time to tarry. He pushed doggedly on from Carlisle to Gettysburg, his exhausted riders falling asleep in the saddle. Stuart finally reached the field on the afternoon of July 2—the second day of the battle. His long absence had considerably damaged Lee's chances of success.[79]

If the Confederate cavalrymen were out on the periphery of the combat arena, Buford's Union cavalry division was moving toward the vortex. On the morning of June 30, the brigades of Gamble and Devin advanced via Emmitsburg toward Gettysburg. The country through which Buford's men rode presented a striking picture of peace and plenty. Magnificent farmhouses, large red barns, and outbuildings dotted the landscape. The fields of golden waving grain were ready for the scythe. Here, in startling contrast to the ravaged areas of Virginia, was a land untouched by the destruction and waste of war.[80]

Buford's command arrived at Gettysburg about noon on June 30.[81] Leading the column into the town were the 8th and 9th New York regiments.[82] The sturdy blueclad cavalrymen were wildly cheered by the townsfolk of Gettysburg, who had just several days before seen gray soldiers marching through their square.[83] The happy and generous citizens provided the Federal riders with the usual friendly handouts of bread and butter and cups of cold water.[84] For a time Buford's headquarters were located in the Eagle Hotel, owned by a Mr. Tate.[85]

Early on the same morning—June 30—the brigade of Brigadier General James J. Pettigrew, of Heth's division, Hill's Third Corps, commenced its march toward Gettysburg, in search of shoes and other provisions.[86] It arrived along the Chambersburg pike in the vicinity of Gettysburg at approximately 10:00 a.m., and halted on an elevation known as Seminary Ridge, three-quarters of a mile west of town.[87] Pettigrew took time to deploy into a line of battle about a mile and a half in length along Seminary Ridge, with his pickets moving forward to the western edge of Gettysburg. The officers spent more time peering through their field glasses, studying the town.[88] Eventually, the Confederate officers spotted Buford's long blue lines entering the community from the south. Not feeling authorized to advance further and engage the Federals, Pettigrew ordered his brigade back toward Cashtown along the pike over which it had advanced earlier in the day.[89] His failure to remain on Seminary Ridge was to cost the Confederates dearly the following day. He left his advanced pickets about four or five miles from Gettysburg, along the Chambersburg road.[90]

One of Pettigrew's officers, Captain W.F. Dunaway, Company I, 40th Virginia regiment, reported the near-encounter with Buford to Heth, the division commander. Heth replied to Dunaway, "Tell General Pettigrew not to butt too hard, or he'll butt his brains out." [91] Hill, the commander of the Third Corps, learning from Heth of the presence of Buford's cavalry at Gettysburg, relayed the information to General Lee, who found it difficult to believe.[92]

Buford had noted, upon entering Gettysburg, the strategic importance of the place, with the ten roads radiating from it. His trained military eye also could not have escaped seeing the prominent heights south of the town—a superb defensive position from which to fight a large-scale battle. He determined to make his dispositions so that he could retain control of the town, if possible.[93] His headquarters were moved to the Lutheran Theological Seminary, which was situated on Seminary Ridge between the Chambersburg and Hagerstown roads, about three-quarters of a mile west of town.[94] The Seminary building was crowned by a cupola and afforded the best observation point in the whole area.

On the 30th of June, Meade's Left Wing, comprising the First, Eleventh, and Third Corps, all under the command of Reynolds, moved northward toward Gettysburg. The left of the Army of the Potomac was resting at Marsh Creek, four miles from Gettysburg, the center near Littlestown, and the right near Manchester.[95] On the same day, Meade issued the following order, so stringent that it was deemed by some Federal soldiers as a reflection on their proven courage and totally unnecessary: "Corps commanders are authorized to order the instant death of any soldier who fails in his duty at this hour." [96] The unappreciative but fun-loving boys in the ranks suggested that the rank and file should in return dispatch a manifesto to the commanding general, "expressing the hope that he would show more ability and judgment than his predecessors had shown when conducting a great battle, and above all, avoid issuing appeals or circulars reflecting the slightest doubt on the courage of the men." [97]

But if this was an unwise order on Meade's part, his somewhat slow and measured advance would conserve the strength of his troops, while Lee was driving his men hard in the effort to concentrate first. In another order on the 30th, the Union commander said that he did not desire "to wear the troops out by excessive fatigue and marches, and thus unfit them for the work they will be called upon to perform." [98] In another dispatch, sent at 4:30 p.m. to Halleck, Meade declared, "I fear that I shall break down the troops by pushing on much faster, and may have to rest a day." [99]

During the course of the day, on the Confederate side, Johnson's division of Ewell's corps was moving from Carlisle on the western side of the mountains, and had been obliged to attach itself to the rear of the long column of Hill's and Longstreet's corps, which were coming across the South Mountain range via the Chamberburg-Gettysburg turnpike.[100] At Heidlersburg, Ewell had received the instructions from Lee to march to Cashtown or Gettysburg, as circumstances might develop. When Ewell subsequently received a dispatch from Hill saying he was then at Cashtown,[101] Ewell issued instructions to Early to march his division on the following morning—July 1—to Cashtown, where Lee intended to concentrate his army.[102]

General Hill, after hearing from Heth that a Union force had been sighted at Gettysburg, determined, in the absence of the Confederate cavalry, to ascertain by a reconnaissance in force the strength of the unknown enemy at this point.[103] Therefore, on the evening of June 30, when Heth said to Hill, "If there is no objection, I will take my division tomorrow and go to Gettysburg and get those shoes," the latter answered, "None in the world." [104] Hill's laconic four-word reply touched off events that were to be momentous.

Hill was justified in trying to find out what size force was in his front; but his movement with the two divisions of Heth and Pender, with most of the Third Corps artillery, away from Cashtown, Lee's intended point of concentration, was against the letter and spirit of the specific orders of Lee not to bring on a general battle at that time. His precipitate action, like that of a number of Prussian subalterns in 1870, took the control of affairs out of the hands of the commanding general of the army.[105] Hill's somewhat irresponsible action was similar to that of Stuart, who had also abused the discretionary power often accorded top ranking subordinates by Lee.[106]

Meanwhile, Couch, commanding the Union Department of the Susquehanna, had the pressure taken off his 15,036 militiamen[107] by the orders of Lee which directed Ewell's corps to concentrate at Cashtown or Gettysburg. On the evening of June 30, Couch sent from his Harrisburg headquarters a message to Meade, saying, "My latest information is that Early, with his 8,000 men, went toward Gettysburg or Hanover, saying they expected to fight a great battle there." [108] Meade received also a dispatch from Buford, who was at Gettysburg, to the effect that Hill's Confederate corps was concentrated near Cashtown, and that Ewell was reported to be crossing the mountains from Carlisle.[109]

Meade's farthest-reaching antennae on June 30 were Buford's two cavalry brigades at Gettysburg. Late that night, Buford discussed the developing situation with his Second Brigade commander, Colonel Devin. The latter confidently asserted that he would take care of any Confederates who attacked him on the morrow. But Buford disagreed vociferously. "No, you won't," he declared, in what turned out to be a remarkably accurate prognostication. "They will attack you in the morning; and they will come 'booming'—skirmishers three deep. You will have to fight like the devil to hold your own until supports arrive. The enemy must know the importance of this position, and will strain every nerve to secure it, and if we are able to hold it we will do well." [110]

At nightfall on June 30, the dispositions of the units of the two armies indicated that Lee still had the advantage.[111] The Army of the Potomac was still rather widely dispersed over the region south, southeast, and southwest of the road-hub of Gettysburg, while the Army of Northern Virginia was rapidly concentrating near Cashtown and Gettysburg.[112] A look in some detail as to exactly how the two armies were situated on the eve of the greatest battle ever fought on this continent is essential to appreciate just how the various units approached the fighting on the first day at Gettysburg.

After the hard marching of June 30, the Confederate units were bivouacked as follows: Pender's and Heth's divisions of Hill's corps were at Cashtown, eight miles west of Gettysburg; Anderson's division of the same corps was at Fayetteville, between Chambersburg and Cashtown;[113] Rodes' division of Ewell's corps was encamped at Heidlersburg, nine miles north-northeast of Gettysburg; Early's division of the same corps was three miles outside of Heidlersburg;[114] Johnson's division of Ewell's command was bivouacked at Scotland;[115] Hood's and McLaws' divisions of Longstreet's corps were at Fayetteville; Pickett's division of the same corps remained at Chambersburg; Stuart's cavalry was at Jefferson; and Imboden's cavalry brigade was at Hancock.[116]

Turning to the Army of the Potomac, it was situated as follows on the evening of June 30: Army Headquarters were at Taneytown, fourteen miles south of Gettysburg; Doubleday's First Corps was at Marsh Creek, five miles southwest of Gettysburg; Hancock's Second Corps was encamped at Uniontown, twenty-two miles south of Gettysburg; Sickles' Third Corps was bivouacked at Bridgeport, twelve miles southwest of Gettysburg; Skyes' Fifth Corps was at Union

Mills, fifteen miles south of Gettysburg; Sedgwick's Sixth Corps and Gregg's cavalry division were at Manchester, twenty-two miles south of Gettysburg; Slocum's Twelfth Corps was encamped at Littlestown, nine miles south of Gettysburg; Gamble's and Devin's cavalry brigades of Buford's division were at Gettysburg; Kilpatrick's cavalry division was halted at Hanover, thirteen miles east-southeast of Gettysburg; and the Artillery Reserve was parked at Taneytown.[117]

Late on the evening of June 30, after his units were bivouacked for the night, Meade issued orders for army movements on July 1. The First Corps was ordered to Gettysburg, the Eleventh Corps to Gettysburg or within supporting distance of the First, the Third Corps to Emmitsburg, the Second Corps to Taneytown, the Fifth Corps to Hanover, the Twelfth Corps to Two Taverns, with the Sixth Corps remaining at Manchester.[118] It must be kept in mind, however, that as these orders were being issued by the Federal commander, he was still considering, as an alternative, fighting a defensive battle at the surveyed Pipe Creek line, just south of the Mason and Dixon Line, if his information about the Confederate dispositions should prove inadequate, or if these dispositions should prove to be unfavorable to the Union offensive.[119]

Meade delayed rather a long time—probably while awaiting developments of Lee's plans—in issuing his orders to his Left Wing commander. Consequently, Reynolds did not hesitate to act largely on his own responsibility, and this action met with Meade's approval.[120] Earlier in the week, at Poolesville, Maryland, Reynolds had remarked to Doubleday that in order to prevent the Confederates from appropriating enormous quantities of foodstuffs, horses, cattle, and other provisions, it would be necessary for the Army of the Potomac to assume a vigorous offensive policy.[121] The decisions and movements which the aggressive Reynolds made on the morning of Wednesday, July 1, 1863, were to bear out this previously announced conception.

CHAPTER 2

The

Meeting of the Ways

In order to comprehend the fighting on the First Day's Battle of Gettysburg, a clear, somewhat detailed description of the physical features of the country which comprise the battlefield is essential. The accidents of terrain often play a key role in the progress and outcome of a military contest, and Gettysburg is no exception to this axiom. A hill here, a wood there, a stream coursing through the arena of combat, the lack of a natural or man-made bastion on which to anchor a flank—these and other physiographic features might well have a decisive effect on the development of a battle. Generals try to take advantage of the roads which are available for reinforcement, of high ground, of wooded areas, of good fields of fire, and of bodies of water which might serve as defensive moats. And, too, the imponderable of luck, of good fortune, coming to one side or the other at a crucial moment, must never be ignored by the careful and thorough commander. Few battles are more illustrative of these military facts of life than the combat of July 1, 1863.

The first thing that strikes the eye upon looking at the Gettysburg battlefield (which area surrounds the town and includes it) is the complex network of ten roads which radiate from the town like spokes from the hub of a wheel. The various roads, and the directions from which they approach Gettysburg, are as follows: the Chambersburg pike,[1] from the west-northwest; the Mummasburg road, from the northwest; the Carlisle road, from the north; the Harrisburg road, from the northeast; the York pike,[2] from the east-northeast; the Hanover road, from the east-southeast; the Baltimore pike, from the south-east; the Taneytown road, from the south; the Emmitsburg road, from the south-southwest; and the Hagerstown road, from the west-southwest. Running parallel with, and approximately 200 yards north of the Chambersburg pike, was an unfinished railroad grading, forming a series of cuts and fills with the various ridges and intervening ground west of town. At the time of the battle in 1863, the roadbed was graded but no rails had as yet been placed in position. Gettysburg was, therefore a notable meeting of the ways, with more roads radiating from it than from any other town or city in the entire region, including Harrisburg, York, Chambersburg, and Carlisle.

The soil of the country around Gettysburg, although showing evidence of red clay, was nonetheless excellent for extensive crop cultivation. Orchards dotted the landscape. The country was more open than that of Virginia, where the previous great battles of the war had been fought largely on heavily forested terrain. Copses and small woods, however, were generously sprinkled about the countryside around Gettysburg.

The most interesting feature of the country about Gettysburg was the ridge system. Ten miles west of town the horizon was limited by the "towering bulk of the South Mountain, vanguard of the serried chain behind it." [3] This range ran in a generally north and south direction. Gettysburg was "among the subsiding swells that the South Mountain has sent rippling off to the east." [4] "When the force which folded and raised up the strata that form the South Mountain was in action, it produced fissures in the strata of red shale which cover the surface of this region of country, permitting the fused material from beneath to rise and fill them on cooling with trap-dykes or greenstone and syenitic greenstone. The rock, being for the most part very hard, remained as the axes and crests of hills and ridges when the softer shale in the intervening spaces was excavated by great water-currents into valleys and plains." [5]

The first ridge west of Gettysburg was wooded Seminary Ridge, running north and south, about three-quarters of a mile west of town. It was named for the Lutheran Theological Seminary located thereon between the Chambersburg pike and the Hagerstown road. North of the railroad grading this ridge is known as Oak Ridge, so called because it was largely covered with groves of oak trees. This latter ridge terminated in a prominent knob, known as Oak Hill, which was approximately one and one-quarter miles northwest of Gettysburg.[6] Passing just to the south of Oak Hill was the Mummasburg road. This hill was the key to the entire first day's field.[7]

About 500 yards west of Seminary Ridge (measured along the Chambersburg pike) was McPherson Ridge, named for the McPherson farm buildings which during the battle were located on the ridge some 250 yards south of the pike. McPherson Ridge converged gradually toward Oak Ridge, and they united at Oak Hill. McPherson Ridge was open except for a small orchard near the barn and a much larger triangular-shaped grove of trees south of the farm buildings, known as McPherson Grove.[8] This wood was the playground and picnic area of the town in 1863.[9]

Approximately 900 yards west of McPherson Ridge (again measured along the Chambersburg pike) was Herr Ridge, named for Herr's Tavern, which, at the time of the battle, was situated thereon along the south side of the pike. A narrow crossroad ran along Herr Ridge perpendicular to the pike and crossing it at the tavern.[10] At the time of the battle, Herr Ridge had scattered copses on its slopes and crest.

Between McPherson and Herr Ridges, and running roughly north and south and parallel to them, was Willoughby Run, a small stream fordable at almost any point. It was along the banks of this stream that the battle opened on July 1. Four hundred yards west of Herr Ridge was the Belmont Schoolhouse Ridge, named for the little red brick schoolhouse situated upon it along the north side of the Chambersburg pike.[11] This ridge is about 1,300 yards west of McPherson Ridge.[12] Except for the woods and copses mentioned, the country was largely open, being chiefly meadows and cultivated fields.

North of the town of Gettysburg the ground comprised a level plain. The only elevation worthy of the name was a low knoll, wooded on its eastern and northern sides at the time of the battle,[13] and now known as Barlow's Knoll. It was located on the western bank of Rock Creek, about a mile north-northeast of the town. This plain was open ground, either clover or cultivated fields, and with very few trees on it.

There were several important heights south of the town. About a quarter of a mile south of the edge of town was Cemetery Hill, named for the Citizens' Evergreen Cemetery situated thereupon. This commanding eminence was crossed at its summit by the Baltimore pike.

The summit of the hill—now the Soldiers' National Cemetery[14]—was a cornfield at the time of the battle. That portion of the hill on the east side of the Baltimore pike is known as East Cemetery Hill.

About one-half mile southeast of Cemetery Hill was a rugged, wooded elevation known as Culp's Hill, named for the William Culp farm in the vicinity. At the southeastern foot of Culp's Hill was Spangler's Spring. The eastern foot of the hill was washed by the waters of Rock Creek, which flowed in a southerly direction from Barlow's Knoll. Between Cemetery Hill and Culp's Hill—really a spur of the latter—was a lower rise of ground known as Stevens' Knoll.

Running southward from Cemetery Hill for a distance of about two miles was a low swell or roll of land known as Cemetery Ridge, which terminated in two bold, steep knobs. The more northerly of these important hills was Little Round Top. Just south of this hill was Big Round Top—a small mountain, and the highest point in the entire area. Big Round Top was fully covered with trees, and was practically inaccessible for artillery. Little Round Top was wooded except for its western slope, which, while rock-strewn, had been cleared of timber shortly before the battle. Cemetery Ridge was generally open, except for some woods where it decreases in elevation just north of Little Round Top, and for Ziegler's Grove near the northern end of the ridge.

At the foot of the Round Tops, to the west, was a sluggish stream known as Plum Run, which flowed in a general north and south direction. About 500 yards southwest of Little Round Top was an outcropping of gigantic boulders. They were formed in a weird pattern, some on top of others, as if some giant had tossed them about at random. This Stonehenge-like formation is known as the Devil's Den. A quarter of a mile northwest of the Den was the Wheatfield, scene of sanguinary fighting on the 2nd of July. West of the Wheatfield, and bordering on the Emmitsburg road, was the famed Peach Orchard, also the scene of desperate combat on the second day's battle.

Running parallel with Cemetery Ridge, and approximately one mile west of it, was Seminary Ridge. The former position formed the battle lines of the Army of the Potomac on the second and third days' battles, while the latter ridge was the main position of the Confederate army.

It would have been hard to conceive, at dawn on July 1, 1863, that this peaceful, rural countryside was soon to become the scene of one of the world's greatest battles. "Those who see a divine hand occasionally revealed in national history might say that that great field was providentially assigned, in view of all preceding movements that led to its use, as the place where the Army of the Potomac might win its pivotal victory." [15]

CHAPTER 3

The Early
Morning Fight of Buford

THE MOMENTOUS DAY OF WEDNESDAY, JULY 1, 1863, DAWNED rainy and misty, with scattered showers prevalent across the countryside of southern Pennsylvania.[1] However, as the morning advanced, the weather was to clear, the sun to come out, and the heat to become intense, with high humidity.[2] After the fog and clouds had lifted, a blood-red sunrise, like the storied sun of Austerlitz, was noted.[3] A gentle wind was blowing from south to north.[4]

General Lee, that morning, rode eastward toward Cashtown over the Chambersburg pike. He was accompanied by Longstreet. Despite the concern over the continued absence of Stuart's cavalry, and despite the dread uncertainty over the location of the Federal legions, Lee appeared to be composed and in good spirits.[5] And why shouldn't he be? His orders for a concentration of the Army of Northern Virginia at Cashtown, later switched to Gettysburg by reason of Hill's precipitateness, were bearing fruit, and led to a fortuitous concentration at the latter point—a concentration "that has nothing to compare with it in the annals of modern war."[6] "The time intervals were carefully adjusted as if the whole movement had been rehearsed." [7]

The early morning of July 1 found Rodes' division, accompanied by corps commander Ewell, marching along the Arendtsville road by way of Middletown (Biglersville) for Cashtown—from which destination he was to be diverted later in the day to Gettysburg.[8] Early's division of the Second Corps was supposed to follow on a parallel road by way of Hunterstown, Schrivers, and Mummasburg. But Early had learned that the Hunterstown road was rough and, exercising his discretion as division commander, moved his column to the Harrisburg road at Heidlersburg. From there he moved to Schrivers, and then headed toward the rendezvous at Cashtown (from which he was also to be diverted later in the day to Gettysburg).[9]

Meantime, on the Union side, caution still prevailed. Meade, at army headquarters at Taneytown, sent the following message at 7:00 a.m. to General-in-Chief Halleck: "The point of Lee's concentration and the nature of the country, when ascertained, will determine whether I attack or not. Shall advise you further today, when satisfied that the enemy are fully withdrawn from the Susquehanna."[10] This dispatch differed from Meade's earlier telegram which had stated that Gettysburg was indicated as Lee's probable point of concentration. Meade gave the positions of his various corps in the same message to Halleck, and acknowledged the receipt of Couch's earlier communications from Harrisburg, adding that "these movements [by the Army of the Potomac] were ordered yesterday, before the receipt of advices of Lee's movements."[11]

Then, early on the morning of July 1, Meade promulgated the following circular to his corps commanders:

> From information received, the commanding general is satisfied that the object of the movement of the army in this direction has been accomplished, viz, the relief of Harrisburg, and the prevention of the enemy's intended invasion of Philadelphia, etc., beyond the Susquehanna. It is no longer his intention to assume the offensive until the enemy's movements or position should render such an operation certain of success.
>
> If the enemy assume the offensive, and attack, it is his intention after holding them in check sufficiently long, to withdraw the [wagon] trains and other *impedimenta;* to withdraw the army from its present position, and form line of battle . . . [along] Pipe Creek . . . . The time for falling back can only be developed by circumstances . . . . [Here follows precise instructions as to how the units would move to the Pipe Creek position.]
>
> This order is communicated, that a general plan, perfectly understood by all, may be had for receiving attack, if made in strong force, upon any portion of our present position.
>
> Developments may cause the commanding general to assume the offensive from his present positions . . . .[12]

Meade's circular, describing a possible falling-back movement to the defensive line behind Pipe Creek, probably did not reach Reynolds before the latter left Marsh Creek for Gettysburg.[13] However, Meade sent out additional liberal orders to Reynolds directly on the heels of the above-mentioned circular—orders which gave the competent Left Wing commander considerable leeway and discretion in deciding how to meet the developing situation. These latter orders—a copy of which was sent to Howard—read in part as follows:

> .... The commanding general cannot decide whether it is his best policy to move to attack until he learns something more definite of the point at which the enemy is concentrating. This he hopes to do during the day ....
>
> If the enemy is concentrating in front of Gettysburg or to the left of it, the general is not sufficiently well informed of the nature of the country to judge of its character for either an offensive or defensive position. The numbers of the enemy are estimated at about 92,000 infantry, with 270 pieces of artillery, and his cavalry from 6,000 to 8,000 .... [Meade then states that he would welcome Reynolds' views, as the latter was better acquainted with the country than was the army commander.]
>
> The movement of your corps to Gettysburg was ordered before the positive knowledge of the enemy's withdrawal from Harrisburg and concentration was received.[14]

Probably these orders likewise failed to reach Reynolds before his departure from Marsh Creek for Gettysburg.

In the most sensitive forward position for the Federals was Buford's command of two cavalry brigades at Gettysburg. Preparing to meet the expected advance of the Confederate forces the next morning, Buford said of his activities on the night of June 30: "The night of the 30th was a busy night for the division .... By daylight of July 1, I had gained positive information of the enemy's position and movements, and my arrangements were made for entertaining him until General Reynolds could reach the scene." [15]

By the morning of July 1, Buford had deployed Gamble's First Brigade along the westernmost crest and slope of McPherson Ridge, on the eastern bank of Willoughby Run, facing west, with its left near the Hagerstown road and its right on the railroad grading. Devin's Second Brigade continued Gamble's line northward to near Oak Hill, then eastward, covering the approaches from Mummasburg, Carlisle, Harrisburg, and York.[16] Buford's troopers were dismounted, every fourth man holding at some distance in the rear his own horse and those of three of his fellow cavalrymen.[17] This reduced Buford's effective fighting force by one-fourth, or from some 3,000 to 2,400 men.[18] Vedettes, or mounted pickets, were thrown forward several miles from the main line to watch for the advance of Hill and Ewell along the several roads.[19]

The dismounted troopers were supported by the six three-inch rifles—iron cannon firing explosive shell—of Tidball's Battery A, 2nd United States Artillery—commanded in this battle by Lieutenant John H. Calef. The right section was on the right (north) side of the Chambersburg pike; the left section was on the left side of the pike; and the center section, under Sergeant Charles Pergel, was further to the left toward the Hagerstown road.[20]

As to the Confederate forces, as they were about to move toward Gettysburg on July 1, Anderson was instructed to move early that morning from Fayetteville to Cashtown so as to clear the road leading from Greenwood to Shippensburg for the advance of Johnson's division and Ewell's reserve artillery and wagon trains.[21] The advance pickets of Rodes' division, marching on Gettysburg from Heidlersburg, were delayed before they got to Oak Hill by Devin's dismounted carbineers, with the 9th New York regiment prominent in the Union skirmish line.[22]

At 5:00 a.m.,[23] Hill sent forward from Cashtown Heth's division and the reserve artillery battalions of Major W.J. Pegram and Major D.G. McIntosh.[24] It was a strong reconnaissance in force.[25] The four brigades comprising Heth's division totaled approximately 7,500 muskets.[26] In Heth's column, Brigadier General James J. Archer's battle-tested Third Brigade was in the lead. Archer was followed by Davis' inexperienced Fourth Brigade,[27] and then by Pettigrew's First Brigade. Bringing up the rear of Heth's column was Colonel John M. Brockenbrough's Second Brigade.[28] Prudently, Hill directed Pender's division to follow within supporting distance of Heth. As this long column advanced down the Chambersburg pike toward Gettysburg, some of the Confederate troops noticed an advertisement, which was hardly comforting, in a Charleston, South Carolina, newspaper, carried by one of the men in the ranks. It read, "Good news to soldiers! Air-tight coffins! Good news to soldiers!" [29]

As Buford's cavalrymen watched amidst the clover and wildflowers[30] for Hill's approach from the west, events of moment were transpiring at Marsh Creek, five miles southwest of Gettysburg. At approximately 6:00 a.m., Reynolds informed Doubleday, then commanding the First Corps, that he was going to the aid of Buford with his nearest division—Brigadier General James A. Wadsworth's First. Doubleday was instructed to call in his pickets, limber up the artillery, and start the remainder of the First Corps for Gettysburg as swiftly as possible.[31] Before marching out from their overnight bivouacks, the men of Doubleday's command had a chance to consume their usual breakfast of pork, hardtack, and coffee.[32] In order that no time be lost, hardtack and cartridges were issued to the men in the ranks at the same time that the chaplains were pronouncing their invocations.[33]

Promptly at 8:00 a.m., Wadsworth's division left Marsh Creek for Gettysburg.[34] At the same hour, Howard received orders from Reynolds to start his Eleventh Corps immediately toward Gettysburg.[35] Wadsworth was followed at 9:30 a.m. from Marsh Creek by Brigadier General Thomas Rowley's Third Division (Doubleday's old division).[36]

As the soldiers of the First Corps toiled over the Emmitsburg road toward Buford's relief, "stifling clouds of yellow dust settled on the ranks like a blanket." [37] The quiet pastoral region through which the Federals were marching was soon converted into familiar scenes reminiscent of the war in Virginia. Alarmed residents of the countryside were met on the road, driving their horses and cattle before them, fearful of depredations from the advancing Confederate forces.[38]

Back at Gettysburg, Devin, at first encountering no Confederate forces north of the town, left a few vedettes on each of the roads north and east of Gettysburg, and posted the bulk of his cavalry brigade between the Mummasburg road and the railroad grading—his line extending southward from the foot of Oak Hill to the railroad cut at McPherson Ridge.[39] Devin's cavalry regiments were deployed in the following manner, from right to left: the 17th Pennsylvania (Colonel Josiah H. Kellogg), the 9th New York (Colonel William E. Sackett), the 6th New York (Major William Beardsley), and two companies of the 3rd West Virginia (Captain Seymour B. Conger).[40]

Gamble's cavalry brigade was on Devin's left, continuing the line southward along the western crest and slope of McPherson Ridge. From right to left, Gamble's cavalry regiments were posted as follows: six companies of the 3rd Indiana (Colonel George H. Chapman), four companies of the 12th Illinois (also commanded by Chapman), the 8th Illinois (Major John L. Beveridge), and the 8th New York (Lieutenant Colonel William L. Markell).[41]

At about 5:30 a.m., skirmishing commenced between the advanced vedettes and pickets of Buford's and Heth's divisions.[42] The Confederates, becoming visible out of the early morning mist, were first fired upon by Lieutenant Jones of the 8th Illinois as the graycoats were approaching the Chambersburg pike bridge over Marsh Creek, about three miles west of Gettysburg.[43] Shortly afterward, Corporal Alpheus Hodges, Company F, 9th New York, spotting the enemy nearing the pike bridge spanning Willoughby Run, hastened to send back one of his vedettes to inform Buford of the foe's presence. Hodges then fired at the oncoming Confederates from behind the abutment of the bridge.[44]

By concealing themselves in the tall grass, and firing from behind bushes, trees, and fences, Gamble's skirmish line, composed chiefly of troopers of the 8th Illinois, put on a show of extreme boldness and thereby delayed Heth's advance to the extent that it took the Southerners some two hours to negotiate the distance from Marsh Creek to Willoughby Run,[45] although at no place did the Federals attempt to make a determined stand.[46] The Union cavalry kept up an incessant fire with their breech-loading carbines[47]—a fire that was answered by the Confederate infantrymen with their standard single-shot, muzzle-loading musket.[48] The Southern officers did not know the number of troops which Buford had at his command, and probably thought that the bold Federal carbineers were strongly supported by infantry and artillery in their rear. An ambush was feared by the invaders.

Soon reports began to reach Buford from vedettes of the 17th Pennsylvania, stationed on the Carlisle road, that Ewell's advance had been detected.[49] After watering their horses at Rock Creek, the First Squadron of the 9th New York cavalry, under Captain Hanley, encountered Ewell's advancing pickets at about 8:00 a.m. This meeting occurred near the buildings of N. Hoffman, which were located on the north side of the Mummasburg road, just west of Oak Hill. Hanley withdrew his command to a position close to the J. Forney buildings on the south side of the road, just to the south of the hill. The Confederate pickets came forward and opened fire on the National cavalrymen from behind the Forney farmhouse. Hanley dismounted his men and drove the enemy from the house. As the numerically superior Confederates again advanced, crawling on hands and knees through a wheatfield, a sudden cheer from the Federals caused the Southerners to withdraw hastily, probably fearing a sudden charge from overpowering forces. The battle's first capture was achieved by Perry Nichols, Company F, 9th New York, when he caught a "Johnny Reb" resting behind a tree.[50] The first Union soldier killed was Cyrus W. James, Company G, 9th New York,[51] while the first Confederate to be slain in the battle was Henry Raison of the 7th Tennessee.[52]

Back on the Chambersburg pike, the main grapple was beginning. General Heth, peering through his field glasses, could find no Union line of battle until he and his division reached Herr Ridge.[53] From there, looking across Willoughby Run, he spotted Buford's blue line of dismounted cavalrymen on McPherson Ridge. Heth ordered the brigades of Archer and Davis forward. At about 8:00 a.m. or a little later,[54] a severe struggle began on the banks of the little stream.[55] Firing rapidly and effectively with their carbines, Buford's command disputed every inch of ground as it fell back from the brook very slowly up the western slope of McPherson Ridge.[56] For about two hours Buford's outnumbered cavalrymen held in check the brigades of Archer on the south side of the Chambersburg pike and Davis on the north side of the road.[57] The first Confederate prisoners to be brought in were seen to be shaking their heads in dismay and saying, in respect to the carbines used by Buford's troopers, "What you all do—load on Sundays and fire all week"? [58]

After a bit of difficulty in locating good firing positions, Pegram's Confederate artillery battalion, of Colonel R. Lindsay Walker's artillery reserve, went into action just west of Herr Ridge on the Belmont Schoolhouse Ridge, north of the Chambersburg pike.[59] Pegram's battalion was composed of the following five batteries: Captain T.A. Brander's battery ("The Letcher Artillery"), two bronze Napoleons —firing twelve-pound solid iron cannon-balls or canister (iron balls sprayed from a can)—and two ten-pounder Parrotts—firing explosive shell;[60] Captain Joseph McGraw's battery ("The Purcell Artillery"), four Napoleons;[61] Lieutenant William E. Zimmerman's battery ("The Pee Dee Artillery"), four three-inch rifles;[62] Crenshaw's battery, two Napoleons and two twelve-pounder howitzers—firing high-trajectory projectiles;[63] and Captain E.A. Marye's battery ("The Fredericksburg Artillery"), two Napoleons and two ten-pounder Parrotts.[64]

Later, Pegram was reinforced by the artillery battalion of McIntosh, also of the artillery reserve, which went into action on Pegram's right, south of the Chambersburg pike.[65] McIntosh's battalion comprised the following four batteries: Lieutenant Samuel Wallace's battery ("The Second Rockbridge Artillery"), four three-inch rifles;[66] Captain W.B. Hurt's battery ("The Hardaway Artillery"), two Whitworths and two three-inch rifles;[67] Captain R.S. Rice's battery ("The Danville Artillery"), four Napoleons;[68] and Captain M. Johnson's battery ("Johnson's Virginia Battery"), two Napoleons and two three-inch rifles.[69]

Noting the protected position of McPherson's Grove, and suspecting that Union forces might be lurking beneath the trees, Heth ordered his batteries to shell the woods for thirty minutes.[70] The first Confederate artillery shot was touched off at approximately 9:00 a.m. —fired from a gun in Marye's battery, posted on the south side of the Chambersburg pike in front of the schoolhouse.[71] At this hour the fighting became quite heavy between Archer's infantry brigade and Gamble's dismounted cavalrymen.[72] It was not until about 10:00 a.m., however, that Heth's men were safely across Willoughby Run, and threatening Buford's line near the westernmost crest of McPherson Ridge.[73]

Immediately after Marye's first Confederate artillery shot came over, three more Southern shells were fired before Calef's Battery A, 2nd United States Artillery, posted in the pike, replied[74]—the range between the opposing guns being about 1300 yards.[75] This first Union artillery shot was fired by Lieutenant John William Roder.[76] During the opening minutes of the artillery duel, Battery A's six guns were being opposed by twelve Confederate cannon.[77] Calef, successfully maintaining the splendid reputation the battery had won in the Mexican War (when it was known as "Duncan's Battery"),[78] replied most effectively against the heavier weight of Confederate metal.[79]

While Heth's Third and Fourth brigades were disputing with Buford the control of Willoughby Run, events of a strategic nature were transpiring to the north of Gettysburg. Early was on his way from Heidlersburg to Cashtown, and his route for a few miles was over a straight road running in the direction of Gettysburg. While on this stretch, Early received a message from his corps commander, Ewell, instructing him to keep on toward Gettysburg, since Federal troops had been seen at that place and since Hill was en route there also in order to ascertain the size of the Union force present. Early was informed also that Rodes' division was marching southward from Carlisle and Heidlersburg to Gettysburg. Hence, Ewell himself was directing the march of two of his divisions toward Gettysburg by two almost parallel roads.[80]

These two Confederate divisions were to arrive on the battlefield of Gettysburg at exactly the right point and at precisely the right time. Both Lee, by his overall strategic combinations, and Ewell were responsible, in part, for this fortunate Confederate concentration at Gettysburg. However, it might be noted that Ewell and especially Hill practically ignored Lee's order to the effect that he "did not want a general engagement brought on until the rest of the [Confederate] army came up."[81] Perhaps Hill's interpretation of Lee's orders was not as perspicacious as it might have been because of the fact that Hill was quite sick during the early morning of July 1.[82]

While Buford, whose superior position and firearms offset somewhat his disadvantage in numbers, was "hotly engaged" along the banks of Willoughby Run,[83] he was undoubtedly aware of a directive which had arrived from cavalry headquarters at Taneytown. It stated, "The cavalry will dispute every inch of ground."[84] The Union troopers at Gettysburg were doing just that. If pressed too hard, and in danger of capture or anihilation, Buford was to fall back toward Taneytown and then Middleburg.[85] Only after two hours of heavy fighting, when about to be relieved by Reynolds' infantry, were Buford's men "literally dragged back a few hundred yards to a position more secure and better sheltered."[86]

The invaluable service rendered by John Buford in keeping in check the Confederate forces until the arrival of Reynolds and the First Corps enabled the impregnable heights south of the town of Gettysburg to be preserved for the Federals' use after the blue units could arrive and concentrate thereon. From these heights the successful battles of July 2 and 3 were fought by the Army of the Potomac.

Buford also sent Meade the first information that the army commander received of the clash at Gettysburg. This dispatch, sent before Buford was relieved by the arrival of the First Corps, read as follows:

> The enemy's forces are advancing on me at this point, and driving my pickets and skirmishers very rapidly. There is also a large force at Heidlersburg that is driving my pickets at that point from that direction. General Reynolds is advancing; and is within three miles of this point with his leading division. I am positive that the whole of A.P. Hill's force is advancing.[87]

Perhaps Buford knew almost as much of Hill's movements as did Lee. As the Confederate army commander, accompanied by Longstreet on the Chambersburg pike, reached the summit of the South Mountain range—passing Johnson's sweating troops toiling up the western slope—he suddenly heard the booming of cannon in the distance.[88] Lee displayed signs of annoyance and impatience at this unexpected firing, and acknowledged that he had been in the dark as to the Union movements since he had crossed the Potomac, owing to the absence of Stuart's cavalry.[89] Lee immediately bade Longstreet goodbye, and rode swiftly forward to Cashtown, where he met A.P. Hill. However, Hill could give the gray chieftain little additional or comforting information as to the nature of the distant firing.[90] Soon, to Lee's painful surprise, the sound of heavy musketry volleys was added to the distant rumble of artillery pieces.[91] To the trained ears of the Confederate leader, the battle seemed to be mushrooming alarmingly in size and intensity. It was all contrary to his wishes and expectations.

CHAPTER 4

Reynolds

Climaxes His Career

THE COMMANDER OF THE UNION LEFT WING WAS ANXIOUS TO
march to Buford's assistance with the leading elements of Doubleday's
First Corps. But before leaving Marsh Creek for Gettysburg early on
the morning of July 1, several duties occupied John Reynolds' attention. These he performed in his customary meticulous way. First he
read to Doubleday the messages he had received in recent hours. Then
Reynolds indicated to the First Corps leader the locations of the various units of the Army of the Potomac. Finally, he discussed the marching orders which these units had received, and pointed out their des-
tinations for the day's movements. Only then did the Left Wing
commander depart for the battlefield.[1]

Riding along the Emmitsburg road toward Gettysburg, Reynolds'
trained military eye could not have escaped noting the strong Cemetery Ridge heights south of the town, and at this time he apparently
formulated plans to keep the enemy away from these elevations until
the remainder of the Army of the Potomac could arrive and concentrate on them.[2] Upon entering Gettysburg, Reynolds met Peter Culp,
a Union scout, at the Eagle Hotel. After briefly conferring with him
about the developing situation, Reynolds asked Culp to direct him to
Buford's headquarters at the Seminary.[3]

There had been tenseness at Federal cavalry headquarters west of
Gettysburg during the early daylight hours on July 1. Buford's troopers were being hard pressed by the superior Confederate numbers, and
reinforcements were breathlessly awaited. Buford's signal officer had

been stationed in the cupola of the Seminary building, and was eagerly watching for the appearance of Reynolds and the infantry of the First Corps.[4] When the signal officer shouted down the news of Reynolds' approach, Buford rushed up into the cupola to see for himself.[5]

At 9:00 a.m., or a little thereafter,[6] Reynolds rode up to the Seminary. Dismounting, he called up to Buford in the cupola, "What's the matter, John?" "The devil's to pay!" Buford replied to his friend and superior.[7] Reynolds then asked Buford if he and his embattled cavalrymen could hold out until the infantry of Doubleday's First Corps could arrive. "I reckon I can," Buford answered.[8]

Reynolds then dispatched Captain Stephen Weld, an aide-de-camp, to General Meade with the following message, which the army commander received at 11:20 a.m.: "The enemy is advancing in strong force, and I fear he will get to the heights beyond the town before I can. I will fight him inch by inch, and if driven into the town I will barricade the streets, and hold him back as long as possible." "Good!" exclaimed Meade. "That is just like Reynolds, he will hold out to the bitter end." [9] Other orders were sent by Reynolds to Doubleday to hasten to the front.[10] Howard's Eleventh Corps was instructed to press forward with the utmost speed, and to move into position in reserve of

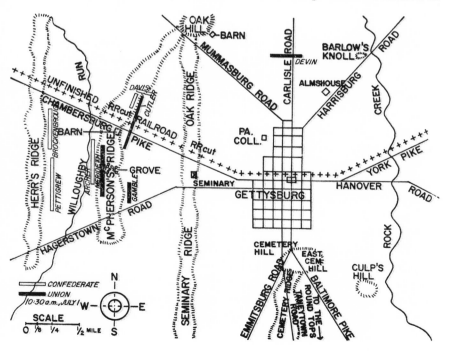

the First Corps, which would arrive on the field before the Eleventh.[11]

Reynolds' decision to fight west of the town was a momentous one. It also happened to be the correct one. For the Federals to have fallen back in the morning to the heights just south of Gettysburg would have been disastrous, in all probability. The Confederate forces, superior numerically to the Union forces present, and being augmented faster than the Northern troops, would have had the better part of the day to drive the Federals from the Cemetery heights, which would then have been occupied by the Southerners. In this position, the better-concentrated Army of Northern Virginia would be at the apex of the three roads to the south of town upon which the more widely-scattered National army was approaching Gettysburg. Additional hours of daylight would have been available for the Confederates, and defeat in detail of the Federal forces would have been quite likely. Probably the entire result of the battle and campaign would have been different. Hence, it can be seen that Reynolds' decision to sacrifice, if necessary, his First Corps, and even the Eleventh, while taking as heavy a toll of Lee's soldiers as possible, was the wise and soldierly move to make. About 8,200 infantrymen of the Union First Corps[12] were therefore soon to be pitted against almost three times that number of Confederates of Heth's, Pender's, and Rodes' divisions.

As Reynolds was conferring with Buford at the Seminary, the units of Doubleday's First Corps were marching swiftly along the Emmitsburg road toward Gettysburg. The sun was breaking through the early morning mist, and was forcing white, fleecy clouds up the side of Big Round Top.[13] The temperature was already mounting at a rapid rate. Leading the First Corps column was Brigadier General Lysander Cutler's Second Brigade of Wadsworth's First Division. Cutler was followed by Captain James A. Hall's Second Maine battery of artillery, and by the First Brigade—the famous "Iron Brigade" of Groveton renown—commanded by Brigadier General Solomon Meredith.

General Reynolds, directed possibly by constable John Burns,[14] rode out the Emmitsburg road to direct his approaching infantry to Buford's assistance. He met the head of the column at the N. Codori farm buildings, a little over a mile from town. There, in order to expedite the movement to succor Buford, Reynolds, seated upon his horse on the west side of the road, directed Wadsworth's division to oblique through the fields on the double-quick, in a direct line to the Seminary.[15]

The 76th New York regiment was in the advance of the column, and as it turned off of the road through the fields a number of fine cherry trees were passed, laden with fruit. The boys in the ranks eyed the trees eagerly, but remembered their orders against pilfering fruit from the farmers' orchards. As they were hesitating, with drooling mouths, their commanding officer, Major Andrew J. Grover, made a brief speech to the regiment concerning those cherry trees: "Boys, the General charges you to be very particular to keep strictly within the rules, and not meddle with those cherry *trees!* Be sure you don't break the *trees* down!" While the Major and other officers then turned their backs, the men of the regiment proceeded to denude the trees of cherries, although being careful not seriously to injure the *trees!*[16] During this brief pause at the Codori buildings, orderlies were met riding to the rear with dispatches. These couriers informed Wadsworth's men of the scarcely pleasant news that "the Rebs were thicker than blackberries beyond the hill."[17]

As the infantry left the road, the pioneers—foot soldiers detailed to clear the way of impediments—swinging their flashing axes, leveled the fences along the road and in the fields beyond.[18] Double-quicking across the fields, Wadsworth's division arrived at the Seminary, and was then rushed forward to the west along the Chambersburg pike. The blueclad infantrymen reached McPherson Ridge at approximately 10:00 a.m.[19] Buford's troopers had been compelled by this time to fall back to the rear, or easternmost, elevation of the ridge.[20] Cutler was the first to arrive on the field, followed immediately by Hall's 2nd Maine battery and then by Meredith's Iron Brigade.[21] These units numbered some 3,600 effectives[22] and were, at first contact, to be confronted with about the same number of enemy soldiers.

Reynolds personally placed Hall's battery in position on the Chambersburg pike on the westernmost crest of McPherson Ridge.[23] Hall relieved Calef's Battery A, 2nd U.S. Artillery. After instructing Wadsworth to place his three other regiments in position on the right (north) of the pike, Reynolds ordered the 95th New York (Colonel George H. Biddle) and the 14th Brooklyn (Colonel Edward B. Fowler) into position between the pike and McPherson's Grove.[24] These two regiments, comprising a demi-brigade under the command of

Fowler, were placed in this position to support Hall's battery, and to check Archer's left regiment—the 7th Tennessee (Lieutenant Colonel S.G. Shepard)—near the toll gate.[25] Advancing up the slope and through an orchard, these two regiments relieved the weary but undaunted troopers of Gamble's cavalry brigade, which had been contesting the ground for two hours with Archer. The 14th Brooklyn was to the right of the 95th New York. As they fell back, the carbineers shouted the following words of encouragement to the infantrymen moving forward: "We have got them now. Go in and give them hell!" [26] The timely arrival of the two Federal regiments at this point prevented the further menacing advance of Archer between the pike and McPherson's Grove.

Doubleday, riding forward to receive instructions from Reynolds, was directed to "hold on to" the Hagerstown road on the Union left, while Reynolds would "hold on to" the Chambersburg pike on the right.[27] Although no Confederate forces were to arrive via the Hagerstown road during the course of the day's battle, Doubleday nonetheless had apprehensions to this effect throughout his fight west of town.[28] He saw at once that the key position on that part of the field was the triangular-shaped McPherson's Grove, situated about halfway between the Chambersburg pike and the Hagerstown road.[29]

Now personal tragedy and military triumph capped the illustrious career of the Union Left Wing commander. Seeing the right regiments of Archer's brigade crossing Willoughby Run and advancing into the woods, Reynolds, accompanied by an orderly, Sergeant Charles H. Veil, escorted the 2nd Wisconsin (Colonel Lucius Fairchild) and possibly the 7th Wisconsin (Colonel William W. Robinson) forward into the grove.[30] Reynolds shouted to these soldiers, "Forward! men, forward! for God's sake, and drive those fellows out of the woods!" [31] While riding with these troops into the southeastern corner of the grove, and while turning around in his saddle to see how his other regiments were coming up, Reynolds was killed almost instantly by a minie ball—probably a stray shot. The bullet entered the back of the head of the forty-three-year-old general, and came out under the eye.[32] The time was approximately 10:15 a.m.[33] When he fell, Reynolds was in front of, and almost on a line with, the left of the 2nd Wisconsin and the right of the approaching 7th Wisconsin as they entered the grove.[34]

Upon the death of Reynolds, the command of the field devolved upon Abner Doubleday.[35] Fortunately, the bulk of the Federal troops did not see Reynolds fall.[36] As the lifeless body was carried off the field, captured Confederate soldiers of Archer's command "manifested their marked respect for the fallen Union General." [37] Reynolds was carried first to the Seminary and then to a small stone cottage on the Emmitsburg road at the edge of town.[38] The Left Wing commander had been one of the most distinguished and best-liked men of his rank in the Army of the Potomac.[39] His loss was a severe blow to Meade, who had relied heavily upon Reynolds since assuming command of the army.

Doubleday determined to continue the policy which his gallant predecessor had already laid out for him. He knew the vital importance of the great road-hub of Gettysburg, and the strategic value of the heights south of the town.[40] He would strive to make sure that Reynolds had not given his life in vain in his endeavor to hold back the hard-pressing Confederates until Meade's forces could arrive and concentrate on Cemetery Ridge.

CHAPTER 5

The First Affair
at the Railroad Cut

GENERAL WADSWORTH'S FIRST DIVISION OF SOME 4,000 FEDER-
al troops[1] had arrived on the field, as noted, at 10:00 a.m., and was
put into action on McPherson Ridge almost simultaneously on both
sides of the Chambersburg pike. While Reynolds was placing the 14th
Brooklyn and 95th New York in position on the ridge to the left
(south) of the road, Wadsworth had been instructed to deploy the
other three regiments of Cutler's brigade on the right (north) of the
railroad grading, which was almost 200 yards north of the pike.[2] Hall's
2nd Maine battery had arrived on the field a few minutes before Cutler's brigade, and had relieved Calef's battery, which was almost out
of ammunition.[3]

Without having had time to take the precaution of advancing a
skirmish line on reconnaissance, Wadsworth rushed the remaining
three regiments of Cutler's brigade into line of battle on McPherson
Ridge just north of the railroad grading. As the infantry relieved
Devin's cavalry brigade, the exhausted carbineers moved off to the
right to patrol the roads leading into the town from the north and east,
along which was expected the early arrival of Ewell's command.[4] The
three right regiments of Cutler's brigade were deployed as follows
from right to left: the 76th New York (Major Andrew J. Grover),
the 56th Pennsylvania (Colonel J.W. Hormann), and the 147th New
York (Lieutenant Colonel Francis C. Miller).[5] Of these three Union
regiments, the 147th New York was the last to get into line. Owing to
a delay in receiving orders, it was halted from three to five minutes

near the paling fence of McPherson's garden, on the south side of the pike, "a few rods east of the stone basement barn" of McPherson's.[6] The regiment then crossed to the north side of the pike, in the hollow draw between the two crests of McPherson Ridge, changed front to the left (west) and advanced up the slope to the westernmost crest of the ridge into line of battle, with the 56th Pennsylvania on its right-rear and the railroad grading on its left.[7]

Opposing Cutler was Davis' Fourth Brigade of Heth's division, minus the 11th Mississippi, which had been detached for guard duty with the wagon train of the division.[8] The two contending brigades each numbered about the same—some 2,000 effectives.[9] Davis deployed his regiments from right to left in the following order: the 42nd Mississippi (Colonel H.R. Miller), the 2nd Mississippi (Colonel J.M. Stone), and the 55th North Carolina (Colonel J.K. Conally).[10]

As Cutler's line approached the crest of the ridge, Davis' men were concealed in the high grass just over the brow.[11] When the heads of the Federals appeared over the crest, the Confederates greeted them with a murderous fire. So unexpected was the shooting from this quarter that Major Grover, commanding Cutler's right regiment—the 76th New York—at first thought it to be coming from Union troops who were blasting at him by mistake. Grover thus allowed the Southerners to pour home several musketry volleys on his right flank before returning the fire.[12] Furthermore, Cutler's right flank was in the air, and the 55th North Carolina was overlapping the right of the 76th New York.[13]

It was approximately 10:15 a.m.—before Cutler's regiments were fully aligned—when Davis' men opened fire upon them.[14] The 56th Pennsylvania was the first of the National infantry regiments to open fire.[15] Immediately afterward, the 76th New York and 147th New York fired their first volleys; and, in furious fighting, Davis' initial thrust was halted for the time being.[16] Almost instantly, in these opening fusilades, Major Grover, commanding the 76th New York, was struck and killed.[17] He was succeeded in command of the regiment by Captain John E. Cook. In this vicious half-hour combat, the 76th lost 234 officers and men out of 370 engaged.[18]

Meanwhile, the 147th New York, advancing through a wheatfield to the left of the other two regiments, and somewhat in advance of their line, moved up the slope of the westernmost crest of McPherson Ridge against a galling fire from the 42nd and 2nd Mississippi regiments. The men were falling as fast as the full wheatheads in the hail of lead. The 147th New York pushed on until it was about six or eight rods in the rear and to the right of Hall's 2nd Maine battery, which was posted just across the railroad grading from it. Hall was working his guns feverishly, and between them the Federal infantry and artillery halted the Confederates for a short time.[19]

But the Southerners were undaunted. After the momentary check, Davis renewed his attack. The 42nd and 2nd Mississippi attacked Cutler in front (from the west), while the 55th North Carolina, marching past Cutler's right flank, wheeled to the south and took the 76th New York in flank, threatening its rear.[20] The enfilading fire of the 55th North Carolina was most effective, and forced drastic action on the part of the Nationals to avoid annihilation. After several unsuccessful attempts, the right wing of the 76th New York managed to change front to the right (north) to meet this fire—a most difficult and trying maneuver to accomplish under fire in the immediate presence of the enemy.[21] But the Confederate pressure remained unrelenting.

Seeing Cutler's three right regiments thus menaced, Wadsworth felt he had no alternative but to order the brigade back to Seminary Ridge. These orders, however, failed to reach the 147th New York, whose left was on the railroad grading, or the 14th Brooklyn and 95th New York, to the left of the pike.[22] Thus, the right flank of these three regiments was threatened when the 76th New York and 56th Pennsylvania, obeying Wadsworth's order, withdrew swiftly to the shelter of Seminary Ridge.

In about half an hour, Hall's 2nd Maine battery, located between the pike and the railroad grading on the westernmost crest of McPherson Ridge, was charged by Davis' right regiments, which were protected by the railroad fill that traverses Willoughby Run valley.[23] The Confederates, approaching to within sixty paces of Hall's right piece, compelled the battery commander to change front to the right (north) with his center and right sections, which then opened with canister on the advancing graycoats. The left section continued to fire on the Confederate batteries behind the crest of Herr Ridge.[24] Hall lost twenty-two men killed and wounded, and thirty-four horses.[25] Although still supported on his right by the 147th New York,[26] he was impelled nonetheless to retire his battery from the field by sections,[27] and was forced temporarily to abandon the gun on the extreme *left* at the pike.[28] Had the 147th not held its ground in close support of the 2nd Maine battery, Hall's guns in all probability would have been captured, since the Confederates of Davis' brigade were almost on top of him.[29] The 76th New York and 56th Pennsylvania fell back in fairly good order to the eastern slope of Seminary Ridge near the railroad grading, while Hall and the 147th New York alone were contesting the ground with Davis.[30]

During the withdrawal of Hall's battery, there occurred one of those sublime acts of personal heroism found on the battlefield. One of the guns was being charged closely by the Confederates, when an artilleryman finally managed to hitch the horses to the gun and prepared to mount and ride off with the piece to safety. A Southern lieutenant placed his hand on the cannon, and demanded that the Federal gunner surrender the piece. The artilleryman, however, grabbed the reins and prepared to dash off to the rear, heedless of the warning to yield. The gray officer, seeing his determined foe about to ride off anyhow, placed a cocked revolver at the gunner's head, and reiterated his demand that the Federal soldier capitulate. Nonetheless, determined to save the piece if possible, the cannoneer made a sudden dash forward. The Confederate officer took aim and shot him in the back at close range. But the gritty Union artilleryman managed to stay astride the horse and bring the gun safely within his own lines, before toppling to the ground. He was listed simply as "killed in action." [31]

Another incident, illustrative of the melodramatic aura of the period as well as of the desperate courage which abounded on both sides during this fierce clash, occurred in the front line of the 6th Wisconsin when that regiment was moving to halt Davis at the railroad cut. A young soldier of manly bearing approached Lieutenant Colonel Rufus R. Dawes, commanding the regiment, came to attention, and saluted. Expecting that the man had a message to communicate, the Colonel turned toward him, when the soldier said, in deliberate and measured words, "Tell my friends at home I died like a man and a soldier!" He then ripped open his coat with both hands, revealing a ghastly chest wound, and fell dead at the feet of the colonel.[32]

While several of Cutler's regiments rallied and regrouped behind Seminary Ridge, an episode of cowardice occurred which demonstrated that, amidst numerous scenes of gallantry, there were nonetheless a few cases of serious deficiencies in intestinal fortitude. As the 76th New York approached Seminary Ridge in its temporary retrograde movement, Captain Pierce, Company A, discovered a man neatly rolled up in a blanket behind a stone wall, his head completely covered. The captain instructed the man to get up at once and take his place in the ranks. The soldier said that he couldn't move, that he was wounded. When asked where, he replied in his side. An inspection revealed no wound. The soldier kept changing the location of the wound, but after finding no blood the exasperated Captain shouted to the cringing faintheart, "Get up, you coward! Fall in!" The terrified man sprang to his feet and rushed into the front line of the regiment, where the stalwarts of Company A kept him for the remainder of the bloody day.[33]

After the withdrawal of the 76th New York and 56th Pennsylvania from the right and Hall's 2nd Maine battery from the left, the 147th New York, not having received the order to retreat, continued to fight on alone in the wheatfield just north of the railroad grading. Approaching from the west was the 42nd Mississippi, and from the north, on the 147th's right flank, the 2nd Mississippi.[34] At this time, Lieutenant Colonel Miller, commanding the 147th New York, was hit in the throat and the command devolved upon Major George Harney.[35] The right companies of the 147th, being menaced on their right flank, changed front to the north behind a rail fence in the field, and opened fire against the 2nd Mississippi.[36] The two opposing lines were at times no more than six or eight rods apart.[37] The 2nd Mississippi was soon joined on its left by the 55th North Carolina, which was now in the right-rear of the isolated 147th New York. Here, under a galling fire, a Confederate officer corrected the alignment of his command as cooly as if on dress parade. The spectacle was said by some Union officers to have been the finest they had seen during the war.[38] At this time, a blueclad officer approached the maelstrom from Seminary Ridge, and waved his cap for the 147th to retire from its isolated and dangerous position. This order was augmented by one delivered by Wadsworth's adjutant general, Captain T.E. Ellsworth, who rode daringly into the angle formed by the two hard-pressed wings of the 147th.[39]

The unordered but invaluable fight of the 147th New York delayed Davis for sufficient minutes to enable Colonel Fowler's 14th Brooklyn and 95th New York, on the left (south) of the pike, to be brought over to thwart Davis a few moments later in the affair at the railroad cut, about to be described. Had this stand of the 147th not been made, it seems likely that Hall's battery would have been captured, and the right and rear of Meredith's Iron Brigade menaced at the same time it was heavily engaged with Archer in its front.

46

The right wing of the 147th New York was finally obliged to fall back on the north side of the railroad to Seminary Ridge, where it was reformed with the other two regiments. The left wing of the 147th, accompanied by the regimental colors, fell back along the pike to Seminary Ridge, where it was soon reunited with the right wing of the regiment.[40] During this vicious thirty-minute combat on McPherson Ridge, the 147th New York lost 220 men killed and wounded out of 380 engaged. The casualties of the regiment for the whole day would total 301.[41] It was later found that the first order for the 147th to withdraw was never carried out because the regiment's commander, Lieutenant Colonel Miller, was shot in the throat just as he was about to transmit the order for execution. Therefore, his successor, Major Harney, not having received any order to retire, assumed that he was expected to fight on that line until compelled to fall back.[42] His stand with the 147th New York was a highlight of the first day's battle.

As the left wing of the 147th New York moved along the Chambersburg pike in its withdrawal to Seminary Ridge, the color-bearer, Sergeant William A. Wyburn, was struck by a bullet and fell on the colors as if dead. Captain Volney J. Pierce attempted to pull the color staff away from him, but the supposedly-dying Sergeant clung to it with grim tenacity. The captain ordered him to release his grasp on it at once. But, to the astonishment of the officer, Wyburn said, "Hold on, I will be up in a minute." He then rolled over and staggered to his feet and carried the colors throughout the battle. Wyburn was commissioned for his bravery and devotion.[43]

Meanwhile, Cutler's other regiments were covering themselves with glory. Seeing the danger to their exposed right, and being relieved of their duties in their front by the arrival of Meredith's Iron Brigade, Cutler's 14th Brooklyn and 95th New York, posted between the pike and McPherson's Grove, performed an about-face and commenced marching eastward. Davis, after repulsing Cutler's three right regiments, was also marching eastward, north of the railroad grading, in pursuit of the three Federal regiments. As Colonel Fowler's 14th Brooklyn and 95th New York suddenly changed front to the north and began moving against Davis' right, these Confederates changed front quickly to the right (south), and took shelter in the deep railroad cut at the easterly crest of McPherson Ridge.[44] Davis felt that from the railroad cut, in almost complete safety, he could bring to bear a heavy fire on the two National regiments. With the 14th

Brooklyn on the left and the 95th New York on the right, Fowler's men crouched along the southern edge of the pike. Here they were soon joined on their right by the Iron Brigade's 6th Wisconsin (Lieutenant Colonel Rufus R. Dawes), which had been in reserve first at the Seminary and then to the left-rear of Meredith's left regiment.[45]

At the command from Colonel Fowler, the three Union regiments, with a cheer, surged forward across the fences along the pike. As they did so, they were greeted with a storm of lead from Davis' men, some of whom were lying down on the southern rim of the railroad cut, and the rest of whom were in the cut itself.[46] The units of Davis which were in the cut were the 2nd Mississippi, in the eastern part, and the 42nd Mississippi, in the western section.[47] In this charge to the cut, of the 420 men who left the pike in the 6th Wisconsin only about 240 remained unhurt when it reached the railroad grading, only 175 paces from the road.[48] A hand-to-hand combat between the advancing Federals and those Confederates along the southern rim of the cut resulted in the latter being driven back into the cut.[49]

Early in the clash at the railroad cut, Colonel Biddle, commanding the 95th New York, was wounded and forced to retire from the field. He was succeeded in command of the regiment by Major Edward Pye, who was aided by the senior captain, James Creney.[50] The 6th Wisconsin lost all of its color-guard, killed and wounded, and the only way in which Colonel Dawes could keep his command together was by continually shouting, "Close up on that color!" Finally, two companies of the 6th, under Adjutant Brooks, were thrown across the eastern end of the cut, thus enfilading the two Confederate regiments therein. The colors of the 2nd Mississippi in the cut proved to be a tempting prize, and Corporal Eggleston, Company H, 6th Wisconsin, leaped forward to seize them. He was shot dead the moment his hand touched the Confederate flag. Furious at the slaying of his comrade, Private Anderson swung his clubbed musket and, with a terrific blow, split the skull of the graycoat who had dispatched Eggleston.[51] The colors of the 2nd Mississippi were then seized by Corporal Francis A. Waller of the 6th Wisconsin.[52]

Colonel Dawes was master of the situation. From the top of the cut he demanded that the Confederates below surrender or face a crushing fire in front and flank. Seeing the hopelessness of their plight, Major John A. Blair of the 2nd Mississippi and about 250 men capitulated to Dawes.[53] The latter collected "a bundle" of swords from yielding

48

Southern officers. Further to the Union left, the 95th New York and 14th Brooklyn also took prisoners. But some Confederates at the western end of the cut succeeded in making good their escape. Dawes, however, picked up "at least 1,000 abandoned Confederate muskets" in the cut.[54] At the time of the Southern repulse—about 11:00 a.m.[55]— Davis' brigade had lost all of its field officers but two in this fearful debacle.[56]

After the termination of the action at the cut, one of Hall's officers brought up horses and a limber, and moved an artillery piece into position at the eastern end of the cut.[57] This would permit the Federals to enfilade any new Confederate line of battle which might reappear along the railroad grading. Upon the conclusion of the successful Union action at the cut, Cutler's three badly mauled regiments—the 76th New York, the 56th Pennsylvania, and the 147th New York— which had regrouped near the railroad grading behind Seminary Ridge, came forward and assumed their position north of the cut on the more easterly crest of McPherson Ridge.[58] Furthermore, the gun which Hall had been obliged to abandon to the enemy was recaptured.[59] The fighting then subsided for a time in this portion of the field,[60] with Wadsworth so far victorious over his opponents.

Davis' shattered regiments fell back in disorder to Herr Ridge. They were in such a crippled condition that Heth hesitated to bring them into action again that day.[61] However, later in the afternoon, Davis' remnants aided Brockenbrough in the final Confederate attack on Doubleday.[62]

In this first infantry clash of the battle, the Confederates "found out that their sudden attacks *en masse* were more dangerous and difficult of execution along the open country of Pennsylvania, than among the thickly wooded settlements of Virginia, where they did not stand in dread of slanting fires." [63] In fact, the First Day's Battle of Gettysburg illustrates better than most combats of the Civil War the employment of the tactical flank attack with its corresponding enfilading fire and crossfire on two fronts. Both sides strove to use this maneuver frequently on the first day, and the side which succeeded first in outflanking its foe won the joust in that section of the field.

CHAPTER 6

The Iron Brigade

in McPherson Grove

WHILE THE FEDERALS WERE STRIVING AND FINALLY WINNING out to the north of the Chambersburg pike, their fortunes were taking a similar turn to the south of that road during the forenoon of July 1st. It will be remembered that Wadsworth's Union division had turned off the Emmitsburg road at the Codori buildings about 9:30 a.m. Cutler's Second Brigade and Hall's 2nd Maine battery, leading the column, had been followed through the fields to McPherson Ridge by Brigadier General Solomon Meredith's First Brigade—the so-called "Iron Brigade." As Cutler and Hall were swinging into action north of the Chambersburg pike, Meredith's command was coming up on the left (south) of the road, in the rear (east) of McPherson's Grove. Nearing the woods, the Iron Brigade encountered some stray solid-shot, which the Confederate batteries just beyond the crest of Herr Ridge were propelling through the tree-tops above the heads of the Federals.[1] Just as Meredith was going into action, Doubleday himself arrived. From daybreak, the latter had been assembling and starting his First Corps units from Marsh Creek to follow Reynolds to Gettysburg, and had been obliged to ride forward swiftly in order to reach the field in time for the opening of the Iron Brigade's combat in Mc-Pherson's Grove.[2]

The Iron Brigade had a reputation in both armies for its staunch fighting qualities and for its unusual headgear. When the brigade was mustered into Federal service, the stock of regular kepi-type caps was temporarily exhausted, and the men of this brigade were issued black felt hats with wide brims. After the splendid fight of the Iron Brigade near Groveton, Virginia, during the Second Manassas campaign, the men of the brigade came to be known as "The Black Hats." [3] It might be noted that one of the regiments now attached to the Iron Brigade —the 24th Michigan (Colonel Henry A. Morrow)—was entering its maiden battle.[4] It was to acquit itself, however, in a manner worthy of the other seasoned regiments of this notable brigade.

Advancing at the double-quick, Meredith relieved the hard-pressed troopers of Gamble's cavalry brigade.[5] Gamble then formed on Meredith's left, toward the Hagerstown road, where he was neutralized by Archer's later detachment of the 5th Alabama battalion to watch him.[6] Doubleday, assisting Reynolds in deploying the Iron Brigade regiments before Reynolds' demise, beseeched the Federal soldiers as they moved past him to hold the grove "at all hazards." Their reply to him was, "If we cannot hold it, where will you find the men who can?" [7]

Rushing into the woods, the soldiers of the Iron Brigade were obliged to load their muskets and fix bayonets on the run, so desperate was their need to halt Archer's advance across Willoughby Run.[8] Meredith's right regiment, the 2nd Wisconsin (Colonel Lucius Fairchild), was slightly in advance of the regiments on its left. It dashed into the right edge of the grove, its right companies passing through the grounds of the McPherson farmhouse.[9] Meredith's alignment from right to left was as follows: the 2nd Wisconsin, the 7th Wisconsin (Colonel William W. Robinson), the 19th Indiana (Colonel Samuel J. Williams), and the 24th Michigan.[10]

The troops opposing Meredith were regiments of Brigadier General James J. Archer's Third Brigade, Heth's division. Archer's deployment was as follows from right to left: the 1st Tennessee (Major Felix G. Buchanan), the 13th Alabama (Colonel B.D. Fry), the 5th Alabama battalion (Major A.S. Van de Graaff), the 14th Tennessee (Captain B.L. Phillips), and the 7th Tennessee (Lieutenant Colonel S.G. Shepard).[11]

With their famed high-pitched, staccato yelp, Archer's men surged across Willoughby Run and, moving up the western slope of McPherson Ridge into the grove, ran head-on into Meredith's advancing regiments.[12] The clash was instant and desperate. Archer got in the first volley, a terribly effective one, when the two lines were but forty or fifty yards apart.[13] In this initial fire, Meredith, the commander of the Iron Brigade, was wounded by the fragments of a shell, "which exploded in front of his horse." The command of the brigade then devolved upon Colonel William W. Robinson, of the 7th Wisconsin, who was in turn succeeded in the command of his regiment by Major Mark Finnicum.[14] The blue line was staggered for a moment, but immediately pressed on. Archer's men, recognizing the distinctive headgear of their opponents, cried with dismay, "There are those damned black-hatted fellows again! 'Taint no militia. It's the Army of the Potomac!" [15] Apparently these Confederates had been told that they would encounter only hastily gathered militiamen.

The fight was bruising and cruel. The 24th Michigan and 19th Indiana, moving up in part through the fields bordering on the southern edge of McPherson Grove, advanced their front faster than the regiments on their right, which had to penetrate the dense woods.[16] The 24th and 19th then wheeled to the right (north) and opened fire. Since Meredith's left overlapped Archer's right, the latter found himself caught between the two sides of a right angle.[17] He was in a cramped position under the brow of McPherson Ridge, with Willoughby Run in his immediate rear, and with his right regiment, the 1st Tennessee, completely enveloped on its right-rear.[18]

Against a crushing frontal and flank fire, Archer's line slowly and grudgingly retired from its point of farthest advance near the center of the grove, and withdrew finally across Willoughby Run, closely pressed by Meredith's victorious regiments.[19] During the action on McPherson Ridge, the flag of the 24th Michigan was downed no less than fourteen times, as nine men of the regimental color-guard were killed and wounded. Sergeant Abel Peck, the original color-bearer of the regiment, was killed almost as soon as contact was made with Archer's soldiers.

Pursuing the retreating Southerners, the four Iron Brigade regiments swept across Willoughby Run and up the slope some 100 yards beyond.[20] Several hundred grayclad prisoners were taken.[21] Among those captured, about thirty paces west of the run,[22] behind a clump of willows,[23] was General Archer himself, who was exhausted by the extreme heat and by strenuous exertion.[24] Archer was overtaken and actually captured by Private Patrick Maloney, of Company G, 2nd Wisconsin;[25] but the General offered his sword to Captain Charles Dow, standing nearby.[26] Dow replied, "Keep your sword, General, and go to the rear; one sword is all I need on this line." [27] Archer finally delivered up his sword to Lieutenant D.B. Bailey, an insistent and somewhat belligerent aide on Meredith's staff.[28] The first general-grade Confederate officer captured since Lee had assumed command of the Army of Northern Virginia,[29] Archer was brought before Doubleday, who recognized him as an old West Point classmate. With extended hand, Doubleday greeted him, saying, "Good morning, Archer! How are you? I am glad to see you!" The disgruntled Southerner, however, refused to shake hands with the Union First Corps commander, and snapped, "Well, I am not glad to see you, by a damned sight, Doubleday." [30] The command of Archer's brigade devolved upon Colonel B.D. Fry, of the 13th Alabama.[31]

The costly advance and repulse of Archer was followed by the placing of his remnants on the extreme right of the Confederate line to guard against a flank attack by Gamble's Union cavalry brigade, near the Hagerstown road.[32] Archer's brigade had been so badly cut up that it was of little service to Heth for the remainder of the day's battle. The combat between the Iron Brigade and Archer had lasted barely an hour; yet an example of the nature of the severe fighting on this portion of the field before noon is shown by the shooting down of 116 men in the 2nd Wisconsin—a loss of thirty-eight percent.[33]

Doubleday, seeing that the Iron Brigade regiments, pursuing the Confederates across Willoughby Run, were becoming too far advanced and exposed, ordered them back to the stronger position in McPherson Grove,[34] but left a skirmish line along the bushes on the bank of Willoughby Run.[35] In the realignment in the grove, the 7th Wisconsin moved to the right of the brigade, the 2nd Wisconsin was placed on the left of the 7th, the 19th Indiana changed places with the 24th Michigan, the 19th now being on the extreme left of the Iron Brigade, and the 24th Michigan on the left of the 2nd Wisconsin.[36] The right wing of the 24th Michigan bent back a little to connect with the left of the 2nd Wisconsin in the grove, thus forming a slightly convex line toward the large Confederate forces to the west.[37]

Quiet now ruled the field of strife. As the lull following the clash between Meredith and Archer continued,[38] Heth regrouped his four brigades for a new onslaught. Reinforcements were eagerly awaited by both sides. In the meantime, there was only desultory fighting along the skirmish lines, and at times fairly heavy firing from the Confederate artillery batteries behind the crest of Herr Ridge.[39] While Hurt's two effective Whitworth guns, just south of the pike, were lobbing projectiles on the Federals in McPherson's Grove,[40] Captain V. Maurin's Donaldsonville artillery battery of Garnett's battalion,

Heth's division, relieved one of the batteries of Pegram's battalion which had expended its ammunition.[41] The Confederate artillerymen were using lunettes and foxholes so as to better protect themselves and their guns from Union counterbattery fire.[42]

While all this fighting was going on in the morning of July 1st, the National commander, as well as the Confederate, was absent. Doubleday was expecting Meade momentarily to ride to the front himself to ascertain personally what was transpiring.[43] But the Federal leader was not to make his appearance on the field until after midnight, although he was only fourteen miles away at army headquarters at Taneytown. Lee, who was to the west on the Chambersburg pike, was not to arrive on the field until the late afternoon, when the combat was largely over for the day. Hence, the fate of the day, and perhaps of the whole battle and the campaign itself, rested in the hands of aggressive subordinates. Theirs was a stupendous responsibility.

CHAPTER 7

Reinforcements
Come Forward

THE ONE THING WHICH COMMANDERS IN BATTLE EVER LOOK FOR is reinforcements. And it was true of Doubleday and Heth in the late morning hours of 1 July 1863. In the first fierce infantry clash just west of Gettysburg, Cutler's and Meredith's brigades of Wadsworth's Union division had thus far won a decided advantage over two of Heth's brigades—Davis' and Archer's—and had driven them back in confusion. Heth still had two additional brigades of his division to commit to battle, and he knew that behind him to the west on the Chambersburg pike, within supporting distance, was the strong division of Pender. Also, Heth was aware that powerful elements of Ewell's Second Corps were expected to arrive shortly from the north and northeast, which would place them on the right flank or right-rear of the Federal forces on McPherson Ridge then contending with Heth. On his part, Doubleday realized the vast forces converging against him, and looked anxiously for the arrival on the field from the south of the remainder of his own First Corps, as well as for the expected appearance of Howard's Eleventh Corps from the same direction. The fate of the day might well depend upon which side's reinforcements arrived first, and exactly where upon the field they could be quickly committed to battle. Meantime, the lull which had occurred in the combat about 11:00 a.m. continued, broken only by sporadic artillery firing.

Finally—and it must have seemed like hours to the tense Union commanders already fighting—about 11:15 a.m. or a little later,[1] the remaining divisions of Doubleday's corps arrived on the field. These were Brigadier General John C. Robinson's Second Division and Brigadier General Thomas A. Rowley's Third Division. The two infantry divisions—numbering together about 5,800 to 6,000 men[2]—were accompanied by the four artillery batteries of Colonel Charles S. Wainwright's First Corps artillery brigade.[3] These batteries were Captain Gilbert H. Reynolds' Battery L, 1st New York Light Artillery, four three-inch rifles;[4] the 5th Maine Light Battery, commanded by Captain Greenleaf T. Stevens, six twelve-pounder bronze Napoleons;[5] Battery B, 1st Pennsylvania Light Artillery, Captain James H. Cooper commanding, four three-inch rifles;[6] and Lieutenant James Stewart's Battery B, 4th United States (Regular Army) Artillery, six Napoleons.[7]

It was determined by Doubleday to hold Robinson's division in reserve at the Seminary for the time being. Several of Ewell's Confederate divisions were known to be approaching Gettysburg from the north and northeast, and, should Howard's arrival with the Federal Eleventh Corps be delayed, Robinson would be needed to oppose Ewell's advance and consequent threat to the right flank and rear of the Union troops then fighting Heth on McPherson Ridge. But while Robinson was left to cool his heels for the moment at the Seminary, Doubleday did send forward the First Brigade of Rowley's division, commanded by Colonel Chapman Biddle, and the Second Brigade, led by Colonel Roy Stone, to McPherson Ridge to assist Wadsworth. The Third Brigade of the division, commanded by Brigadier General George J. Stannard, was absent on detached duty.

Having arrived at the grove adjoining the western face of the Seminary building, Stone's brigade was halted for a short time to allow the men to catch their breath.[8] The brigade numbered approximately 1,315 effectives.[9] While resting for a few moments at the Seminary, Stone's soldiers were addressed by Rowley and Doubleday, who reminded them that they were on the soil of their native Pennsylvania, and that the eyes of the world were upon them.[10] As the brigade prepared to move forward from the Seminary to McPherson Ridge, the order was given to unsling knapsacks. Then Colonel Langhorne Wister, commanding the 150th Pennsylvania, gave the order, "Forward!" when a chorus of voices reminded him that he had forgotten to give first the order to load muskets. This operation was then executed amidst some merriment and banter on the parts of both the Colonel and the men in the ranks.[11]

It was decided to split Rowley's division: Stone's brigade was deployed about 11:30 a.m. on the western crest of McPherson Ridge, connecting with Meredith's right near the grove, and with its own right on the Chambersburg pike;[12] while Biddle's brigade was ordered into position at about the same time on Meredith's left-rear, on the eastern crest of McPherson Ridge, with its left extending toward, but by no means reaching, the Hagerstown road.[13] However, before Biddle finally got in the position where Doubleday wanted him, several complicated movements were performed.

Biddle's brigade first marched out the Hagerstown road until it reached the ridge on the *western* side of Willoughby Run. There it was halted in a piece of woods, and put into line of battle in the road, facing northward, with its right near the run.[14] The brigade then marched northward some 300 yards in the direction of the Finnefrock buildings; and then, discovering itself in the presence of large enemy infantry and artillery forces, moved by the right flank eastward across Willoughby Run between the Hagerstown road and the Herbst buildings. The brigade noticed that some of Gamble's cavalrymen were still jousting with Confederate skirmishers. Biddle then moved to the crest of McPherson Ridge between the grove and the Hagerstown road, where he deployed into line of battle in the open fields, facing westward toward the run, with the Iron Brigade to his right-front.[15] The 151st Pennsylvania (Lieutenant Colonel George F. McFarland) had been left temporarily in reserve at the Seminary.[16] Biddle's other three regiments were posted as follows from right to left: the 142nd Pennsylvania (Colonel Robert P. Cummins), the 80th New York State Militia (Colonel Theodore B. Gates), and the 121st Pennsylvania (Major Alexander Biddle).[17] Cooper's guns came into battery between the 80th New York and the 142nd Pennsylvania,[18] and Gamble's troopers took position to the left of and slightly in front of Biddle's left flank.[19]

Then, after taking position as indicated, Biddle's brigade, for reasons unknown, was ordered down into the ravine of Willoughby Run. The Nationals marched westward, unsupported, a short distance to reach this low area. Here, in a cramped position, Biddle received a heavy fire from the Confederates, stationed in a grain field and behind a fence on the western side of the run. The Federals were unable to reply to these enemy volleys, and the brigade was soon ordered back to its original position on the crest of McPherson Ridge. Thus far, while Biddle had not distinguished himself in the direction of his brigade, it was largely the fault of Rowley, who seems to have exercised little effective control of his brigades, was possibly drunk, and who was later court-martialed.[20]

It should be noted that, although Biddle's left appeared to be protected by the remnants of Gamble's cavalry brigade, such was really not the case. This was due to the fact that, later in the afternoon, Lane's Confederate brigade was able to neutralize Gamble, thus permitting Perrin's brigade to swing around Biddle's left and then to "roll up his line." [21] Hence, with his left regiment, the 121st Pennsylvania, having no natural defensive position on which to rest its left, Biddle's left flank may be said to have been in the air, despite Gamble's presence. The 121st was instructed to lie down in the grass just behind the crest of the ridge in order better to escape detection, and thereby perhaps to suffer less severely from enemy artillery fire from Herr Ridge to the west.[22] The Confederate artillery practice was particularly heavy at this time, with ten batteries in position just beyond the crest of Herr Ridge.[23]

The interval in Biddle's brigade made by Cooper's battery caused Colonel Biddle to direct Colonel Gates of the 80th New York to assume command of the left wing of the brigade, including his own 80th and the 121st Pennsylvania, thus forming a demi-brigade. Biddle, the overall commander of the brigade, retained direction of the 142nd Pennsylvania and of the soon-to-arrive 151st Pennsylvania. This was a sound, expedient decision on the part of Biddle, given the situation he was to face later in the afternoon. The two wings of his brigade were not to be reunited until about 4:00 p.m. on Seminary Ridge, near the close of the day's struggle.[24]

Meanwhile, before the renewal of the combat in earnest, Doubleday's artillery was being juggled in order to bolster the Union infantry. Calef's battery, after replenishing its ammunition, relieved Hall's battery in the Chambersburg pike on the western crest of McPherson Ridge.[25] Calef, in turn, was soon relieved by Reynold's battery, which had been parked previously in a field near the Seminary.[26] Early in the fight, while this battery was going into action, Captain

Reynolds was not only wounded in the left side, but suffered the loss also of his left eye, and the command of his guns devolved upon Lieutenant George Breck. Reynolds, although in great pain, refused to leave the field, and remained at his cannon, inspiring his men to greater effort.[27] The positions of this battery were as follows: Lieutenant Wilber, with one section of the battery, was in the orchard just south of the McPherson buildings; the other four pieces were sent to the south of the grove to support Biddle's brigade.[28] Colonel Wainwright, commanding the artillery brigade of the First Corps, placed his other batteries in the following positions: Cooper's battery, as noted, was posted in an oatfield approximately 350 yards south of the Chambersburg pike, supporting Biddle; Stewart's battery was stationed on both sides of the railroad cut at Seminary Ridge; and Stevens' battery was placed in position near the Seminary.[29]

And to the north of McPherson's Grove Doubleday's line was being augmented also. Stone's Pennsylvania "Bucktail" brigade[30] was hustled out from the Seminary to take position on the westerly crest of Mc-Pherson Ridge, between the Chambersburg pike and the grove. As they deployed into line of battle, the Bucktails chanted, "We have come to stay!"[31] and many of them remained forever at Gettysburg. When Stone arrived, Cutler's brigade had already returned to its initial position on the easterly crest of McPherson Ridge, north of the pike.[32] It should be noted that this more easterly position of Cutler was in line with Biddle's brigade, well to the south; but it was to the right-rear of Stone and Meredith, who were on the westerly crest of the ridge. It must further be remembered that, while Stone's and Biddle's brigades were taking position on McPherson Ridge, Robinson's division remained in reserve at the Seminary, where barricades were thrown up in the woods in front of the western face of the Seminary building.[33]

Stone deployed his regiments from right to left as follows: the 149th Pennsylvania (Lieutenant Colonel Walton Dwight), between Mc-Pherson's stone-basement barn and the Chambersburg pike; the 143rd Pennsylvania (Colonel Edmund L. Dana), in the lane between Mc-Pherson's house and barn, in the center of the brigade; and the 150th Pennsylvania (Colonel Langhorne Wister), on the left of the brigade, between the house and the northern edge of McPherson's Grove.[34] The three regiments faced west at first, the brigade front being perpendicular to the pike. A small quarry was immediately in front of the center of the brigade, and this formed an obstacle that compelled some of the Confederate attackers later in the day to oblique to the south, toward McPherson's Grove.[35]

Immediately upon deployment, Stone ordered a skirmish line to be thrown forward to watch for any enemy advance across Willoughby Run. This line was formed by detaching one company from each regiment.[36] These pickets soon engaged similarly deployed soldiers in gray on the western slope of McPherson Ridge, along a fence, and drove the Southerners back across the run. The infantrymen in the hostile skirmish lines then plied their wares vigorously across the waters of the little stream.[37]

A little later in the afternoon, after the arrival of Rodes' Confederate batteries on Oak Hill, north of the line of the Bucktails, and after Cutler's brigade was compelled to fall back again to Seminary Ridge owing to enemy infantry pressure and the enfilading fire from these cannon, Stone was obliged to shift the positions of his three regiments.[38] The 150th Pennsylvania would continue to face westward along the westerly slope and crest of McPherson Ridge, between the pike and the grove; the 149th Pennsylvania's left wing would join the right flank of the 150th, both facing westward, while the right wing of the 149th would be refused—that is, bent backward at an angle—eastwardly along the pike facing northward, at right angles to the left wing of the regiment on the ridge; and the 143rd Pennsylvania would extend the line along the pike to the right of the 149th.[39] These movements would be made under a destructive cross-fire from the Confederate guns to the west on Herr Ridge (especially Brander's battery) and from those on Oak Hill to the north.[40] Against the artillery fire of approximately sixty enemy guns, Doubleday would be able to muster but thirty-six Federal pieces.[41] However, since no immediate Confederate assault was evident when Stone's brigade first deployed, Colonel Wister ordered the 150th Pennsylvania to take temporary shelter from the hot Southern artillery fire by moving to the cover of the McPherson stone barn.[42]

It was at this time, just as the 150th Pennsylvania was about to move to the shelter of the barn, that a famous incident occurred—one witnessed but rarely on the American field of battle since the days of the Revolutionary War. The men of the 150th noticed a singular figure approaching the battlefield from the direction of town. The man wore a dark, swallow-tail coat, with shiny metal buttons, a light buff-colored vest, and dark trousers. He carried a musket at "trail arms." As he neared the artillery-swept position of McPherson Ridge, he commanded the attention and respect, if incredulity, of the men in the Union ranks. This man was seventy-year-old John Burns, patriot of the War of 1812, in which he had fought with Winfield Scott at Lundy's Lane. Asking for the commander of the 150th Pennsylvania, Burns requested permission to fight in the line of battle. After displaying to the colonel his coat-pockets bulging with ammunition, he was granted permission, the colonel saying that he wished there were more patriotic Northern citizens like him. Burns fought for a brief time with the 150th Pennsylvania, then moved into the shade of the grove and assisted the men of the 7th Wisconsin and 24th Michigan of the Iron Brigade. Eyewitnesses attested to the old man's coolness and deliberation under fire, saying that he exchanged shots with the foe until he was wounded three times, and disabled. Only then was he carried to the town, where his unusual physical constitution, despite his advanced age, pulled him through. His presence and bearing were an inspiration to the boys in blue. John Burns won special recognition and high tribute in Doubleday's official report of the battle.[43]

When the thunder from the first cannon of the battle was heard, Brigadier General John C. Robinson's Second Division of Doubleday's First Corps was three miles from the battlefield.[44] Robinson began at once to gather his units into marching order and start them for the field. The men were urged forward at a faster cadence by the artillery reports, as well as by false rumors to the effect that their beloved former army commander, Major General George B. McClellan, was again in command of the Army of the Potomac.[45]

At a little after 11:00 a.m., Robinson's command arrived at the Seminary,[46] where it was halted for a short time by Doubleday to act as his reserve. The First Brigade of this division, commanded by Brigadier General Gabriel R. Paul, was put to work immediately constructing temporary breastworks in the grove in front of the western face of the Seminary building.[47] The usefulness of these slight defensive works in the fighting later in the day will be duly seen.

While resting briefly near the Seminary, an incident occurred illustrative of the tragic nature of war as noted on the First Day's field at Gettysburg. A number of spent, solid-shot cannon balls, fired from Confederate guns on Herr Ridge, were noticed rolling slowly along the ground toward the Seminary. A soldier from a Wisconsin regiment was seen by Robinson's men suddenly to put his heel gleefully out to try to stop a ball which was rolling toward him, expecting to have no difficulty in so doing. The men witnessing this supposed sport on the part of the Wisconsin lad, shouted at him to desist. It was too late, however, for in an instant the soldier's extended leg was severed completely. In his extreme pain, the man's grief was evident, as he wept like a child at the loss of his member through such ignorant carelessness. It would have been better, he felt, to have lost his leg in close-quarter combat. The manner in which the accident occurred impelled the soldier to cry out, "I shall always be ashamed to say how I lost it!" Unfortunately, the latent force in such rolling cannon balls was not known to this new recruit.[48]

In the fighting in which Paul's First Brigade was to be heavily engaged later in the day, this unit was to be under the command of five successive commanders, all of whom were wounded: Brigadier General Gabriel R. Paul, the original brigade leader; Colonel Samuel H. Leonard, commander of the 13th Massachusetts; Colonel Adrian R. Root, of the 94th New York; Colonel Richard Coulter, commanding the 11th Pennsylvania of Brigadier General Henry Baxter's Second Brigade, which regiment was transferred to the First Brigade in the afternoon; and Colonel Peter Lyle, of the 90th Pennsylvania, also of the Second Brigade.[49]

At about noon,[50] Major General Robert Emmett Rodes' large Third Division of Ewell's Confederate Second Corps arrived on the field from the north. Rodes had approximately 8,125 effectives[51] as he moved forward to the environs of Oak Hill. He at once ordered Major Blackford's sharpshooter battalion and General Doles' crack Georgia brigade to move to his left (east) to the Carlisle road, to watch for the arrival of Early's Confederate division, and to keep Devin's Union cavalry brigade in check.[52] Rodes had been marching toward Cashtown from Heidlersburg early in the morning, when he had been diverted to Gettysburg by Hill's message saying that Federal forces in strength had been encountered at the last mentioned point.[53] Rodes' division was composed of the following brigades: the First Brigade, commanded by Brigadier General Junius Daniel; the Second Brigade, led by Brigadier General Alfred Iverson; the Third Brigade, Brigadier General George Doles commanding; Brigadier General Stephen D. Ramseur's Fourth Brigade; and the Fifth Brigade, commanded by Colonel Edward A. O'Neal.

Accompanying Rodes was the division artillery battalion, commanded by Lieutenant Colonel Thomas H. Carter, which comprised the following batteries: Captain W.P. Carter's battery ("The King William Artillery"), two ten-pounder Parrotts and two twelve-pounder Napoleons;[54] Captain W.C. Fry's battery ("The Orange Artillery"), two ten-pounder Parrotts and two three-inch rifles;[55] Captain R.C.M. Page's battery ("The Morris Artillery"), four Napoleons;[56] and Captain W.J. Reese's battery ("The Jeff Davis Artillery"), four three-inch rifles.[57]

Rodes' timely arrival at Oak Hill, the commanding eminence on the First Day's field, was unperceived by the Unionists at first, because of the heavy woods, and at once constituted a grave menace to the right flank of Doubleday's line.[58] The Federal force most immediately threatened was Doubleday's right brigade—Cutler's—located on the easterly crest of McPherson Ridge, just to the north of the railroad cut, and within very easy range of any enfilading enemy guns which could be placed on the summit of Oak Hill. Doubleday's right flank was exposed also to any Confederate infantry attacks from the direction of Oak Hill, while it was expected that any assault Rodes might make would be supported by renewed thrusts from Hill to the west. With the later arrival of Howard's Union Eleventh Corps on the plain north of town, "Rodes formed a block to the welding of the two Federal corps." [59] The fortunate Confederate concentration was to see, later in the day, still another Southern force arrive on the field at a crucial time, and again directly on the Union right flank!

CHAPTER 8

The Arrival and Deployment of

the Eleventh Corps

DURING THE LULL IN THE FIGHTING, ABOUT 11:00 A.M., DOUBLE-day was anxiously observing the build-up in strength and the concentration of the Confederate forces opposed to him. The Union First Corps commander was eagerly awaiting the arrival from the south of the Federal Eleventh Corps, Major General Oliver Otis Howard commanding. Howard would bring with him a total of some 9,500 effectives,[1] and they would be desperately needed on the field to try to check the preponderant enemy forces being arrayed against the National soldiers.

At about 8:30 a.m., Howard, at Emmitsburg, Maryland, had received Reynolds' order to move immediately to Gettysburg to succor Buford and Doubleday. The Eleventh Corps commander had put his divisions in motion at once to comply with this directive. In order to expedite movements, Brigadier General Francis Channing Barlow's First Division, and one artillery battery, moved to Gettysburg via the Emmitsburg road; while Brigadier General Adolph von Steinwehr's Second Division, Major General Carl Schurz' Third Division, and the remaining four artillery batteries of Major Thomas W. Osborn's artillery brigade traveled eastward by a cross-road from the Emmitsburg road to the Taneytown road, and thence by the last-named highway to Gettysburg.[2] After directing that the infantry and artillery be hurried forward to the front as rapidly as possible, Howard himself rode on ahead toward Gettysburg to see what was transpiring.[3] At about 11:00 a.m., he received the sad tidings of Reynolds' death from

Major William Riddle, aide-de-camp of the late Federal Left Wing commander.[4]

General Howard himself arrived on the battlefield at approximately 11:15 a.m.[5] Being the senior officer present, he succeeded Doubleday in command of the whole field, the latter retaining command of the First Corps west of town. Schurz now became temporary Eleventh Corps commander, while his Third Division was turned over to Brigadier General Alexander Schimmelfennig. The command of Schimmelfennig's First Brigade was given to Colonel George von Amsberg, and the latter's 45th New York regiment was commanded, in turn, by Lieutenant Colonel Adolphus Dobke.

Howard immediately set up his headquarters on East Cemetery Hill, across the Baltimore pike from the citizens' Evergreen Cemetery.[6] Then he went to the top of the Fahnestock building, at Middle and Baltimore streets, to survey the situation.[7] While observing the lines of battle from there, Howard evidently saw a temporary retrograde movement of several regiments of Cutler's brigade, and prematurely reported to Meade the erroneous intelligence that the whole First Corps was crumbling. This hasty and ill-considered action by Howard was unjustified. It led, in part, to Meade's replacing Doubleday in command of the First Corps with Major General John Newton of the Third Division, Sixth Corps, despite the very capable handling of the First Corps by Doubleday throughout the day—generalship and dexterity that were superior to that shown by Howard himself during the First Day's battle.[8]

The Eleventh Corps commander soon had instructions for Doubleday. To a messenger, Howard said, "Tell Doubleday to fight on the left, and I will fight on the right." The order further instructed Doubleday to try to hold the Seminary Ridge line if forced back from McPherson Ridge.[9] That was all. Howard, in fact, exercised little effective control of the tactical situation during the remainder of the day's battle, and his directives to Doubleday were few in number and of little help. After his examination from atop the building in town, Howard rode back to his headquarters on Cemetery Hill near the cemetery gate. Here he met Schurz, who was now in temporary command of the Eleventh Corps, and who had ridden forward ahead of his troops to learn of recent developments on the field.[10]

The task assumed by Howard was a difficult one for an officer who had had as yet little chance to observe closely the battle lines then established, who posssessed little information as to the nature of the fighting which had taken place on the field so far, and who had little detailed information of the movements of the various Confederate units. Howard, nevertheless, saw and appreciated the splendid defensive position of the Cemetery heights south of Gettysburg. He determined to make every effort to hold them, thereby pursuing the policy already so successfully sustained by Buford, Reynolds, and Doubleday. For this decision, Howard alone received the official thanks of the United States Congress.

Meantime, the Eleventh Corps units were marching swiftly toward Gettysburg. At 10:30 a.m., Schurz' division had progressed as far as Horner's Mills.[11] Soon after Howard himself had reached the field, the 45th New York infantry regiment arrived as advance guard of the corps.[12] It had covered the last few hundred yards on the double-quick, and was "panting and out of breath."[13] This was owing to the fact that Howard had probably seen several of Cutler's brigades temporarily falling back and felt that every possible Eleventh Corps regiment was needed on the field as quickly as it was possible to get them there. Almost immediately, Colonel Amsberg ordered the four right companies of this regiment, under Captain Francis Irsch, to advance out the Mummasburg road to the north-northwest of town, the objective being the large red barn of M. McLean on the east side of the road at the foot of the eastern slope of Oak Ridge.[14] Skirmishers were to be thrown out to the right toward the Carlisle road as far as possible The other companies of the 45th New York were to follow the preceding four as soon as they caught their breath.[15]

As the four advance companies moved out the Mummasburg road, the only fire they initially encountered was from Page's Confederate battery, located near the McLean barn. The deploying of skirmishers to the right in a wheatfield proceeded satisfactorily. Soon, however, the four companies received hostile fire from Blackford's Alabama sharpshooter battalion of Rodes' division, which lay "stretched along the lane at the foot of Oak Hill to the apple orchard, at or near Hagy's farm" near the Mummasburg road on the left and in the rye and wheatfield in the front.[16] The combined Confederate artillery and sharpshooter fire began to take casualties in the four New York companies.

Soon, the four advance companies of the 45th New York were augmented by the remaining six of the regiment, and by the six Napoleons of Captain Hubert Dilger's Battery I, 1st Ohio Light Artillery. Dil-

66

ger unlimbered his guns on the flat ground behind the right of the 45th, and replied effectively to the Confederate guns on the eastern slope of Oak Hill near the McLean barn.[17] Dilger himself sighted and fired one of his pieces, the resulting shot being said to have temporarily disabled an enemy gun.[18] It was reported also that five Confederate gun carriages were destroyed.[19] The Southern guns on the eastern slope of Oak Ridge were reinforced later, while Dilger received the support of Lieutenant William Wheeler's 13th New York Light Battery, comprising four three-inch rifles.[20]

The four companies of the 45th New York continued to advance, soon noticing, however, that skirmishers from O'Neal's brigade of Rodes' division were moving "stealthily" down the lane at the base of Oak Ridge. These Confederate soldiers were attempting to penetrate the gap between the left of the 45th New York and the right of Robinson's division, which had been moved by Doubleday into position on Oak Ridge just west of the Mummasburg road, facing westward. The 45th was soon reinforced on its right by the arrival, at about 1:00 p.m., of the 61st Ohio (Colonel Stephen J. McGroaty) and the 74th Pennsylvania (Colonel Adolph von Hartung), both of Amsberg's brigade. These regiments were soon to become engaged in a desperate combat with Doles' Georgia brigade, Rodes' division, which was deploying on O'Neal's left near the Carlisle road.[21]

The fire that the four companies of the 45th New York poured into O'Neal's left flank and rear helped to slow down that Confederate advance. The other six companies of the 45th obliqued to the left to try to fill the gap between the First and Eleventh Corps. Their fire was soon opened against O'Neal, who, chiefly from Robinson's volleys, was repulsed with severe loss.[22] O'Neal's remnants retreated toward the eastern slope of Oak Hill, near McLean's barn. Page's Confederate battery limbered up and withdrew further up the slope. The four companies of the 45th charged the fleeing Southern stragglers, and finally captured the barn and some 300 graycoats, who belonged chiefly to the 5th and 6th Alabama regiments, which had temporarily occupied the fields near the barn.[23]

As the 45th New York was sending its prisoners to the rear, it was seen that Iverson's brigade of Rodes' division was moving against the ridge from the northwest and the west. From the barn, the four companies of the 45th opened fire on Iverson's left flank. This long-range musketry helped somewhat in the repulse of Iverson, who was in turn charged by a number of Federals, including some men of the 45th. About 300 more prisoners were captured and sent to the rear to the vicinity of Pennsylvania College.[24] Most efficacious was the fighting done here at this phase of the First Day's Battle by the 45th New York; it was a well-handled regiment of the Eleventh Corps.

At approximately 12:30 p.m., the Eleventh Corps brigades began arriving at Gettysburg,[25] with Brigadier General Alexander Schimmelfennig's brigade in the lead.[26] A number of the regiments covered the last few miles to town on the double-quick, and were considerably exhausted before ever entering the combat.[27] The Second Division, commanded by Brigadier General Adolph von Steinwehr, was posted by Howard in reserve on Cemetery Hill, supported by Captain Michael Wiedrich's Battery I, 1st New York Light Artillery.[28] When Wiedrich's guns came into battery on East Cemetery Hill, Howard addressed the cannoneers, saying, "Boys, I want you to hold this position at all hazards. Can you do it?" The unanimous, enthusiastic rejoinder was, "Yes, Sir!" [29]

Three regiments of Colonel Orland Smith's Second Brigade, Steinwehr's division, were posted at the northern base of Cemetery Hill, and occupied some houses at the edge of town.[30] The First Brigade, commanded by Colonel Charles R. Coster, was posted on the summit of the hill, from where it was rushed, later in the afternoon, to try to slow the victorious advance of Early's Confederates. Howard's decision to maintain a reserve force on Cemetery Hill, as a rallying point in the eventuality that his forces to the west and north of town should be overwhelmed and obliged to retreat, was one of foresight and sagacity.[31] He sought to hold the Confederates away from the strategic and defensibly formidable heights south of the town until the scattered units of the Army of the Potomac could arrive and concentrate thereon.

Upon the arrival of Schurz's two divisions, commanded by Barlow and Schimmelfennig—some 6,000 effectives in all[32]—Howard ordered them to move through Gettysburg to the plain north of town. There they were to connect with Doubleday's right flank on Oak Ridge, and also to guard against the expected arrival of Early's Confederate division from Heidlersburg. Howard himself accompanied Barlow's First Division as it deployed onto the level ground north of Gettysburg. He rode to the left along his Eleventh Corps line, and then proceeded to inspect briefly the line of the First Corps.[33]

The Eleventh Corps artillery brigade was commanded by Major Thomas W. Osborn, and comprised a total of twenty-six guns. The batteries making up the unit were as follows: Captain Michael Wiedrich's Battery I, 1st New York Light Artillery, six three-inch rifles;[34] the 13th New York Light Battery, commanded by Lieutenant William Wheeler, four three-inch rifles;[35] Battery I, 1st Ohio Light Artillery, six Napoleons, commanded by Captain Hubert Dilger;[36] Captain Lewis Heckman's Battery K, 1st Ohio Light Artillery, four Napoleons;[37] and Battery G, 4th United States (Regular Army) Artillery, six Napoleons, Lieutenant Bayard Wilkeson commanding.[38]

Heckman and Wiedrich were in reserve early in the afternoon on Cemetery Hill.[39] Dilger became engaged, as previously noted, alongside the Mummasburg road, about 500 yards from the edge of town. As seen, when the duel between Dilger and the Confederate guns on Oak Hill became more severe, Wheeler's battery went to the assistance of Dilger—both Federal batteries being positioned between the Mummasburg and Carlisle roads. The Confederate battery opposing the two Union batteries was Page's, located on the eastern slope of Oak Hill. Page suffered the severe loss of thirty men and seventeen horses before being succored by the batteries of Reese and Carter. The reinforced Southern guns, having the advantage of position, then regained the supremacy over Dilger and Wheeler. In the meantime, the left section of Wilkeson's battery was detached and sent to the Almshouse on the western side of the Harrisburg pike, while the other two sections, under the immediate command of Wilkeson himself, went into action on Barlow's Knoll, further out the Harrisburg road near the bridge over Rock Creek.[40]

Howard's intention was that Schimmelfennig's division should extend Robinson's right northward along Oak Ridge, facing to the west; while Barlow's division was either to come into line of battle also along the ridge, to Schimmelfennig's right, or else was to form a second line *en echelon* to the right-rear of Schimmelfennig.[41] This design appeared to have been feasible at the time it was ordered. However, the movement was actually impracticable, owing to the fact that Rodes' Confederate division had already moved into position on Oak Hill but, being behind the crest of the hill and screened by the woods thereon, was not visible to Schurz on the plain below.[42]

Instead of holding the line of the Almshouse, Barlow pushed the two brigades of his First Division of some 3,200 effectives[43] forward to the north. Further, Barlow failed to follow Schurz' order to place Colonel Leopold von Gilsa's First Brigade in the right-rear of Brigadier General Adelbert Ames' Second Brigade, in order to meet a possible flank attack from the right-front, where Early's Confederate division was expected to arrive momentarily. Barlow instead posted his two brigades in a straight line with each other. Since Barlow's left, under Ames, was now pushed forward in advance of Schimmelfennig's right, Schurz was impelled to order Schimmelfennig's division forward into line with Barlow.[44] At the same time, Schurz called for one of Steinwehr's two brigades on Cemetery Hill to be placed in a reserve position near the railroad station to protect his right flank and rear.[45] Howard, however, did not permit this reinforcement to go forward until later in the afternoon, when it was too late to do much good. The deployment of Schurz' two small divisions north of the town, at about 2:00 p.m.,[46] did, however, prevent Doles' Georgia brigade from joining in the attack made on Robinson at Oak Ridge by O'Neal's and Iverson's brigades.[47]

Gilsa's brigade was posted on Barlow's right on the eastern and northern slope of the low elevation later known as Barlow's Knoll, along the bank of Rock Creek near where it is crossed by the Harrisburg pike bridge. Gilsa's deployment from right to left was as follows: the 54th New York (Major Stephen Kovacs), the 68th New York (Colonel Gotthilf Bourry), and the 153rd Pennsylvania (Major John F. Frueauff).[48] The 41st New York (Lieutenant Colonel Detleo von Einsiedel) was absent on detached duty at Emmitsburg. On Gilsa's left was Ames' brigade.

After the brief pause near the Almshouse, Schimmelfennig's Second Brigade, commanded by Colonel Wladimir Krzyzanowski, was pushed forward in support of Ames' left. While moving out, the 75th Pennsylvania lost its colonel, Francis Mahler, and the command of the regiment devolved upon Major August Ledig.[49] Krzyzanowski's regiments were posted in line of battle from right to left as follows: the 26th Wisconsin (Lieutenant Colonel Hans Boebel), two companies of the 58th New York (Lieutenant Colonel August Otto), the 119th New York (Colonel John T. Lockman), the 75th Pennsylvania, and the 82nd Ohio (Colonel James S. Robinson).[50]

Advancing along the Harrisburg road from near the Almshouse, with four companies of the 17th Connecticut thrust ahead as skirmishers, Ames' Second Brigade, First Division, took position on the western slope of Barlow's Knoll, connecting on the right with Gilsa's left, and on the left with Krzyzanowski's right.[51] Ames' deployment from right to left was as follows: the 17th Connecticut (Lieutenant Colonel Douglas Fowler), the 25th Ohio (Lieutenant Colonel Jeremiah Williams), the 75th Ohio (Colonel Andrew L. Harris), and the 107th Ohio (Colonel Serephim Meyer).[52] The 25th and 75th Ohio were in support of Wilkeson's battery.[53]

On the extreme left of the Eleventh Corps line on the plain north of town, with its left resting near the Mummasburg road, was Schimmelfennig's First Brigade, commanded by Colonel George von Amsberg. Amsberg's right connected with Krzyzanowski's left, but the left of the First Brigade was unable to make contact with Robinson's right, fully a quarter of a mile distant to the front-left on Oak Ridge. Amsberg's deployment was as follows from right to left: the 61st Ohio (Colonel Stephen J. McGroaty), the 82nd Illinois (Lieutenant Colonel Edward Salomon), the 74th Pennsylvania (Colonel Adolph von Hartung), the 45th New York (Lieutenant Colonel Adolphus Dobke), which had returned from near the McLean barn at Oak Hill to its place in the line, and the 157th New York (Colonel Philip P. Brown, Jr.).[54]

As Schurz' two divisions relieved the troopers of Devin's cavalry brigade, which had been holding the position since early morning, Devin took position, for a time, mounted, on Schurz' right and rear.[55] While statioined there, the Union troopers were mistaken for Confederates by the Union gunners on East Cemetery Hill. The batteries there opened fire on their own cavalrymen, but fortunately the firing was halted before any Federals were struck down.[56] Perhaps this incident encouraged the blueclad troopers to withdraw from support of Schurz before they normally would have done so.

When Barlow moved forward from the Almshouse to the knoll that bears his name, he encountered some of Doles' enemy skirmishers. These were brushed aside without difficulty.[57] When Barlow decided on this aggressive movement, it appeared to him to be the correct thing to do. Subsequent developments, however, were to demonstrate that the movement was a bad mistake, as it exposed Barlow's right flank to the devastating attack soon to be made by Early. This movement also necessitated a corresponding advance by the Third Division in order to protect Barlow's left. The original line based near the Almshouse, where there was additional timber, was a stronger one than the new line which Barlow adopted. His two brigades were supported by Wilkeson's battery.[58] These guns were the first to occupy the advanced position on the knoll, and were soon to be supported by Gilsa and then by Ames.[59] After discovering that Barlow had moved forward without orders, Schurz determined nonetheless to support him to the best of his ability. Schimmelfennig was directed to advance and assume line of battle on Barlow's left. As noted, Krzyzanowski was the first to come into position, connecting with the left of the First Division.[60] By 2:00 p.m., Schurz' deployment of his two divisions on the plain north of Gettysburg was completed.[61]

It should be emphasized that the Eleventh Corps fought on terrain of an extremely disadvantageous nature. The ground was flat, affording no elevations (except for the low Barlow's Knoll) which would benefit the National artillery and infantry. The fields of ripe golden grain provided the Confederates with cover in which to move up close to the Federal lines without detection. "The numerous roads and open country stretch[ed] to the aid of the strongest battalions." [62] On the other hand, although outnumbered, Doubleday's First Corpsmen did have the advantage of position, being posted on the slight ridges. But the Eleventh Corps was terribly handicapped by its inability to connect with Doubleday's right flank on Oak Ridge, the gap between the two corps being about one-quarter of a mile.

Before the arrival of Early's Confederate division along the Harrisburg road, Schurz was confronted at first by O'Neal's sharpshooter battalion, commanded by Major Blackford. Shortly thereafter, Blackford was reinforced by Brigadier General George Doles' crack Third Brigade, Rodes' division, which deployed into line of battle across the fields near the Carlisle road, facing southward, in the following manner from right to left: the 21st Georgia (Colonel John T. Mercer), the 44th Georgia (Colonel S.P. Lumpkin), the 4th Georgia (Lieutenant Colonel D.R.E. Winn), and the 12th Georgia (Colonel Edward Willis).[63] It must be remembered that the Confederate divisions and corps were approximately twice as large as their Union counterparts, and a Southern division was almost as big as a Federal corps. This is explained in part by the fact that Confederate divisions often contained more brigades (and Southern brigades more regiments) than did the Union.

At approximately 2:00 p.m., just as the deployment of the Eleventh Corps had been completed, Howard inspected Schurz' lines from right to left. He then continued along and hastily examined the positions of the First Corps, possibly ordering Doubleday, in the event of defeat, "to fall back to Cemetery Hill." [64] Seeing that Rodes had arrived on Oak Hill ahead of him, Howard decided not to attack him, probably owing to the fear of Early's imminent arrival on the field from the northeast. Meanwhile, the Eleventh Corps regiments, "without shelter of any kind," were being subjected to a punishing artillery fire from Carter's, Reese's, and Page's batteries on Oak Hill. [65]

It will be noted that Schurz' line was too long to be held adequately by the relatively small number of men under his command. Another weakness was the fact that his right flank, near the Harrisburg road, was in the air. Schurz' difficult dilemma was well summed up in his own words:

> Of the enemy we saw but little, and had no means of forming a just estimate of his strength. Either the enemy was before us in small force, and then we had to push him with all possible vigor, or he had the principal part of his army there, and then we had to establish ourselves in a position which would enable us to maintain ourselves until the arrival of reinforcements. Either of these cases being possible, provision was to be made for both. [66]

The severe and sometimes caustic critics of the Eleventh Corps in its fight north of Gettysburg are either unversed in the handicaps under which it fought, or else are blindly prejudiced against this unfortunate unit of the Army of the Potomac.

Barlow, now advanced to the knoll which bears his name, was apparently not aware that Early's division was close at hand on his right flank. He watched with relish the advance of Doles' single brigade, feeling confident that he could swing Gilsa's brigade around to the left, and thereby envelop Doles' left-rear. [67] Such a maneuver seemed plausible and inviting of success, and may well have succeeded had not Early made his opportune arrival on the field at almost the same time. When Amsberg's brigade was thrown forward toward Doles' right flank, Doles avoided the threat by rapidly changing front to the right. [68] During this early skirmishing, the artillery batteries on both sides were heavily engaged. The Confederate batteries on Oak Hill inflicted a severe loss on Schimmelfennig's regiments, while Doles' infantrymen suffered less heavily, owing to the fact that the Federal guns were engaged in counterbattery fire against the Southern cannons, instead of firing at the grayclad infantry.

As Doles' brigade was coming to grips with Schimmelfennig's division, an incident occurred which was illustrative of the dangers to which high-ranking officers were subjected on the battlefields of the Civil War. General Doles' horse suddenly became crazed with fear, or else was struck by a bullet. The terrified steed bolted straight for the Union lines, and neither the General nor anyone else could cope with him. Doles escaped death or capture only by falling off the animal in a wheatfield, just before the beast reached the Federal lines. The General was only mildly shaken up by the incident.[69]

Then the new and greater danger reared its ugly head to Schurz. This menace was the sudden appearance of Early's Confederate division on the field from the northeast—directly on the right flank of the Federal line. This feat of Early's was to duplicate the earlier one of Rodes, who had likewise appeared at a critical point in the battle on the right flank of Doubleday's forces.

CHAPTER 9

The Advent of Early

and

His Fight with Schurz

THE UNION DEFEAT AT CHANCELLORSVILLE WAS ALL THE ELEVenth Corps' fault—so said many of the critics of this unfortunate body of troops; and O.O. Howard and Fighting Joe Hooker were the particular malefactors in that dreadful fiasco. The Eleventh Corps had been stationed on the extreme right wing of the Army of the Potomac at Chancellorsville in early May of 1863, and had been overwhelmed by the ferocious flank attack of Stonewall Jackson. It had, fairly or unfairly, received a bad name in the press and in the army for its inability to stay Jackson's thunderbolt. Now, on July 1, two divisions of Howard's corps, commanded by Schurz, were again to encounter a mighty onslaught against the right flank of a Union line of battle, this time on the plain to the north of Gettysburg. Could these ill-starred Federals—composed of large numbers of German-American soldiers—repel the surging grayclads, or would they again cave in and thereby endanger the entire National battle position? The decision would soon be forthcoming.

While Doubleday's First Corps was contending with the Confederate divisions of Heth, Rodes, and then Pender, the Eleventh Corps was seeking to rout Doles to the north of town. The fate of the field, however, was to be decided by the fortuitous arrival on the Union right flank of Early's First Division, Ewell's corps. "Old Jube," marching via the Harrisburg road, came onto the field a little before 3:00 p.m.,[1] with about 6,300 effectives under his command.[2] Early's advance had been detected by Devin's blue cavalry vedettes sometime before in the afternoon,[3] causing Howard to throw two of his three Eleventh Corps divisions onto the plain north of town. Unfortunately for the Federals, owing to the presence of Doles' and O'Neal's Confederate brigades and two enemy batteries on the eastern slope of Oak Hill, Howard and Schurz were unable to make connection of their left with Robinson's right on Oak Ridge.

Early deployed his brigades—facing southwestward—across the Harrisburg road, north of the bridge over Rock Creek. On his right was Brigadier General John B. Gordon's Fourth Brigade, to the right (west) of the road. Gordon aligned his regiments from right to left as follows: the 60th Georgia (Captain W.B. Jones), the 31st Georgia (Colonel Clement A. Evans), the 13th Georgia (Colonel James M. Smith), the 61st Georgia (Colonel John H. Lamar), and the 38th Georgia (Captain William L. McLeod).[4] Gordon's 26th Georgia regiment (Colonel E.N. Atkinson) was detached to support Jones' artillery battalion.[5]

Posted on Gordon's left was Brigadier General Harry T. Hays' First Brigade, which was deployed as follows from right to left: the 5th Louisiana (Major Alexander Hart), the 6th Louisiana (Lieutenant

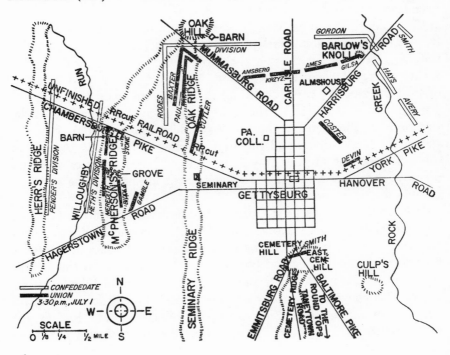

Colonel Joseph Hanlon), the 9th Louisiana (Colonel Leroy A. Stafford), with its right wing to the west of the Harrisburg road and its left wing to the east of the road, the 7th Louisiana (Colonel D.B. Penn), and the 8th Louisiana (Colonel T.D. Lewis).[6]

On the left of Hays' brigade was Brigadier General Robert F. Hoke's Second Brigade, commanded in this battle by Colonel Isaac E. Avery. Avery threw his regiments into line of battle on the left (east) side of the Harrisburg road in the following order from right to left: the 6th North Carolina (Major S.M. Tate), the 21st North Carolina (Colonel W.W. Kirkland), and the 57th North Carolina (Colonel A.C. Godwin).[7]

In reserve, supporting the division artillery batteries, and not actively engaged, was the Third Brigade, commanded by Brigadier General William ("Extra Billy") Smith. Smith deployed his regiments on the left of the Harrisburg road, well to the rear of Hays' and Avery's brigades, in the following manner from right to left: the 52nd Virginia (Lieutenant Colonel James H. Skinner), the 49th Virginia (Lieutenant Colonel J. Cattlett Gibson), and the 31st Virginia (Colonel John S. Hoffman).[8]

Accompanying Early's infantry was his divisional artillery battalion, commanded by Lieutenant Colonel H.P. Jones. Jones' batteries went into position on the eastern side of the Harrisburg road, about one-half mile north of the bridge over Rock Creek. His batteries were posted as follows from right to left: Captain James M. Carrington's battery ("The Charlottesville Artillery"), four Napoleons;[9] Captain A.W. Garber's battery ("The Staunton Artillery"), four Napoleons;[10] Captain C.A. Green's battery ("The Louisiana Guard Artillery"), two ten-pounder Parrotts and two three-inch rifles;[11] and Captain W.A. Tanner's battery ("The Courtney Artillery"), four three-inch rifles.[12] These Southern guns were to play a significant role in the impending clash with the two Eleventh Corps divisions.

General Early was bustling about as his troops came forward into position, supervising the formation of his lines of battle preparatory to assaulting Schurz' thin line on the right flank at Barlow's Knoll. Old Jube's ostrich feather on his hat never appeared jauntier as he rode amongst his eager troops. But if the Confederate division commander was all business, several of his men in the ranks were not. Personal foraging was evidently a sine qua non, regardless of impending unit action. One of the division's young pioneer corpsmen was seen "carrying under each arm a great round Dutch loaf of bread about the size of a cart-wheel, giving him, upon a side view, the appearance of rolling in on wheels." [13]

At approximately 3:30 p.m., Early commenced his skillful attack against Gilsa's brigade on Barlow's Knoll.[14] Gordon was to assail Gilsa in front and on the immediate right flank, while Hays and Avery were to move past Gilsa's right and threaten to take his line in reverse. The outcome of the day's battle—so far definitely in the Federals' favor—would probably be determined by the success or failure of Early's movement, now unfolding.[15] Unhesitatingly, Old Jube threw his brigades forward against the enemy.

As Gordon moved ahead, he received valuable artillery support from the twelve guns of Garber's, Green's, and Tanner's batteries, posted on the slightly higher ground to the east of the Harrisburg road, where they were able to pour a terrible enfilading fire at easy range on Barlow's right flank and along his entire line.[16] No troops ever arrayed for battle could withstand for long such a fearful artillery fire, when it was combined with such a spirited infantry assault.

The artillery duel which ensued quickly resolved itself in the Confederate favor, owing chiefly to their heavier weight of metal. Wilkeson's splendid Battery G, 4th U.S. Artillery, posted on Barlow's Knoll, replied as best it could to the more numerous Confederate guns, and inflicted some casualties on Jones' cannoneers. Garber lost one man wounded, and Green two men killed and five wounded.[17] In turn, Wilkeson himself was mortally wounded (the command devolving upon Lieutenant Eugene A. Bancroft), and his battery suffered the loss of one officer and one man killed, eleven men wounded, four men missing, and thirty-one horses killed.[18] Wilkeson expended 1,400 rounds of ammunition against the Southern artillery and infantry.[19] Among Jones' batteries, Garber used 106 rounds, Green 161, Tanner 595, with Carrington's expenditure unreported.[20] It must be remembered, too, that the Eleventh Corps units—infantry and artillery—were being pounded not only by Jones' guns, but were also being fired upon with effect by Carter's batteries on Oak Hill.

Although they were inflicting serious damage upon the Union forces, Jones' batteries themselves were experiencing several unfortunate incidents. One of Garber's bronze Napoleon twelve-pounders was struck in the muzzle or on the face by a Federal solid shot, and was bent and disabled.[21] This piece was replaced later by one captured from the Nationals, probably from Heckman's battery.[22] One of Green's ten-pounder Parrotts had to be retired owing to "a shot too large lodging half way down the bore, which [was] found impossible to force home." [23] Two additional pieces, likewise, were disabled by faulty ammunition wedging in the tubes.[24]

The stark, naked horror of the battlefields—often ignored by military historians who concentrate chiefly on matters of strategy and tactics—might well be illustrated by an episode which occurred in Jones' Confederate artillery battalion during the battle. When a Union shell burst among the guns, a wheel on one of the field-pieces was damaged. An impatient Southern officer walked up and inquired of the battery commander, "Why don't you change that wheel?" Replying that too many of his men had been killed or wounded, or were otherwise too actively engaged to do so, the artillery officer pointed to a singular mangled mass which had once been a man. The investigating officer took a closer look. He sadly recorded what he saw: "There lay our noble comrade, each several limb [sic] thrice broken, the body gashed with wounds, the top of the skull blown off and the brain actually fallen out upon the ground in two bloody, palpitating lobes." [25]

Just prior to Early's attack, as Barlow had moved out to the knoll, Doles shifted his gray brigade to the left in order to meet him frontally.[26] Then, Gordon moved forward and to the right to support Doles, and to connect with his left.[27] As Schimmelfennig advanced with Amsberg's brigade against Doles' right, the latter changed front partially to the right and extended his right wing in an effort to outflank Amsberg's left.[28] This, however, stretched Doles' line rather thin, and exposed his own left flank to the threat of an attack from Krzyzanowski and Ames.[29] With Early's arrival, the Eleventh Corps line—especially the right under Barlow—was caught as in a vise, and a Union attack against Doles did not develop. Gilsa had been skirmishing with the advance line of Doles, which was advancing near the fork of the two roads at the Blocher smithy.[30] But this was all that the intrepid Doles actually had to contend with of an offensive nature from the Nationals, although he did not know it at the time.

The serious pressure on Doles was relieved in time by Gordon's sudden charge.[31] After swiftly deploying his units, Early wasted no time in putting them in motion against Barlow's front and right flank. Gordon's brigade led the way. As Gordon was moving toward the Federal lines, Hays' and Avery's brigades, on Gordon's left, were advancing rapidly toward Barlow's right-rear.[32] With a chorus of savage, unearthly yells,[33] Gordon's 1500 Georgians[34] surged toward Barlow's line in magnificent array, with great dash,[35] "swinging lines of bright muskets gleaming among the trembling wheat."[36] A British officer present described the stirring scene in these words: "Like the sickles of a great line of reapers the sharp bayonets came nearer through the ruddy gold of the ripening wheat to emerge unbroken and unhesitating from the willows which lined the little stream" of Rock Creek.[37]

The clash was instant and desperate. Barlow's guns were belching double charges of grape and canister at Gordon; while Wheeler, further to the left, turned his right section on him also. The Federals were unable, however, to check the impetuous Confederate assault.[38] Gilsa fought stubbornly, but with the disadvantage of having his right flank, which was in the air, enveloped in a devastating manner. His efforts to change front to the right were futile,[39] but he struggled on. At times the swaying lines were barely fifty paces apart,[40] and the musketry volleys were continuous. The fight at a few points was a furious hand-to-hand one.[41] General Gordon was mounted on a magnificent black steed, and was observed by a Confederate artilleryman to be "standing in his stirrups, bare-headed, hat in hand, arms extended ... voice like a trumpet, exhorting his men." [42] The 82nd Ohio of Krzyzanowski's brigade, supporting Dilger's battery, moved forward 125 yards to threaten Gordon's right; but, encountering Doles' frontal fire, it was forced to yield and recoil to its starting point.[43]

Under the trying, impossible conditions, Barlow's position became untenable, even critical.[44] The dangerous situation of the Unionists was heightened by the severe wounding of Barlow himself, and his being made a prisoner.[45] The command of the First Division devolved upon Adelbert Ames, who was thus thrust into a thankless and hopeless task. And Barlow was not the only Federal officer rendered hors de combat. Lieutenant Bayard Wilkeson, commanding the Union battery on Barlow's Knoll, "had a leg nearly severed from his body by a shell." The nineteen-year-old officer himself coolly amputated the dangling member with his penknife, and dragged himself to the Almshouse barn, where he soon expired.[46]

But Early's graycoats were not to be denied, even by such enemy gallantry. Gordon's irresistible assault drove Gilsa's regiments to the left and rear and through the ranks of Ames' brigade, "creating considerable confusion." [47] Although some of Gilsa's soldiers maintained fairly good order in their retreat, a rather hurried rush to the rear generally ensued. [48] The 45th New York was withdrawn at about 3:45 p.m. from its advanced position near McLean's barn to support the 157th New York, "which had gone gallantly forward to the right against Gordon." [49] But it was all in vain. The forced retrograde movement by Gilsa exposed Ames' right to attack by Gordon, who was thus vouchsafed a golden opportunity to rout Barlow's entire First Division. [50] The Southerners completed this enterprise with dispatch.

Barlow's men fell back to the line of the Almshouse, about 500 yards to the rear, with their right on the Harrisburg road and their left near the Carlisle road. [51] This new position, based on the masonry buildings of the Almshouse, was a somewhat better defensive line than was the exposed and advanced one at the knoll. [52] But Barlow's defeat left Doles free to assail Schimmelfennig, [53] whose plight now became critical. And the Confederate artillery was not backward in its eager attempts to come to closer grips with the foe. Jones ordered Carrington's battery forward to support Gordon's advancing line, but the retreat of Barlow was too swift to permit the guns to come into battery. [54] The hoped-for stand by the Federal First Division—now commanded by Ames—at the Almshouse line was not possible for long, owing to the persistent pressure on the Union right by Hays and Avery, as well as that being exerted by Gordon on the front. [55] The time was now approximately 3:45 p.m. [56] At this point, seeing that Hays and Avery comprised sufficient force to insure Ames' continued withdrawal, and perceiving the possible use of the Fourth Brigade against Schimmelfennig's right, Gordon halted near the Almshouse. [57]

The relentless advance of Hays and Avery on the east of the Harrisburg road was delayed for a few minutes by Devin's Union cavalry brigade, [58] before the blueclad troopers were forced to retire. These precious moments thus purchased enabled Steinwehr's First Brigade, [59] commanded by Colonel Charles R. Coster, to double-quick from Cemetery Hill to a point northeast of the railway depot just north of Stevens' Run, near some houses on the outskirts of Gettysburg. [60] The 73rd Pennsylvania (Captain Daniel F. Kelly) was posted near the railroad station in the rear of the small brigade. Heckman's Ohio battery moved into position on the Carlisle road near the college grounds, well to the left of the brigade. [61]

Coster deployed the 134th New York (Lieutenant Colonel Allen H. Jackson) on the right in a wheatfield, the 154th New York (Lieutenant Colonel Daniel B. Allen) in the center, and the 27th Pennsylvania (Lieutenant Colonel Lorenz Cantador) on the left near a brick house.[62] Higher ground rose near the position of the 154th New York and extended past the brick house and across a lane beyond. While this terrain feature protected the left of the brigade somewhat, it permitted the left regiment—the 27th Pennsylvania—to fire only obliquely to the right. The left of the brigade should have been advanced to this higher ground, and probably would have been ordered there had time permitted, and had not a stout post-and-rail fence intervened.[63]

Hardly had Coster deployed into line of battle than Hays' and Avery's brigades came down upon him from two directions, against his front and right flank.[64] Despite this overwhelming pressure and grave menace, Coster's small brigade managed to delay the Southerners long enough to allow Ames to withdraw his First Division from its threatened and critical poistion at the Almshouse line.[65] In buying this invaluable time, however, Coster's men suffered fearful casualties from the severe enemy fire.

An incident illustrative of the nature of the fighting men in action on the Gettysburg battlefield that hot July day occurred here in the fight of the 154th New York. "A dead soldier was found on the field after the battle was over, and in his hand was an ambrotype picture of three children upon whose faces his last look had been fixed, and on which his sightless eyes were still directed." [66]

So savage and overbearing was the Confederate pressure on Coster that each of his regiments had time to fire but from six to nine musketry volleys before being impelled to fall back.[67] In attempting to succor the hard-pressed infantrymen of Coster's brigade, Captain Heckman's Battery K, 1st Ohio Light Artillery, in action well to Coster's left, fired 113 rounds of canister at the enemy for thirty minutes before being compelled to withdraw.[68] Heckman suffered a loss of two men killed, eleven wounded, and two missing.[69] In addition, in retreat, two of his pieces were captured by the 6th North Carolina of Avery's brigade.[70]

Seeing his front and right flank threatened, Coster sought to disengage and fall back, but his attention was suddenly called to the fact that his left was also being menaced. Coster would have to fall back swiftly from the nutcracker or his line of retreat would be cut off.

Especially severe was an enfilading fire from the right that was decimating his regiments.[71] Therefore, like the others of Barlow before him, Coster's Federals now hurried to the rear, hopeful of extrication.

In the retreat of Coster's blueclads, several events are worth noting. The national and state colors of the 134th New York, found lying on the ground, were carried off safely by the wounded Captain M.B. Cheney of the 154th New York; while the national flag of the 154th, in turn, was borne successfully from the field by a soldier of the 134th! [72] A mounted Union officer, trying to rally his men, shouted, "Don't run, men; none but cowards run!" A number of Confederates, cheering his gallantry, called out, "Don't shoot that man!" But a fusilade of musketry dropped him horizontal, despite these generous pleas.[73] In the repulse of Barlow and Coster, the Southern brigades of Hays and Avery suffered relatively small loss—far less combined casualties than those inflicted upon Gordon, which were not heavy.[74] Incidentally, Hays' was the only one of Early's brigades as such permitted to enter the town in pursuit of Schurz' shattered legions (although probably a small number of men from Avery's brigades also got into Gettysburg).[75] This was perhaps owing to the fact that Gordon's and Avery's brigades were more disorganized, even in victory, than Hays' and to the likelihood that Early possibly felt that more than one brigade might well get mixed up and in the way of another in the narrow streets of the town.

The sudden collapse of Barlow on the right isolated Amsberg's and Krzyzanowski's brigades on the left of Schurz' line, and made it difficult for Schimmelfennig to withdraw them from Doles' front.[76] Severe casualties were suffered in the fighting withdrawal of the Third Division which followed. Once more, the Confederate artillery played an important part in driving the Federal forces back.[77] This final repulse of Amsberg and Krzyzanowski decided the fate of the entire field north of the town.[78] The two Eleventh Corps divisions were obliged to yield their ground again, and this time the retreat became a rout through the streets of Gettysburg and on toward the rallying point on Cemetery Hill.

In the last action, as the 157th New York was opposing the advance of Doles' 44th Georgia, the latter regiment lost its commander, Lieutenant Colonel S.P. Lumpkin. He was succeeded in command by Captain Peebles. Captain J.H. Connolly of Company E, 44th Georgia, seeing Lieutenant Gates of the 157th New York lying severely wounded on the ground, generously gave him a canteen of water as the Southern line swept past.[79] The bulk of the high Union casualties occurred in about thirty minutes of furious action.[80] Schimmelfennig fell back first to a cross-road, 500 yards in the rear. Here a brief halt was made to reform the Union lines.[81] Schimmelfennig, in a futile attempt to try to stop Doles—who was now also threatening Robinson's rear on Oak Ridge—posted Dilger's battery near the point where the Mummasburg road enters the town.[82] But when the Confederate onslaught turned Schimmelfennig's right flank, he was compelled to continue the retreat into the town.[83] In this combat north of Gettysburg, and in the retreat which followed, Krzyzanowski's brigade lost every one of its regimental commanders.[84] This last attack on the Eleventh Corps occurred at approximately 4:00 p.m.[85] Only when the Confederates were closing a pincer in his rear did artilleryman Wheeler strive to withdraw his four three-inch rifles from Schimmelfennig's front. He successfully evaded capture, and again came into battery near the edge of town in order to keep the pursuing grayclads at a respectful distance. While unlimbering in this second position, a Confederate shell dismounted one of Wheeler's pieces. "Slinging the gun under the limber with the prolonge rope, he carried it some distance until the prolonge broke, whereupon he was obliged to abandon the piece." [86]

Doles' handling of his single brigade in its fighting against three Federal brigades (although it must be remembered that a Confederate brigade was almost twice as large as a Union one) was an outstanding feat of generalship. When Gilsa had been broken by Gordon, Doles had struck Ames on the left flank, causing him to fall back, pursued by Doles' left. This advance had led to Doles' own right being threatened by Krzyzanowski's right. So, turning his complete attention to Schimmelfennig, Doles had been able to rout the former's two brigades, aided greatly by the destructive fire of the Confederate artillery on Oak Hill and on the east of the Harrisburg road.[87] But, despite Doles' able maneuvers, Schimmelfennig fell back only after Barlow's First Division had folded, thereby exposing Schimmelfennig's right flank.[88]

The Eleventh Corps retirement was fairly deliberate and orderly until the streets of the town were reached; then confusion prevailed. Large numbers of National soldiers were captured in the avenues and alleys of Gettysburg by the pursuing Confederates.[89] The vociferous

84

Southerners were shouting exultantly, "Shoot the Yankees! Lay down your arms! Don't let one escape!" [90]

The gallant fight of the Eleventh Corps on the plain north of Gettysburg had been doomed to failure from the start. The conditions under which it had tried to stem Doles' and Early's impetuous and well-directed thrusts were impossible. The Federal defeat was perhaps quickened by the inexpert handling of the First Division by Barlow, although other Union generalship in Schurz' two divisions was fairly competent.

Let us leave for the moment the Eleventh Corps troops fleeing through the streets of the town of Gettysburg, and turn our attention to the events that were occurring on the right of Doubleday's First Corps at the same time that Schurz was striving in vain to halt Early.

CHAPTER 10

The Oak Ridge Combat

of

Robinson and Rodes

EARLY'S SWIFT AND STRIKING SUCCESS AGAINST THE ELEVENTH Corps did not mean that similar good fortune would fall to the Confederates attacking the First Corps—far from it. While Schurz' two divisions were striving futilely to maintain their position on the plain north of Gettysburg, Doubleday's new right wing, under Robinson, on Oak Ridge, was gallantly resisting the heavy pressure of Rodes. The arrival at the Seminary of Robinson's Second Division, First Corps, at approximately 11:00 a.m.[1] has already been noted. Robinson's two brigades were the First, commanded by Brigadier General Gabriel R. Paul, and the Second, Brigadier General Henry Baxter commanding. Together they numbered 3,000 effectives.

When word was received of the appearance near Oak Hill of Rodes' large Confederate division of some 8,125 effectives, Baxter was ordered at about 12:30 p.m. to move along the northern extension of Seminary Ridge, called Oak Ridge north of the railroad cut, to contest Rodes' threat to the present right flank of Doubleday's line on McPherson Ridge.[2] Baxter had present for duty a little over 1,200 men.[3] Paul's brigade was not sent to the right until later in the afternoon, when Baxter was encountering serious opposition.[4]

While the other regiments of Baxter's brigade were halted for a time at the Seminary, the 11th Pennsylvania (Colonel Richard Coulter) and the 97th New York (Colonel Charles Wheelock) were ordered to proceed at once northward along Oak Ridge "to a point near the Mummasburg Road."[5] Colonel Coulter of the 11th Pennsylvania was

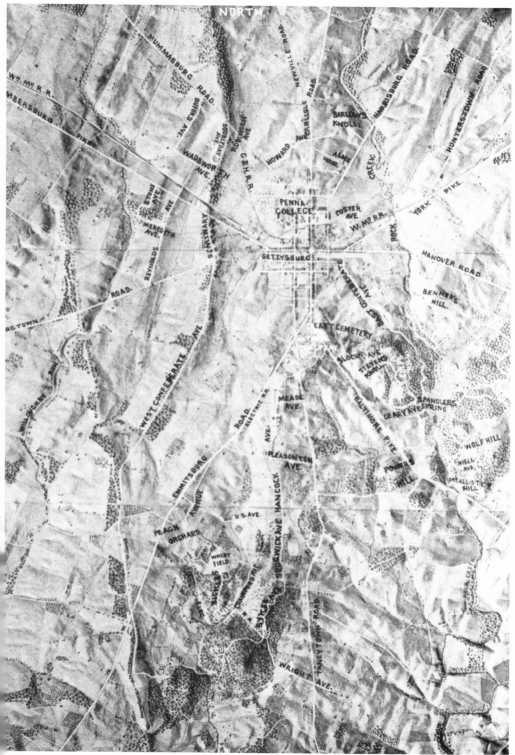

Topographical Relief Map of Gettysburg showing all major roads (B & L).

Marker of the 26th Pennsylvania Emergency Regiment near Marsh Creek on the Chambersburg Pike (GNMP).

26th Pennsylvania Emergency Regiment Monument and narrative tablet on the south side of Chambersburg Street (GNMP).

View near Cashtown looking west on the Old Cashtown Pike. This is the route much of the Confederate Army took to

Monument where the first shot was fired along the Chambersburg Pike, circa 1900 (GNMP).

Theological Seminary. General Buford directed the opening of the battle from this cupola (GNMP).

GEN JOHN F REYNOLDS

Major John F. Reynolds, lithograph bust from a portrait by A.H. Richie (GNMP).

Reynolds' Woods from Reynolds' Ave. (GNMP).

Confederate General Henry Heth (MOLLUS-MASS/USAMHI).

View of the railroad cut. The scene of the capture of the Confederate Brigade (GNMP).

Portrait engraving of Solomon Meredith of the Iron Brigade (GNMP).

Engraving of John L. Burns, "The Old Hero of Gettysburg" (B & L).

Lt. Bayard Wilkeson holding his battery to work in an exposed position (B & L).

The south side of Chambersburg Street at the center of Gettysburg (1863) (GNMP).

Entrance to the Evergreen Cemetery on Cemetery Hill (MOLLUS-MASS/USAMHI).

Major General Winfield Scott Hancock, Commanding the 2nd Army Corps at Gettysburg (B & L).

placed in charge of the two regiments.[6] This movement began at approximately 12:30 p.m., and somewhat later the remainder of the Second Brigade joined the 11th Pennsylvania and 97th New York on Oak Ridge, just south of the Mummasburg road.[7] The division commander, Robinson, and his staff probably "hurried after Baxter" at this time.[8] The brigade first moved into position on a line near and along the southern edge of the Mummasburg road, facing northward, on the eastern slope of Oak Ridge.[9]

At approximately 2:00 p.m., or a little earlier, Rodes' gray division was in position on Oak Hill to attack Baxter.[10] But the intense heat and exertion in moving along the wooded and rocky ground north of the hill had caused considerable suffering among Rodes' infantrymen, many of whom had fainted from heat exhaustion.[11]

Preceding the infantry of Rodes was his divisional artillery battalion, commanded by Lieutenant Colonel Thomas H. Carter, which moved into action on Oak Hill. Carter posted his four batteries as follows: on the southern crest of Oak Hill were Captain W.P. Carter's battery ("The King William Artillery"), two ten-pounder Parrotts and two Napoleon twelve-pounders,[12] and Captain C.W. Fry's battery ("The Orange Artillery"), two ten-pounder Parrotts and two three-inch rifles;[13] while on the eastern crest of Oak Hill were Captain R.C.M. Page's battery ("The Morris Artillery"), four Napoleons,[14] and Captain W.J. Reese's battery ("The Jeff Davis Artillery"), four three-inch rifles.[15] Carter's and Fry's batteries began firing southward against the right flank of the First Corps line on McPherson Ridge, enfilading the entire line and causing grievous discomfort.[16] Page's and Reese's batteries engaged the advance of the Eleventh Corps units on the plain north of town.[17] Later in the afternoon, Captain Carter's battery augmented those of Page and Reese, while Fry continued to fire southward.[18]

The cannonading from Carter and Fry caused Cooper's Union battery to move southeastward to a point in a meadow between Mc-Pherson Ridge and Seminary Ridge, where Cooper was obliged to change front to the north and engage these Confederate batteries.[19] Meanwhile, Page and Reese were engaged with the Eleventh Corps batteries of Dilger and Wheeler. In this artillery duel, Captain Carter lost four men killed and seven wounded, while expending 572 rounds of ammunition.[20] Fry's losses were not reported, but he fired 882 rounds—a prodigious outpouring of metal.[21] Page suffered the heavy loss of four men killed, twenty-six wounded, and seventeen horses killed or disabled, with the battery expending 215 rounds.[22] Reese's casualties were not reported, but his battery fired 229 rounds.[23] Nonetheless, Schurz's men were fearfully battered by this Confederate artillery bombardment.

In the meantime, during the lull in the battle, Heth was planning to retrieve the morning defeats which he had suffered in the repulse of the brigades of Archer and Davis. Seeing the arrival of Rodes on the field, Heth asked General Lee, who had just come up in the Confederate rear, if he (Heth) might resume his attack on Doubleday. Lee replied, "No; I am not prepared to bring on a general engagement today; Longstreet is not up." However, seeing that Robinson's division in his front at the Seminary was moving northward to confront Rodes, Heth repeated his request to Lee for permission to attack. This time the great Confederate chieftain nodded in assent.[24] So Heth began moving his other two brigades—Brockenbrough's and Pettigrew's—into position to renew the assault on Doubleday's battle-weary but thus far victorious Federals on McPherson Ridge. This took some time, and gave the center of the stage to Rodes.

With at first only one brigade deployed, Rodes moved southward unopposed along Oak Ridge until he was obliged to flush out some of Devin's lingering cavalrymen. He then deployed on a front of three brigades. Proceeding southward in this alignment for about one mile, Rodes reached Oak Hill, the commanding eminence northeast of the Mummasburg road opposite the Forney house.[25] He placed Brigadier General Alfred Iverson's Second Brigade on his right in the fields, Colonel Edward A. O'Neal's Fifth Brigade in the center on the ridge, Brigadier General George Doles' Third Brigade on the left on the plain at the foot of the eastern slope of Oak Ridge, Brigadier General Junius Daniel's First Brigade in the second line on the right-rear of Iverson, and Brigadier General Stephen D. Ramseur's Fourth Brigade in reserve behind O'Neal.[26] Doles' 1,369 effectives[27] were engaged with the Eleventh Corps, and their fight has been described above. Seeing the Eleventh Corps approaching on his left, and knowing that Early's division was soon to arrive on Schurz' right, Rodes determined to hold with his left and attack with his right and center.[28]

Unable to withstand, in the open ground, the destructive short-range fire from Carter's batteries on Oak Hill, Cutler withdrew his brigade from the eastern crest of McPherson Ridge to the woods on Seminary (Oak) Ridge just north of the railroad cut.[29] Cutler still suffered in this new position from Carter's guns, which continued to pour on his line a severe enfilading fire. In addition, Heth's numerous batteries on Herr Ridge to the west were in constant action against Doubleday's thin and badly mauled line. Thus, the cross-fire of Confederate artillery neutralized Cutler to such an extent that his usefulness was largely impaired.

In order to contain Rodes' threat at right angles to Doubleday's right flank,[30] Baxter's line was formed for a time perpendicular to and across Oak Ridge, and behind a stone wall which ran parallel with and close to the southern edge of the Mummasburg road. As will be seen, Baxter, after throwing back some Confederate skirmishers, would repulse O'Neal's attack from this first position, then would change front to the left (west) and advance up Oak Ridge to the crest, where Iverson would be hurled back with fearful loss.[31] In his initial deployment along the Mummasburg road, Baxter's alignment was as follows from right to left: the 90th Pennsylvania (Colonel Peter Lyle), the 12th Massachusetts (Colonel James L. Bates), the 88th Pennsylvania (Major Benezet F. Foust), the 83rd New York (Lieutenant Colonel Joseph A. Moesch), the 97th New York (Colonel Charles Wheelock), and the 11th Pennsylvania (Colonel Richard Coulter).[32]

In the immediate front of Baxter, northward across the road from him, near the big red barn of McLean, was O'Neal's Confederate brigade and Page's artillery battery.[33] O'Neal's line "extended from [the] plain up the slope of the ridge." [34] The regiments of O'Neal's brigade were deployed from right to left as follows: the 3rd Alabama (Colonel A.C. Battle), the 12th Alabama (Colonel S.B. Pickens), the 26th Alabama (Lieutenant Colonel John C. Goodgame), the 6th Alabama (Colonel J.N. Lightfoot), and the 5th Alabama (Colonel J.M. Hall).[35]

Rodes' deployment was probably unavoidable in the short time available to him, but it was unfortunate for the Southerners that the battle-tested brigades of Ramseur and Doles were not in action initially against Baxter, and that the brunt of the assault had to be borne by O'Neal and Iverson, who were more inexperienced and less iron-nerved than their fellow brigade commanders. Ramseur did his best to assist O'Neal, however, and ordered the 2nd North Carolina (Major D.W. Hurtt) and the 4th North Carolina (Colonel Bryan Grimes) to support him.[36] In order to bridge a gap between Doles' right and O'Neal's left, caused by the nature and configuration of the terrain,

Rodes ordered the 5th Alabama—O'Neal's left regiment—not to participate in the attack, but to remain where it was. Rodes intended later to direct its movements personally. The 5th Alabama covered this gap by thinning its line—an action which almost doubled the length of its front.[37] Rodes also recalled Colonel Battle's 3rd Alabama on O'Neal's right, which was too far advanced, and pulled it back on a line with Daniel's brigade. Daniel was given discretionary orders either to support Iverson or to attack on the right.[38]

Although O'Neal had present approximately 1,794 effectives,[39] he found himself, through misunderstanding, carelessness, or bad management, attacking with but three of his five regiments, the 5th Alabama remaining motionless in the gap between Doles' right and O'Neal's left, and the 3rd Alabama not moving forward on his right, but being instructed to operate with Daniel's brigade.[40] The arrangement which Rodes had evolved was not good. When he finally did advance, O'Neal did so in some confusion and disorder and not exactly along the line personally indicated to him by Rodes.[41] In this assault, O'Neal was embarrassed on his left by the musketry of the 45th New York and by the fire from Dilger's battery, both of the Eleventh Corps. He expected to be supported on his right by Iverson's brigade, but the latter had halted his forward motion while Carter's guns shelled the Union position. This delay prevented Iverson from synchronizing his forward movement with that of O'Neal,[43] and it was a fatal error.

Throwing his regiments against Baxter's line, posted behind the stone wall which ran just south of and parallel with the Mummasburg road, O'Neal was repelled with heavy loss.[44] Seeing that O'Neal, with his three regiments, could not drive Baxter, Rodes turned back personally to get the 5th Alabama, which he had left motionless on O'Neal's left flank to guard the gap between O'Neal and Doles. To Rodes' astonishment, he discovered that O'Neal himself had remained in the rear with the 5th Alabama instead of directing in person his three attacking regiments! [45] The 5th Alabama finally moved forward and had the dubious honor of "sharing in the repulse of O'Neal's Brigade engaged at the McLean buildings." [46] Rodes' first thrust, therefore, had been parried, but he determined to make ready a new onslaught with Iverson's brigade against Baxter's left flank. The arrangements were made, and Iverson's men were ordered forward.

But the Nationals were ready. Being apprised of the approach of Iverson's brigade across the Forney fields from the west against his left flank on Oak Ridge, Baxter hurried his regiments up along the crest of the ridge behind a stone wall, having to change front to the left (west) to execute the maneuver.[47] At the apex of the angle made by the Mummasburg road and Oak Ridge, Baxter placed the 90th Pennsylvania, with its right wing refused along the road and its left wing resting along the ridge. The other regiments—now facing westward—took position along the ridge to the left of the 90th in this order from right to left: the 12th Massachusetts, the 88th Pennsylvania, the 83rd New York, the 97th New York, and the 11th Pennsylvania.[48] On Baxter's left—though not directly adjoining it—at this time was Cutler's brigade.[49] Stewart's battery was in position at the railroad cut in Seminary Ridge, supported by the 14th Brooklyn and 6th Wisconsin.[50]

From his field headquarters on Oak Hill,[51] Rodes ordered the continued firing of the batteries of Captains Carter and Fry on that part of the First Corps line which extended southward along Oak Ridge to the railroad grading.[52] Soon, this destructive artillery fire was played also on Meredith's and Biddle's lines south of the Chambersburg pike on McPherson Ridge. While the Iron Brigade was more sheltered in McPherson's Grove, Biddle's brigade in the open suffered more heavily from this bombardment. Consequently, Doubleday ordered Biddle temporarily to change front to the north so as to escape more of the screaming projectiles.[53] Likewise, Cooper's and Reynolds' batteries changed front to the right and opened fire upon Carter on Oak Hill, inflicting some damage.[54]

Iverson, preparing to move against Baxter's line on Oak Ridge, deployed his regiments from right to left as follows: the 12th North Carolina (Lieutenant Colonel W.S. Davis), the 23rd North Carolina (Colonel D.H. Christie), the 20th North Carolina (Lieutenant Colonel Nelson Slough), and the 5th North Carolina (Captain Speight B. West).[55] Ramseur ordered two of his regiments, the 14th North Carolina (Colonel R. Tyler Bennett) and the 30th North Carolina (Colonel Francis M. Parker) to support Iverson.[56] The latter had present approximately 1,470 effectives.[57]

Iverson's advance at about 2:30 p.m.[58] was from the west-northwest through a field of timothy,[59] with the Forney buildings between his left and O'Neal's right.[60] Having noticed a gap between his left and O'Neal's right when the latter was advancing, Iverson bore to the left a little as he moved forward to attack Baxter. This uncovered Daniel's left and compelled his three left regiments to follow Iverson's line for some distance. At the same time, Daniel's right was under fire from Stone's Bucktail regiments, situated along the Chambersburg pike at right angles to Daniel.[61]

As Iverson's line neared Oak Ridge, Cutler's brigade wheeled ninety degrees to the right (north), bringing the Unionists into line facing Iverson's exposed right flank, and raked the advancing Southerners as they swept past to the north of Cutler.[62] But the Confederates pressed on. It seems apparent that Iverson did not see Baxter's soldiers, who were crouching, with hooded colors, behind the stone wall along the crest of Oak Ridge, facing westward.[63] Iverson's men charged up to within some seventy-five paces of the wall, when Baxter's men rose up and delivered into the face of the gray line one of the most decimating musketry volleys ever seen on a field of battle.[64] The Confederates were blasted off their feet where they stood by this withering fire. Five hundred dead and maimed on a line as straight as a dress parade marked the position which Iverson's line had occupied.[65] The horrible yet striking scene was described by an eyewitness: "Iverson's line was indicated by the ghastly row of dead and wounded men, whose blood trailed the course of their line with a crimson stain clearly discernible for several days after the battle, until the rain washed the gory record away." [66]

Iverson committed another regrettable error—which could have had serious repercussions—when he informed his division commander, Rodes, of the untrue story "that one of his regiments had raised the white flag and gone over to the enemy." [67] He later exonerated those of his shaken troops who had raised white handkerchiefs in token of surrender in order to halt the merciless shooting by Baxter's men. Iverson's shattered regiments gamely regrouped, however, and attempted a second assault, only to be beaten back again by the crashing Federal musket volleys. They withdrew to a little gully about 100 yards to the rear, where they opened a steady and fairly effective fire upon Baxter's line posted behind the stone wall.[68]

On this portion of the field occurred an incident which exemplifies the nature of the severe fighting there. A Sergeant Evans, Company B, and Private John Witmoyer, Company H, both of the 88th Pennsylvania, crouched side by side behind the stone wall, firing steadily at the Confederates in the gully. When a Southern flag-bearer boldly flaunted his colors in plain sight, Evans said to his comrade, as he snapped his musket to his shoulder, "John, I will give those colors a whack." Before he could fire, Witmoyer heard the dull and sickening thud of a lead slug striking bone and flesh near him. He turned and asked Evans if he had been hit. Keeping his eyes straight ahead, the sergeant slowly lowered the musket from his shoulder, and without uttering a word, toppled over dead at Witmoyer's feet. His heart had been pierced by a Rebel bullet.[69]

Seeing that this was the time for a counter-stroke, Baxter hurled the 83rd New York, 97th Pennsylvania, and 88th Pennsylvania forward almost immediately after Iverson's badly mauled regiments had reached the slight shelter of the gully.[70] A few men of the 12th Massachusetts also participated in the charge.[71] An instant success was scored; nearly 1,000 [72] of Iverson's soldiers were captured, of whom some 400 [73] were retained permanently by the Federals. These Southern prisoners belonged chiefly to the 5th, 20th, and 23rd North Carolina regiments.[74] Also, the 88th Pennsylvania captured the flags of the 23rd North Carolina and the 26th Alabama (the latter of O'Neal's brigade).[75] The colors of the 23rd North Carolina were seized by Lieutenant Levan, who presented them to General Robinson with "an impromptu speech," while the 26th Alabama colors were taken by Sergeant Gilligan.[76] The 97th New York captured the flag of the 20th North Carolina during this charge, the bunting being borne from the field by Corporal Sylvester Riley.[77] This flag, however, was to be recaptured later in the day by Daniel's Confederate brigade.[78] In an incident seldom seen on Civil War battlefields, one of Iverson's regiments, the 12th North Carolina, deviously escaped through some bushes under a white flag of truce or surrender—an act which halted for a few moments the musketry fire from Baxter's men.[79] Nonetheless, Iverson had suffered one of the most crushing defeats ever sustained by a brigade in the Civil War, his final demise in the Union counter-charge coming at approximately 2:45 p.m.[80]

As the shattered remnants of his brigade rolled back like scattered driftwood, Iverson became so unnerved by the experience of his repulses that Captain D.P. Halsey, his assistant adjutant-general, had to assume command of the brigade personally and try to rally the men.[81] The lack of unison and synchronization of motion between Iverson and O'Neal—and perhaps Daniel, too—was probably the only thing that prevented Baxter's small brigade from being overwhelmed by the superior numbers of the Southerners. But O'Neal decided to give it one more effort, alone. He again moved forward against Baxter's refused right at the angle of the Mummasburg road and Oak Ridge;[82] and, although he could not force the main National position, some of his grayclad skirmishers did seize the northern end of the stone wall running along the ridge crest near the road.[83]

With Ramseur moving up in relief of Iverson, and with O'Neal again trying another cast of the dice, Robinson ordered up Paul's First Brigade from the Seminary to bolster the vital Oak Ridge position. Paul had been in reserve up to this time at the Seminary, and occupied only in erecting some slight breastworks in front of the western face of the building. His brigade arrived on Oak Ridge just in time to lend some assistance in the repulse of Iverson.[84] Paul formed on the ridge, a little in the rear of Baxter's first position. His deployment from right to left was as follows: the 13th Massachusetts (Colonel Samuel H. Leonard) on the lower eastern slope of Oak Ridge, facing northward, parallel to and near the Mummasburg road; the 104th New York (Colonel Gilbert G. Prey), on the upper slope to the left of and continuing the line of the 13th Massachusetts up to the crest of the ridge; then, facing westward, came the 16th Maine (Colonel Charles W. Tilden), the 107th Pennsylvania (Lieutenant Colonel James Mac-Thomson), and the 94th New York (Colonel Adrian R. Root).[85] It was about 2:30 p.m. when Paul arrived to support Baxter.[86] With its ammunition being almost exhausted, Baxter's brigade held its position for a time with the bayonet before moving off to the left.[87]

As Paul's regiments were deploying into position, the division commander, Robinson, personally ordered Colonel Prey to form his 104th New York on the *right* of the 13th Massachusetts. As Prey moved obediently toward that indicated position, Robinson—noted for his hardbitten manner—changed his mind as to where Prey should form, and shouted down to him from the crest of the ridge in a stentorian voice, "Colonel Prey, god damn you, where are you going? Form on the *left!*" Without batting an eye, Prey skillfully hustled his men into position on the left of the 13th Massachusetts.[88] It did not pay to argue with the burly General, even if one had been correct in following original directions.

Paul's brigade got a warm welcome at once. Coming into position, it received a heavy fire from the Confederates "sheltered in the grove and behind the stone wall" to the north of the Mummasburg road.[89]

Paul arrived in time to assist in the repulse of O'Neal's second and less serious forward thrust.[90] And it was high time, for the Second Brigade had taken about all the punishment it could stand. Before falling back, Baxter's men, out of ammunition and suffering additional casualties every minute, obtained some replenishments from the cartridge boxes of those soldiers who had fallen.[91] This permitted Baxter to delay for some moments his forced withdrawal. The 11th Pennsylvania of this brigade had already had three successive commanders in the stern fighting: Colonel Richard Coulter, Captain Benjamin F. Haines, and Captain John B. Overmyer.[92] Baxter's regiments had earned a respite, having performed more than their full duty; Paul's would do at least as well.

Shortly after having arrived on the field, General Paul, commanding Robinson's First Brigade, while in the rear of the 104th New York, was shot in the face, the ball carrying away both his eyes.[93] The command of the brigade devolved upon Colonel Leonard of the 13th Massachusetts, whose regiment was in turn taken over by Lieutenant Colonel N. Walter Batchelder. But Leonard was soon wounded, and the brigade command fell upon Colonel Root of the 94th New York, who was in turn wounded himself and later taken prisoner by the enemy. Root was succeeded in command by Colonel Coulter of the 11th Pennsylvania, which regiment was now temporarily attached to the First Brigade. But again the new temporary commander of the brigade was struck down, and Colonel Lyle became the fifth leader of this tenacious, hard-fighting, but ill-fated unit.[94]

The unrelenting Confederate pressure against Oak Ridge continued, and Paul's brigade was in danger of being driven from its vital position in mid-afternoon. If this happened, the flank and rear of both Doubleday's line on McPherson Ridge and Schurz' embattled forces on the plain north of Gettysburg would be fatally compromised. But Paul's stout regiments did not buckle. The Southern fire from the angle of the road and ridge was terrific, however, with seven colorbearers of the 104th New York going down in the hail of lead. Colonel Prey ordered the left wing of this regiment to charge on the stone wall at the angle, telling his men they would all soon be dead if they did not silence the crashing Confederate volleys. For the first time in the war the regiment hesitated. Colonel Prey then stepped in front of his line and shouted, "I'll lead you, boys!" The New York lads instantly surged forward toward the enemy line, and the stone wall near the road was captured and held for a time.[95] Returning to the right wing of his regiment after this successful action, Prey ordered a limited charge of this wing on the Mummasburg road, which netted the Federals "over sixty" additional prisoners.[96] After Ramseur had reinforced Iverson's shattered legions, Paul's brigade made several attacks westward across the fields, but these costly assaults served only to delay temporarily the Confederate offensive from that quarter.[97]

Rodes now selected another of his five brigades to hurl against the stubbornly resisting men in blue. Ramseur's experienced Fourth Brigade numbered approximately 1,090 effectives.[98] His deployment from right to left was as follows: the 14th North Carolina (Colonel R. Tyler Bennett), the 30th North Carolina (Colonel Francis M. Parker), the 2nd North Carolina (Major D.W. Hurtt), and the 4th North Carolina (Colonel Bryan Grimes).[99] The first two of the above-mentioned regiments attacked Paul from the west, while the latter two attacked southward down the ridge from Oak Hill against Paul's right flank. Ramseur was assisted to a small degree by the remnants of Iverson's and O'Neal's crippled brigades.[100] At this time, as Baxter was moving off the field, having been relieved by Paul, Schurz' two divisions of the Eleventh Corps on the plain north of town were being attacked by Early.[101] But Ramseur, too, in his first assault, shared the fate of O'Neal and Iverson, and was thrown back with loss.[102] Quite a number of Confederate prisoners were seized in this initial repulse of Ramseur, and in a limited National countercharge which followed.[103] Eighty-one dead Southerners were counted the next day in position in front of the 94th New York alone.[104] The 13th Massachusetts bagged 132 prisoners in a local bayonet counterattack, but soon found itself almost surrounded, and only extricated itself after a loss of almost three-quarters of its men.[105]

After futilely assailing Paul along the above-mentioned lines, Ramseur tried a new modus operandi. He directed the 14th and 30th North Carolina regiments, assisted by O'Neal's 3rd Alabama, to shift their position and attack Paul's right flank; while Ramseur's 4th North Carolina, aided for a time by several of Doles' regiments, threatened the rear of Robinson's line.[106] All this took time, but as the reinforced Confederates of Rodes' division kept applying increasing pressure, Paul's men began to run low on ammunition. General Robinson himself helped out his rapidly firing musketeers by extracting charges from the cartridge-boxes of the dead and wounded Union soldiers lying so thickly about.[107]

While Paul was hurling back Ramseur's first onslaught, Baxter's battered brigade, out of ammunition, was moving into position with the bayonet in support of Stewart's battery at the railroad cut in Seminary Ridge.[108] Apparently some fresh ammunition arrived in time to aid the regiment in checking the approaching Confederates of Pender's division.[109] As the Southerners rushed forward to capture Stewart's pieces—many of the batterymen already having been shot down—a Federal cannoneer swung his swab at an enemy officer, and laid him low with a broken neck. The swab-wielding Union gunner, however, was soon himself writhing on the ground from several bayonet thrusts through his body.[110]

But there was no surcease for the embattled Nationals. After Ramseur's initial attack had been repulsed, Federal officers on Oak Ridge soon noticed heavy columns of Confederates massing in the McLean woods, and it appeared probable that their overwhelming numbers would compel Paul to yield the ground which he had held so tenaciously thus far.[111] However, before the Southerners could strike again, a local, limited counterattack by the 97th New York netted eighty prisoners from Ramseur's regiments.[112]

Several personal episodes in the combat just described might be noted here in order to show that warfare at Gettysburg was more than just strategy and tactics. Lieutenant Thompson of the 16th Maine was confronted with an experience that was too often allowed to occur without punishment to the guilty party. "Thompson noticed a stranger to the regiment standing about fifteen paces in rear of line, loading and firing independently. Thinking the man might do mischief to his comrades, Thompson went to him, said something in his low peculiar tone, and receiving a reply, immediately knocked him down, and then raising him from the ground by the collar, kicked him rapidly to the rear, much to the merriment and satisfaction of the men, who didn't care to be shot in the back." [113]

Another incident, a bit more bizarre, illustrates the confusion attending even the best drilled regiments when the blood is at fever pitch in a desperate life and death struggle. "Lieutenant G.A. Deering of Company G, 16th Maine, sheathed his sword, and seized a musket from a fallen man, and went into the ranks. He was evidently excited, and every once in a while would forget to return his rammer after loading, hence would send it over to the enemy. The peculiar swishing noise made by the rammer, as it hurtled through the wood was laughable to the boys, and must have been a holy terror to the rebels." [114]

Finally, Ramseur launched another powerful assault, en masse, on Paul's right flank at the angle of the ridge and road, the units attacking this point being chiefly his own 14th and 30th North Carolina regiments and O'Neal's 3rd Alabama.[115] On his right Ramseur was assisted by two of Daniel's regiments, the 43rd North Carolina (Colonel T.S. Kenan) and the 45th North Carolina (Lieutenant Colonel S.H. Boyd).[116] Daniel's remaining regiments were then moving southward against the railroad cut and Stone's brigade on McPherson Ridge. While Ramseur's 14th and 30th North Carolina regiments were attacking on the left of the Mummasburg road, his 2nd and 4th North Carolina regiments were moving on the right of the road against Paul.[117] This Confederate assault was vigorous, well directed, and not to be denied. Paul's men had reached the limit of human flesh and blood.

The end had finally come for the First Brigade. At approximately 4:15 p.m. Robinson ordered Paul's brigade to withdraw from its long held and now critical position.[118] In order to extricate the brigade from the closely pressing graycoats, Robinson personally instructed the 16th Maine to make a suicide stand at the angle of the ridge and road, directing the regiment to hold that position "at any cost." This splendid regiment delayed the Southerners long enough to allow the bulk of the remnant of the brigade to pull out safely, although itself being severely cut up and losing many prisoners. Total casualties of the regiment were 232 men killed, wounded, and missing out of 298 engaged. The retreating survivors of the 16th Maine tore their regimental flag into small bits and distributed these amongst themselves to prevent the colors from falling into the hands of the foe.[119]

Among the prisoners captured by Ramseur were Colonel Wheelock and Lieutenant Colonel Spofford of the 97th New York.[120] The flag of the 97th was saved by Corporal James McLaren, although himself wounded.[121] The flag of the 88th Pennsylvania was carried out of the fight by Color-Corporal Bonnin, who, almost collapsing from loss of blood from a serious wound, turned over the flag safely to the regiment in town.[122] The state flag of the 104th New York was borne off the field to safety by Sergeant David E. Curtis, although he was slightly wounded. The national flag of this regiment was torn from its staff and destroyed by Sergeant Moses Wallace of Company E to prevent its falling into Confederate hands.[123]

The fight made by Robinson's division was a memorable one. His two small, outnumbered brigades had successfully held their important position on Oak Ridge for over two and one-half hours against savage and unrelenting attacks. The handling of these Union brigades—especially Paul's—compared favorably with that of any on the field that day. On the Confederate side, Rodes found that he could not duplicate his victorious feats of Chancellorsville with such ease and co-ordination at Gettysburg. He had suffered enormous losses, but had inflicted staggering ones on the Federals. Two of his five brigades had been shattered, and two others had endured serious casualties. These losses would grievously, and perhaps decisively, impair Rodes' usefulness on the next two days of battle at Gettysburg. The chief responsibility for his failure on the first day's combat seems to have been the pitiful performances of O'Neal and especially of Iverson, plus Rodes' own inability to synchronize their attacks on Oak Ridge. Had this been done, and had these two brigades, and perhaps Daniel's, attacked simultaneously, it is difficult to reject the belief that success would have come much earlier in the afternoon against Robinson than it did, and with far fewer Southern casualties.

As Robinson was withdrawing from Oak Ridge, Cutler moved his brigade to a point near the railroad cut in Seminary Ridge with a view to occupying the cut, facing northward, and holding Rodes in check. Cutler then received an order to send aid to the Seminary building area, whereupon he dispatched the 76th New York, 14th Brooklyn, and 147th New York to that point.[124] It was at this time that Cutler had his horse shot from under him, and another one wounded.[125]

It has now been seen that the determined Confederates, after strenuous fighting, had succeeded in clearing the obstinate Union troops from their defensive positions north and northwest of Gettysburg, and were beginning to pursue them through the streets of the town toward Cemetery Hill. Attention must now be returned to the field west of Gettysburg, in the vicinity of the Chambersburg pike and McPherson Ridge, at a time earlier in the afternoon, when Doubleday was still holding his lines simultaneously with the struggle of Schurz and Robinson. Could the National First Corps commander purchase several more valuable hours' time by partially sacrificing his "Black Hats," taking a heavy toll of the enemy, and thus allowing the scattered Federal divisions approaching the field from the south to arrive in time and concentrate on the strategic Cemetery heights south of town? His answer—a resounding Yes!—forms part of the epic page of July 1, 1863, in the annals of the Army of the Potomac.

CHAPTER 11

The Second Contest

at the Railroad Cut

MOST INVITING TO RODES—EVEN WHILE HE WAS CONTENDING with Robinson on Oak Ridge—was the seemingly exposed right flank of Doubleday's line on McPherson Ridge. But, as Davis' brigade of Heth's division had discovered in the morning, this Union right flank was partly protected by the railroad cuts in the two crests of Mc-Pherson Ridge. In mid-morning, as will be recalled, a great many of Davis' men had been captured or shot down in the cut in the more easterly crest of the ridge. But now Daniel's brigade of Rodes' division determined to renew the experiment at the railroad, with hopes of driving the Nationals back in short order.

Long before the Southern infantry leapt forward to the attack, their brethren manning the cannon had been pounding and softening up the Federals for several hours. The Confederate artillery, in fact, had one of its best days of the war on July 1, 1863; and it played no small part in contributing to the finally successful Southern efforts to drive back Stone's small Bucktail brigade of Rowley's division, posted on the westernmost crest of McPherson Ridge just south of the Chambersburg pike.

The Confederate batteries, as mentioned before, were posted just beyond the crest of Herr Ridge, in a line roughly perpendicular to the pike. On the right (south) was Wallace's battery; then, in order to the left (north) were Rice's battery, Marye's battery, and the two Whitworth breechloading guns near the pike. Continuing the line north of the road were McGraw's battery, Crenshaw's battery, Maurin's battery, and, on Hill's extreme left, on a slight rise of ground east of Willoughby Run, Brander's battery. Later, Johnson's and Hurt's batteries went into position near the Hagerstown road on the extreme Confederate right.[1] With the destructive fire of Carter's batteries on Oak Hill and Jones's beyond Rock Creek added to that of Hill's guns on Herr Ridge, the Federal lines of the First and Eleventh Corps were exposed to the fearful fire of nearly sixty Confederate pieces, while being able to muster only thirty-six in reply.[2]

As O'Neal attacked Robinson from the north—before Iverson moved forward from the west—a gap opened between these two Confederate brigades. Consequently, when Iverson charged forward toward the stone wall on Oak Ridge, he was impelled to bear a bit to the left (north) to try to close this gap. This action resulted in the exposure of the left of Daniel's brigade, which was in support of Iverson on the latter's right-rear. Therefore, both of Daniel's flanks were in the air, although not being menaced then by any likely Federal attack or encircling movement.[3]

Daniel's veteran brigade totaled approximately 2,300 effectives, and its commander—a Tarheel, West Pointer, and Louisiana plantation owner—was himself a seasoned officer.[4] Being about 200 yards in Iverson's right-rear[5] and unable to assist his neighbor directly, Daniel instructed his right wing to change front to the right (south), and to move down to and then along the Chambersburg pike so as to threaten the left flank of Robinson and Cutler.[6] The Confederate brigadier was soon to find that this was easy to order but difficult to achieve, owing to the unyielding resistance of Stone's Union brigade, posted along the pike at the westernmost crest of McPherson Ridge. Actually, Daniel's object of reaching and then moving eastward along the pike to Seminary Ridge, and then falling upon Cutler's or Robinson's left flank was unrealistic.

At first, Daniel's 43rd, 53rd, and 32nd North Carolina regiments remained behind, vainly trying to assist Iverson in dislodging Baxter. While they were thus engaged, Daniel moved southward toward the railroad grading with his 2nd North Carolina battalion (Lieutenant Colonel H.L. Andrews) and 45th North Carolina regiment (Lieutenant Colonel S.H. Boyd).[7] As these two units advanced southward, Cutler's blue brigade, which had been firing northward against Iverson's right, wheeled backward to its line on Oak Ridge facing west, and opened a heavy flanking musketry fire on Daniel's left.[8]

Meanwhile, the steady enfilading fire from Hill's artillery on Herr Ridge to the west inflicted casualties on Stone's 143rd Pennsylvania, and, to its left, the 149th Pennsylvania, which were posted along the southern edge of the Chambersburg pike, facing northward. This caused Lieutenant Colonel Dwight of the 149th to order that his colors be placed "on the eastern edge of a wheatfield a little beyond the left flank of the regiment and somewhat to the front, where the color-bearers and guards sheltered themselves behind a pile of rails." [9] This perhaps unintended ruse was soon to prove most beneficial to the Nationals.

As Daniel neared the railroad cut, he noticed on his right some men of Hill's corps lying idle in position near Willoughby Run. Daniel requested their cooperation and support on his right flank; but the answer he received was that this was an impossible demand, owing to the shattered condition of these troops.[10] The men whom Daniel asked to help him were those of Heth's division belonging to Davis' Mississippi brigade, which had been so badly mauled earlier in the day in the clash with Cutler at the railroad cut in the easterly crest of McPherson Ridge. Despite Daniel's strong plea, it was deemed inadvisable as yet to bring Davis' remnants into battle.

This lack of aid was most disconcerting. It led Daniel later in the afternoon to try to throw his right regiment, the 32nd North Carolina —which was to be ordered down from its position supporting Iverson —astride the cut, facing eastward, while the remainder of the line faced southward.[11] But Daniel's first charges at the railroad cut were to be made solely by the 45th North Carolina and the 2nd North Carolina battalion. Later, he was compelled to call down to support his left the 43rd and 53rd North Carolina, which had been also assisting Iverson.[12] These regiments were recalled by Daniel after Iverson had been repulsed in his attack on Baxter.[13]

Facing Daniel's line were the 149th Pennsylvania along the pike at the westerly crest of McPherson Ridge, and the 143rd Pennsylvania, on the right of the 149th.[14] They opened fire as Daniel's advancing units came into range. The 150th Pennsylvania of Stone's brigade continued to face westward along the ridge, thereby making a right angle at the pike with the 149th. In addition to the small arms fire he received from Stone, Daniel was shelled by Cooper's battery, situated in a meadow near the Hagerstown road, between McPherson Ridge and Seminary Ridge.[15]

Anticipating Daniel's intention to seize and cross the railroad cut, the 149th Pennsylvania was rushed forward (to the north) to the line of the cut. Daniel's men surged forward as far as a fence bordering the adjoining field to the railroad. The Bucktails delivered a volley and then charged *across* the cut, driving Daniel over the fence to the rear. A Confederate battery to the west then enfiladed the 149th Pennsylvania's line, and this bombardment helped lead to the Federals' later withdrawal to their starting position along the southern border of the pike.[16] The success of this Union limited offensive action had been doubted at the time by Doubleday; but it had turned out satisfactorily, with Daniel's first assault on the railroad cut being repelled.[17]

After ordering the 45th North Carolina regiment and the 2nd North Carolina battalion back "some 40 paces to the crest of a hill' for regrouping,[18] Daniel called up his three remaining regiments. He directed the 53rd and 43rd North Carolina regiments to the left, and the 32nd North Carolina to the right to flank the cut.[19] The 149th Pennsylvania was then still crouching in the high grass at the northern edge of the cut, with its colors twenty paces to the left of the left flank of the regiment. As Daniel's reinforced line again swept forward, the 149th delivered a fearful volley of musketry at the graycoats at a distance of little over twenty paces. The Confederate line was staggered and baffled, thinking the Union regiment was more to their (the Confederate) right on the colors.[20]

Recovering, the persistent Daniel came forward again in formidable array. Dwight's 149th Pennsylvania, suffering under the Confederate artillery fire from the west, was compelled to retreat from the northern edge of the cut. This proved difficult to do. The right wing of the regiment got back safely across the railroad grading to the pike, because the cut was shallow at that point; but the left wing of the 149th fared worse, the cut there being quite steep. Many of the men in blue were either shot down as they slipped and slid while trying to scale the precipitate cliffs, or else were captured in the cut. The depleted ranks of the regiment reached their former position along the southern edge of the pike in a somewhat scattered order.[21] But when the Confederates were ready to attack again, they would find the 149th still putting up a bold front to them.

At about this time, in mid-afternoon, the commander of Rowley's Second Brigade, Colonel Roy Stone, was severely wounded in the arm and hip. He was entirely disabled, and forced to relinquish leadership of the brigade.[22] The command devolved upon Colonel Langhorne Wister of the 150th Pennsylvania, who, in turn, handed over the direction of his regiment to Lieutenant Colonel Henry S. Huidekoper.[23]

The colors of the 149th Pennsylvania still remained to the left of the regiment and across the pike on the northern side. They proved irresistable to Daniel, who once again came forward in a determined effort to storm across the railroad cut. But the 149th and 143rd Pennsylvania along the road were augmented now by the right wing of the 150th Pennsylvania, which came into line on the left of the 149th. After delivering what General Daniel termed the most destructive infantry volley he had ever seen, the 149th and the right wing of the 150th charged the cut and once again hurled Daniel back, despite his superior numbers. The 150th recaptured, as will be seen, the colors of the 149th, which had been cut off.[24] But the Federal troops then were obliged to return to their original position on the pike, owing to the pressure of the 32nd North Carolina, which was astraddle the railroad cut and enfilading the Union left wing, and of the Southern guns to the west on Herr Ridge.[25]

An example of the confusion of the fighting here occurred when some Confederates seized temporarily the national flag of the 149th Pennsylvania in its advanced position. Creeping up to the Union color-guard on hands and knees, the enemy squad had overcome the color defenders, and Confederate Sergeant Price, escorted by his fellow soldiers, made off with the flag toward the Southern lines. The blue color-guard, however, recovering, picked up their muskets and fired a number of shots at the running grayclads. They brought down every man save Price, who was bearing off the Federal flag. A lone Confederate staff officer, noticing the dusty, unidentified man carrying the Stars and Stripes, assumed that he was a National soldier, and strove to capture the Union flag. Dismounting, the Southern officer picked up some muskets lying amongst the dead and wounded men in the vicinity and fired several shots at his fellow soldier; but he missed.[26]

A remarkable escape from serious injury occurred about this time, when the left wing of the 150th Pennsylvania was at right angles along McPherson Ridge to its right wing along the pike. The Confederate batteries posted on Herr Ridge had been shelling the Federal line here with a steady and effective fire. Suddenly, Sergeant Major Lyon, of this regiment, had his chest grazed by a large shell "which tore away his clothing, discoloring the skin and causing intense pain, but without lacerating the flesh in the slightest." [27]

The 32nd North Carolina, which was astride the western end of the railroad cut, and which was threatening Stone's left wing along the pike, was neutralized for the time being by the left wing of the 150th Pennsylvania.[28] During the combat at approximately this time, the commander of the 149th Pennsylvania, Lieutenant Colonel Dwight, and Lieutenant Colonel Huidekoper, Major Thomas Chamberlin, and Adjutant R.L. Ashhurst, of the 150th, were wounded, as was Colonel Wister, in temporary command of the brigade. Wister had received a damaging ball through the face and mouth which, while not completely disabling him, rendered it impossible for him to give verbal commands, thus necessitating his relief from command.[29] Dana was succeeded in command of his regiment by Captain James Glenn and later by Captain Irvin of Company B; while Captain Cornelius C. Widdis assumed command of the 150th upon the wounding of Huidekoper and Chamberlin.[30]

Although he had been bloodily repulsed in his several previous sorties against the railroad cut and the pike, the intrepid Daniel determined to try it once again, in an all-out assault. He was now reinforced on his left by the 12th North Carolina of Iverson's brigade, which had escaped being riddled and captured by Baxter by making off under a white flag of truce.[31] Surging forward unrelentingly, Daniel, with the additional aid now of Davis' remnants, crossed the railroad cut finally and pushed irresistibly forward against the steady but waning fire of the 143rd and 149th Pennsylvania regiments along the pike. The 150th Pennsylvania, meanwhile, was being assailed directly from the west by one of Pender's fresh brigades, and outflanked by another newly arrived brigade of that division.[32] The greatly thinned ranks of Stone's little brigade were thus compelled to withdraw toward Seminary Ridge. This they did in perfect order, firing as they went. Calef's battery, which had once again relieved Hall's Maine battery in the pike on the westerly crest of McPherson Ridge, had been obliged to retire a little earlier in the afternoon, at approximately 3:30 p.m.[33]

Noting with approbation the approaching reinforcement of Pender's fresh brigades, Daniel's men came forward "with a chorus of terrific yelps" in their last and successful attack on the Bucktail brigade.[34] After an initial repulse, the 32nd North Carolina of Daniel's brigade, greatly assisted by Hill's men, cleared the area around the McPherson stone-basement barn.[35] The Confederates, therefore, after a costly series of uncoordinated and piecemeal attacks, had finally managed to synchronize their assaults, and their vastly superior numbers deployed against Doubleday determined the outcome.[36]

At 3:30 p.m., Howard ordered the withdrawal of the Eleventh and First Corps to Cemetery Hill, after the former and, especially, the latter, units had held the lines north and west of Gettysburg with grim tenacity and dogged determination. His purpose—like that of Buford, Reynolds, and Doubleday before him—had been to keep the Confederates from occupying the strategic heights south of the town until the bulk of the approaching Army of the Potomac could arrive and take position on those impregnable elevations. The order from Howard—given verbally to a staff officer—never reached Doubleday, however, and the First Corps commander determined to fight on west of Gettysburg in a vain hope of reinforcement, or else of holding the enemy back for some additional time. Howard, in effect, exercised little real control over the field, even though he was responsible for doing so as senior officer present.[37] His performance, in several respects, at Gettysburg, as at Chancellorsville, was distinctly disappointing.

But promises of nearing Union reinforcements were now forthcoming. Major General Daniel E. Sickles, commanding the Third Corps, informed Howard and Meade at 3:15 p.m. that he was moving his corps toward Gettysburg at once, but would be impelled to march via two separate roads. He sent also the following encouraging message to the hard-pressed Howard: "I shall move to Gettysburg immediately." At 3:35 p.m., Howard received, further, the cheering dispatch from Major General Henry W. Slocum, "I am moving the Twelfth Corps so as to come in about one mile to the right [east] of Gettysburg."[38] The Third and Twelfth Corps, if they could arrive at Gettysburg intact, without being defeated in detail by an enemy victorious by mid-afternoon and ensconced shortly afterward on Cemetery Hill at the apex of the several roads upon which these Federals were approaching the town, would tip the numerical scales in favor of the Unionists, and go far toward insuring that the battle should be an eventual Northern victory.

If Doubleday and Howard could hold on a little longer, and keep the desperate Confederates away from the Cemetery heights south of

Gettysburg, the Third and Twelfth Corps would therefore soon arrive and make secure those elevations. Other massive blue units would follow these. Although parts of Early's and Rodes' Confederate divisions were in pursuit of the Eleventh Corps Federals near the town, three of Doubleday's superb divisions, though badly shattered, were still heroically contesting every foot of ground to the west of Gettysburg on both sides of the Chambersburg pike. It was not yet clear by 3:30 p.m. whether they could hold Hill in check long enough to use up sufficient daylight to enable the marching Federal hosts to assemble in time on the Cemetery heights. If Doubleday could keep the determined Confederates from Cemetery Hill until about 4:30 or 5:00 p.m., the legacy he would leave to the Union cause would contribute an imperishable, epic page in American military annals.

CHAPTER 12

The Federals

Lose McPherson Ridge

In the heavy fighting on the morning of July 1, 1863, Abner Doubleday's Union First Corps had done exceedingly well in repelling Heth's early thrusts from the west. Wadsworth's brigades of Meredith and Cutler, before noon, had bloodily repulsed Archer and Davis, and had captured large numbers of men. Then Rowley's brigades of Stone and Biddle came up to reinforce the McPherson Ridge position. And while Schurz' Eleventh Corps divisions were contending in the hours after noon with Doles and Early, other First Corps units were distinguishing themselves. Robinson's two brigades of Baxter and Paul, assisted by Cutler, were throwing back attack after attack launched at Oak Ridge by Rodes. At the same time, in mid-afternoon, Stone's Bucktail brigade was hurling back Daniel's repeated attempts to storm across the railroad cut from Oak Hill.

But Heth was not through yet; he would bring up his two remaining fresh brigades in a final endeavor to rout Stone (already under attack from the north by Daniel), Meredith, and Biddle from McPherson Ridge, and drive them back at least to Seminary Ridge in the rear. Then, Pender's unbloodied division could finish the job by driving Doubleday through the streets of Gettysburg and perhaps even destroy or capture his remaining survivors. So, consequently, at about 2:30 p.m., Heth relieved the decimated brigades of Archer and Davis by his First Brigade, commanded by Brigadier General James J. Pettigrew, and by his Second Brigade, Colonel John M. Brockenbrough commanding. Both of these Southern brigades were deployed south of the Chambersburg pike on Herr Ridge, overlooking the valley of Willoughby Run.

But as Heth was deploying these fresh troops, a thorn was thrust into his right flank, to remain there until later in the afternoon. This was the bold movement of a company of the 80th New York, of Biddle's brigade, commanded by Captain Ambrose N. Baldwin, which drove forward some thirty rods *across* Willoughby Run and routed from the E. Harman farm buildings there a small force of Confederates. Soon, a second Union company under Captain William H. Cunningham reinforced the first company. This audacious action probably led the Southerners to overestimate the number of National troops available for defense on McPherson Ridge. It certainly did embarrass the movements of the Confederate right wing for some time during the course of the afternoon. Only later in the day, during the general Union withdrawal, when almost cut off from its line of retreat, was this Federal force pulled back from the Harman buildings. It then had to move—covered in part by Gamble's cavalry brigade— in a southerly direction through a ravine, then eastwardly through cultivated fields until rejoining the rest of Biddle's brigade on Cemetery Hill.[1]

It has been noted that, by 2:30 p.m., the Confederate artillery batteries had achieved a decided supremacy over the few Union batteries available to Doubleday. Within an hour after this time, Calef's horse artillery battery of three-inch rifles had been obliged to limber up and withdraw from its position on the pike at the westerly crest of McPherson Ridge.[2] Also, Cooper's battery, which had been supporting Biddle's brigade on the easterly crest of McPherson Ridge south of the grove, had been impelled to fall back a bit to a position in front of (that is, just to the west of) the professor's house near the Seminary. Cooper soon became engaged in a gun duel with Fry's Confederate battery on Oak Hill, and with Brander's battery, "stationed on a hill to the north of the railroad cut, on the east side of Willoughby Run." [3] With a marked inferiority in artillery weight of metal supporting them, Doubleday's infantry would be hard pressed by the superior numbers of enemy foot-soldiers arrayed against them.

Looking at the First Corps line posted along McPherson Ridge, it will be seen that the position occupied by Stone's Bucktail brigade, at the southeastern angle of the pike and westerly crest of the ridge, was the key to Doubleday's line.[4] On Stone's left was Meredith's Iron

Brigade, still holding its position in McPherson's Grove. Biddle was posted on Meredith's left-rear, in the open fields, on the easterly crest of the ridge, but with his left by no means reaching the Hagerstown road. A small gap existed between Biddle's right and Meredith's left, near the southeastern corner of the grove, in the vicinity where General Reynolds had been killed in the morning. Rowley, therefore, ordered up the 151st Pennsylvania (Lieutenant Colonel George F. McFarland), which had been in reserve at the Seminary, and directed it to take position in the gap on Biddle's right.[5]

Seeing Heth's two fresh brigades swinging into line of battle on Herr Ridge, supported in their rear by Pender's entire division, and realizing the gravity of the situation confronting him, Doubleday sent an aide, Lieutenant Slagle, to Howard, asking for some reinforcements from Steinwehr's division on Cemetery Hill. Howard, however, felt himself unable to spare any units from his reserve, so none were forthcoming to the anxious Doubleday.[6]

After a heavy cannonade,[7] Heth threw Pettigrew and Brockenbrough across Willoughby Run at the depleted line of Doubleday's First Corps.[8] The time of this movement was approximately 2:30 p.m.[9] Brockenbrough attacked Stone's position between the pike and the grove, while Pettigrew assailed the Iron Brigade in the grove and Biddle in the fields south of the woods toward the Hagerstown road. Brockenbrough's deployment from right to left was as follows: the 2nd Virginia battalion (Major John S. Bowles), the 40th Virginia regiment (Captain T.E. Betts), the 47th Virginia (Colonel Robert M. Mayo), and the 55th Virginia (Colonel W.S. Christian).[10] Pettigrew's 2,000 men[11] were deployed in line of battle as follows from right to left: the 52nd North Carolina (Colonel J.K. Marshall), the 47th North Carolina (Colonel G.H. Faribault), the 11th North Carolina (Colonel Collett Leventhorpe), and the huge 26th North Carolina (Colonel Henry K. Burgwyn, Jr.).[12]

Heth ordered the two brigades forward. Pettigrew crossed the run and moved slowly up the westerly slope of McPherson Ridge.[13] This able Confederate officer was aided somewhat on his right by the remnants of Archer's shattered brigade.[14] Instantly, the hostile lines erupted in furious volleying, as the Southerners, sweating up the slope, came within range of the Union muskets. As Pettigrew neared the crest of the ridge, he found the Iron Brigade in the grove and Biddle's brigade *en echelon* on Meredith's left-rear. This Union arrangement enabled

Pettigrew to flank the left (southernmost) regiment of the Iron Brigade, the 19th Indiana, and force it back a short distance. This uncovered the left flank of the 24th Michigan, which then succeeded in changing front to the left under a murderous fire, and thus extricated itself by a short withdrawal. Meanwhile, Brockenbrough's Virginia brigade was occupying Meredith's attention by exerting considerable pressure in the front.[15]

The 24th Michigan, fighting superbly in its maiden battle, waited until the enemy soldiers were "within 80 paces" before opening fire. The Confederates were so close to the Federal line "that the commands of their officers could be heard." Just in the rear of the gray line was a colonel mounted on a mule, shouting, "Give 'em hell boys!" At that moment, a Federal bullet knocked off his hat. The Confederate colonel, however, caught it before it touched the ground and, undaunted, resumed the vociferous urging on of his line.[16] In this desperate clash, the 24th Michigan lost heavily, though again essentially checking the foe in his initial onslaught. This regiment was to lose, in the course of the day's battle, 363 men out of 496 engaged! [17]

As the 26th North Carolina of Pettigrew's command approached the front of Biddle's right regiment, the 151st Pennsylvania, it received a heavy fire on its left flank from the 19th Indiana, in addition to suffering from the salvoes of Cooper's battery.[18] The Tarheelers came up to within twenty paces of the line of the Pennsylvanians. Then, the two regiments riddled each other at almost point-blank range with annihilating volleys, which produced "losses the most remarkable in the annals of the war!" [19] The 26th North Carolina lost eleven men shot down while bearing the colors.[20] The 151st Pennsylvania lost 337 men out of 467 engaged—a loss of seventy-nine per cent.[21] The commander of this Union regiment, Lieutenant Colonel McFarland, lost a leg in the severe fighting, and was hopelessly maimed in the other.[22] This regiment was composed of schoolboys and teachers from Juniata County, McFarland being the superintendent there of the local academy.[23] On the other side, the 26th North Carolina lost 588 out of 800 engaged—the heaviest loss in the Army of Northern Virginia during the entire battle and campaign.[24] The staggering casualties in these two regiments occurred chiefly within the space of forty minutes.[25] General Heth said of the 151st Pennsylvania, after the Southerners had managed later to occupy the position, "The dead of the enemy marked its line of battle with the accuracy of a line at a dress parade." [26] Pettigrew, however, found that the Federal line was, for the moment, immovable. Doubleday, heavily outnumbered, was making a determined stand.

To Pettigrew's left, Brockenbrough crossed Willoughby Run and headed at first directly for Stone's western front. But as his Virginians splashed across the water to the eastern bank they met with stubborn resistance from Stone's skirmish line, posted 400 yards in front of the main Bucktail line.[27] The 150th Pennsylvania, seeing Brockenbrough's line approaching at about 2:45 p.m., wheeled its line back from the Chambersburg pike to its original line along the ridge, facing westward.[28] It appeared for a moment as if Brockenbrough was going to continue advancing head-on against Stone; but, as the Confederate line neared the westerly crest of McPherson Ridge, the small quarry midway between the pike and the grove compelled most of these Southerners to oblique to their right (south) toward the woods in the direction of Meredith's Iron Brigade. This deflection, however, permitted Brockenbrough's right to link up with Pettigrew's left.[29]

But, like Pettigrew in his initial thrust at the south of the grove, Brockenbrough too was repulsed with loss in his first charge, by the Iron Brigade.[30] Meredith, being in advance of Biddle on the left, was obliged to protect his left by pulling his command back to a less advantageous position in the woods, about 200 yards to the rear.[31] Then, too, Brockenbrough was aided by the attacks made by Daniel from the north against the railroad cut, and by the assistance of the remnants of Davis' brigade on his (Brockenbrough's) left.

A few incidents which occurred in this part of the battle go far toward showing the desperate nature of the fighting. The 150th Pennsylvania flag-bearer, Sergeant Phifer, "fell bleeding from a mortal wound, while proudly flaunting the colors in the face of the foe."[32] The temporary commander of the 150th, Lieutenant Colonel Huidekoper, fell at this time, pierced in the arm and leg. He visited the stone-basement barn for repairs, came back immediately to his regiment, but was too weak from shock and loss of blood to continue in command. He was obliged to retire from the field. The next in command, Major Chamberlin, had been seriously wounded earlier, so the command of the regiment changed for the fourth time, Adjutant Ashhurst assuming command. Ashhurst, too, was quickly wounded, but gamely remained in direction of the regiment on the field.[33]

In the 26th North Carolina, there were three sets of twins. After this furious clash, five of these six individuals were dead.[34] In Company F of this regiment, there were eight officers and eighty-one men. Thirty-nine of them were killed, and every man in the company was hit by a bullet except one, who was knocked unconscious by the concussion of a shell while crossing the run.[35] The 26th North Carolina remnants, out of ammunition, replenished their supply from the Union dead, lying scattered about, mingled with the gray.[36]

Despite the stubborn Union resistance, and the repulses of their first thrusts, the two gray brigades gallantly renewed their advance. Pettigrew's attack on Meredith's left and against Biddle was now steadily gaining ground; Brockenbrough's assault at the northern edge of the grove was progressing also. The Confederates were fresh, while the Iron Brigade soldiers were jaded and much depleted in numbers from the heavy fighting which, for them, had begun at 10:15 a.m. Finally, the right regiment of Meredith's brigade, the 7th Wisconsin, was ordered to retire to Seminary Ridge, which it did slowly and deliberately, firing and reloading step by step.[37] This forced withdrawal endangered the other Federal regiments of the brigade. But before withdrawing to Seminary Ridge, the 24th Michigan formed three separate lines of battle in McPherson Grove. In the ensuing retrograde movement, it was to form two more in the fields between the grove and Seminary Ridge, and a sixth line of battle on Seminary Ridge itself.[38]

In the withdrawal through the fields, the last member of the color-guard of the 24th Michigan having fallen, Colonel Morrow himself grabbed the flag to rally the remnant of his regiment. The staff was seized instantly from his hands by Private William Kelly of Company E, who said, "The Colonel of the 24th Michigan shall not carry the colors while I am alive." In a few seconds, his prostrate form was lying lifeless at the feet of the colonel. Morrow then picked up the colors and only relinquished them when he reached the comparative safety of Doubleday's lines on Seminary Ridge, where he himself fell wounded in the head.[39]

Meanwhile, despite the retreat of the 7th Wisconsin, Brockenbrough could make little immediate impression on Meredith's right regiments in the grove or on the 150th Pennsylvania near McPherson's barn until the Union flanks were turned. Only then would he be able to come forward with better results,[40] assisted by Daniel's persevering attempts to cross the railroad grading and gain the pike.[41] The 150th Pennsylvania, especially, though in the open fields, seemed as immovable as Gibraltar; fifty dead "in a straight line" marked its position distinctly, as noted later by the Southerners.[42]

But further to their right, as the bitter fighting continued, the Confederates were having better fortune. The 52nd North Carolina, Pettigrew's right regiment, outflanked Biddle's left and poured a devastating enfilading fire into his line.[43] The 47th North Carolina, to the left (north) of the 52nd, aided also in crumbling Biddle's unprotected line in the open fields.[44] The range of the musketry fire here was extremely short and deadly.[45] Despite severe losses, and in spite of the attempts of the 121st Pennsylvania, Biddle's left regiment, to change front to the left (south) and check the enemy, Pettigrew prevailed.[46] Colonel Chapman Biddle's horse was shot out from under him, Biddle himself receiving a slight scalp wound from a minié ball.[47] In Pettigrew's 11th North Carolina, one company took three officers and thirty-five men into the battle, and lost two officers and thirty-one men. On the third day's battle, the captain and four men again participated in the combat, with three of them being shot down, leaving just two men of the company on their feet at the end of the three days of battle.[48]

Pettigrew's skillful attack on Biddle's left, which was in the air due to lack of numbers, compelled Biddle to withdraw to the rear to avoid capture or annihilation. Colonel Gates, of the 80th New York, commanding Biddle's left demi-brigade, was the only regimental officer of the brigade remaining on horseback. He himself took the colors of the 80th New York to insure the men's steadiness in the difficult fighting retreat to Seminary Ridge.[49] This rapid but orderly withdrawal of Biddle occurred at approximately 3:45 p.m.,[50] and was followed very shortly afterward by that of Meredith, which was also carried out with precision and discipline.

The forced withdrawal of the Iron Brigade came a few moments before the Bucktails, on its right, were dislodged. Stone fell back, step by step, firing and reloading, and compelling the eager Confederates to stay at arm's length. The brigade reformed in line of battle in a peach orchard on Seminary Ridge south of the pike.[51] Colonel Wister of the 150th Pennsylvania, wounded in the face, was taken prisoner by the enemy, although he was able later to escape from his captors.[52]

An incident illustrative of the devotion of the men in the ranks to their regimental leader occurred when the beloved commander of the 142nd Pennsylvania, Colonel Cummins, was slain. An officer witnessing the event described it:

Three or four of the remnant of the column . . . faithful to their old commander, endeavored to carry his lifeless body along; but the enemy was too close. Several of the boys were shot dead while trying to perform this solemn duty. One was left, and seeing the impossibility to accomplish this purpose himself, he unbuckled the Colonel's belt and came off the field, swinging the Colonel's sword, not, however, escaping being wounded; for, as he passed me the blood was streaming out of his mouth, and the tears down his cheeks. But with the courage of an infuriated lion, he was swearing eternal vengeance on our enemies.[53]

A striking figure in the retreat of the 143rd Pennsylvania to Seminary Ridge was Color-Sergeant Ben Crippen. This intrepid flag-bearer turned around several times and shook his fist in the faces of the Confederates who were closing in on him. He soon fell mortally wounded. Major Conyngham, on the right of the regiment, seeing the flag fall, shouted, "143rd rally on your colors!" The command was obeyed instantly and the colors were saved. Confederate General A.P. Hill witnessed the incident and voiced regret that such a gallant man as Crippen should thus meet his doom.[54]

With Doubleday's whole line in retreat, finally, near 4:00 p.m., toward Seminary Ridge, Hill decided to clinch the decision on the field by committing Pender's division of four fresh brigades to the fray. Could Doubleday seriously hope to delay this new and overwhelming threat to his hastily formed line on Seminary Ridge, or would his battered brigades succumb at once to the massive fresh forces being poured on them relentlessly? His answer, and the magnificent staying qualities of his First Corps soldiers, would astound the daring Hill and his confident subordinates.

CHAPTER 13

Pender's Clash

with Doubleday

on Seminary Ridge

KING NUMBERS WAS FINALLY ASSERTING HIMSELF. PETTIGREW, aided by Brockenbrough and Daniel, had at last succeeded in pressing the stubborn Doubleday off McPherson and Oak Ridges, but at fearful cost to the Southern invaders. It was only when Heth's division had been terribly cut up that Hill decided to throw the four fresh brigades of Major General William D. Pender's Third Division into the conflict. Heth himself had been wounded in the head, his life having been saved by a wad of folded paper—previously placed inside the sweatband of his oversized hat—which had deflected a hostile bullet.

Doubleday saw that the overbearing numbers of fresh Confederate soldiers would inevitably drive his depleted First Corpsmen from the field unless timely reinforcements were forthcoming. Therefore, at about 4:00 p.m., he sent his adjutant general, Halstead, to Howard for reinforcements. But when Halstead told Howard of Pender's approaching lines, "Howard [at first] insisted that Halstead mistook rail fences for troops in the distance." Howard refused then to issue orders for a retreat and would not send additional troops to Doubleday, but instead dispatched Halstead to look for Buford—who had fallen back towards Cemetery Hill—for cavalry support.[1] Once again Howard's unrealistic, imperious attitude and erroneous views were to endanger the embattled Nationals falling back from McPherson Ridge onto Seminary Ridge, while his own Eleventh Corps troops were reeling backward in total defeat through the streets of the town.

The unbloodied troops that Hill had selected to clinch the contest were now being moved into their jump-off positions. Pender—one of Lee's ablest division commanders—deployed Brigadier General James H. Lane's Second Brigade on the Confederate right, Colonel Abner Perrin's First Brigade in the center, and Brigadier General Alfred M. Scales' Fourth Brigade on the left near the Chambersburg pike. Brigadier General Edward L. Thomas' Third Brigade was held in reserve behind the other three, where it supported the massive Confederate artillery array on Herr Ridge.[2] Thomas was to remain out of the action throughout the day, even when the Confederate batteries moved forward from Herr Ridge to McPherson Ridge in the rear of the infantry which was engaged with Doubleday.

The deployment of Lane's brigade, on the Confederate right, was as follows from right to left: the 7th North Carolina (Captain J. McLeod Turner), the 37th North Carolina (Colonel W.M. Barbour), the 28th North Carolina (Colonel John W. Barry), and the 33rd North Carolina (Colonel C.M. Avery).[3] The 7th North Carolina on the extreme right changed front to the right and faced southward against Gamble's Union cavalry brigade.[4] Lane had present 1,355 effectives.[5] It should be noted that when Pender moved forward across Willoughby Run against Doubleday's lines, at about 3:30 p.m.,[6] Lane's brigade of his division overlapped Doubleday's left flank "for a quarter of a mile."[7] This was unavoidable on Doubleday's part because, even after extending Biddle's left wing as far as possible to the south, the Union line was extremely thin, due to lack of numbers. The Confederate threat to his left-rear was a prime factor in eventually compelling Doubleday to yield the field later in the afternoon.

On Lane's left, Perrin's brigade deployed as follows from right to left: the 1st South Carolina (Provisional Army) commanded by Major C.W. McCreary, the 14th South Carolina (Lieutenant Colonel Joseph N. Brown), the 13th South Carolina (Lieutenant Colonel B.T. Brockman), and the 12th South Carolina (Colonel John L. Miller).[8] Although the brigade's 1st South Carolina Rifles (Captain William M. Hadden) was detached on train duty and did not participate in this battle, Perrin nonetheless mustered 1,600 effectives for action.[9]

On Perrin's left, Scales deployed his brigade from right to left as follows: the 16th North Carolina (Captain L.W. Stone), the 22nd North Carolina (Colonel James Conner), the 34th North Carolina (Colonel William Lee Lowrance), the 13th North Carolina (Colonel J.H. Hyman), and the 38th North Carolina (Colonel W.J. Hoke).[10]

The 38th was to the left (north) of the Chambersburg pike, the other regiments to the right.[11] The brigade numbered 1,250 effectives.[12] Scales was aided on his left somewhat by the remnants of Davis' brigade, now augmented by its 11th Mississippi regiment, which had been detached on train guard duty. Davis' brigade had seen little action since its fiasco in the railroad cut early in the morning.[13] Scales was assisted also by the previous unremitting efforts of Daniel's brigade to cross the railroad grading and rout Stone's Bucktail brigade.

Thomas' brigade of Pender's division was in reserve, supporting Hill's tremendous concentration of guns on Herr Ridge. However, Thomas was ready to advance if needed, and was deployed from right to left as follows: the 49th Georgia, the 45th Georgia, the 14th Georgia, and the 35th Georgia.[14]

As Stone's brigade was pulling back toward Seminary Ridge in the face of the overwhelming numbers of Daniel, Davis, and Brockenbrough, backed by Scales, several affairs occurred which demonstrate graphically the desperate fighting and gallantry exhibited on this portion of the field. Adjutant Ashhurst of the 150th Pennsylvania saw First Sergeant Weidensaul of Company D bend over and clutch his body with his hands, as if in great pain. Ashhurst asked him, "Are you wounded?" "No," the Sergeant replied, "killed!" He then fell dead in a half-turning motion away from the adjutant.[15] Being in temporary command of the 150th, Ashhurst relayed to his men an order which he had received to withdraw. Lieutenant Bell of the regiment then came storming up to Ashhurst, protesting vehemently that the forced retrograde movement was "damned cowardice." Despite this emotional outburst, the regiment and brigade had no choice but to fall back or be annihilated.[16]

At approximately 4:00 p.m., Doubleday's thin lines were reformed in a fairly strong defensive position on Seminary Ridge, again to contest the unrelenting Confederate advance from the west.[17] Scales had tried to push through the ranks of Meredith's Iron Brigade in the Union withdrawal to Seminary Ridge, but had been thwarted.[18] In this advance against Doubleday, Pender and Scales were both wounded, the former fatally.[19] The absence of Pender would handicap Lee during the remainder of the battle, for the division commander was a brilliant officer. Pegram's and McIntosh's artillery battalions were advanced by Hill to McPherson Ridge, Doubleday's previous position.[20]

Pender was embarrassed on his right throughout his advance against the First Corps. Buford's mounted cavalrymen, on the Federal left flank, so delayed Lane by their carbine fire that, although suffering relatively light casualties, Lane was obliged to form squares against a possible cavalry charge. This so retarded his advance that he was unable to participate effectively in the final Confederate drive on Doubleday's position on Seminary Ridge.[21]

As Biddle was falling back, just prior to Meredith's and Stone's withdrawal,[22] the 19th Indiana lost its eighth color-bearer. Lieutenant Colonel W.W. Dudley—who was, after the war, to play a rather dubious role in the political campaign of 1888—then picked up the flag and waved it with a cheer, before going down with a severe wound in his right leg.[23] The fighting retreat was difficult, and must have seemed to drag on endlessly to the bluecoats. The distance that the First Corps soldiers had to cover in their withdrawal from McPherson Ridge to Seminary Ridge was about 500 yards.[24] Doubleday's trying task of extricating his force in the face of a closely-pressing, superior-numbered foe, was truly an outstanding feat of generalship, and he made the grimly pursuing Southerners pay dearly for every yard they gained. In doing this, he was following the dictum laid down early in the morning by Reynolds.

On Seminary Ridge, the distance between the Chambersburg pike and the Hagerstown road was approximately 600 yards, with the Seminary building standing about midway between the two highways. The new Union line there was buttressed by artillery batteries posted by Colonel Wainwright.[25] These Federal batteries were, from right to left, Stewart's, Stevens', Cooper's, and Reynolds'.[26] About twenty Union guns were thus ready to open up on the advancing enemy phalanx. A race then ensued between Wadsworth's remnants and Pender's men to reach Seminary Ridge, the Confederates striving earnestly, but futilely, to follow directly on the heels of the retiring Federals in order to escape the deadly Union artillery fire which they knew was about to hit them. But despite the efforts of the Southerners, Wadsworth won the crucial race.[27]

As the battered National First Corps soldiers neared the vicinity of the Seminary building, they were directed into position behind the slight semi-circular rail entrenchments which Paul's brigade had hastily thrown up early in the afternoon.[28] Doubleday now deployed his shattered brigades in the following order from right to left: Paul's,

Cutler's, Baxter's, Stone's, Meredith's, and Biddle's.[29] They did not have long to wait; at approximately 4:15 p.m. Pender's four fresh brigades attacked this last Union line of battle west of Gettysburg.[30]

The Confederate assault was impetuously delivered, but the defense made by the thin blue line was masterful. As the beautifully aligned ranks of Scales' brigade came up the western slope of Seminary Ridge between the pike and the Seminary building, Stewart's battery—one section just north of the railroad cut in the ridge and the other section in Thompson's yard just south of the cut—opened fire on the Confederates when they were about seventy-five or 100 yards away. Stewart's six twelve-pounder bronze Napoleons belched double charges of canister at the gray lines, which melted away under the hail of metal. This decimating fire was undoubtedly the most destructive field artillery fire by a battery of the entire battle—perhaps of the war! Stewart's guns were far enough to the right to enable them to enfilade Scales' left wing and line as the Confederates moved up the slope. The result of these murderous salvoes was that Scales' regiments were broken up and reduced in size to squads, Scales himself being wounded in the leg. The command of the brigade devolved upon Lieutenant Colonel G.T. Gordon of the 34th North Carolina. No troops could have withstood this withering storm of death, and Scales found it difficult even to rally his shattered units after the fearful execution wrought by Stewart's cannon. Only one field officer was left standing in Scales' entire force! That evening, only 500 of the brigade answered the roll call.[31] Yet Lee was to call on this unit—as he would have to do with other commands heavily engaged on July 1st—as a key element in Pickett's charge on the 3rd day's battle. Certainly, after the experience suffered by Scales' brigade on the first day's combat, it was not reasonable to expect that it would be of great service on the 2nd or 3rd.

Indicative of the furious fighting which took place on this portion of the field at this time was an incident which occurred in the 14th Brooklyn, which regiment was supporting Stewart's battery. An aide was giving orders for a slight adjustment in position of the regiment. He had his arm raised, pointing to the new position. Suddenly his extended hand was blown off by a Confederate solid shot fired from a gun which had been zeroed-in on the Federal position.[32]

Scales' right wing was checked, also, for an additional twenty minutes, as Doubleday threw his own headquarters-guard into the

Seminary building as a reinforcement to the hard pressed Union infantrymen and cannoneers.[33] The musketry firing was so concentrated and rapid, said one soldier, that the muskets "grew hot in our hands, and the darkness [from the clouds of smoke], as of night, had settled upon us."

Despite the staggering initial losses they had suffered, the Confederates regrouped and pressed forward again. The color-bearer of the 13th North Carolina, W.F. Faucette, of Big Falls, North Carolina, had his right arm almost torn from the socket by a shell; but, clasping the flag standard under his left arm, with his right arm dangling in shreds, he surged ahead, shouting, "Forward, forward!"[34] Such men, in superior number, were not to be denied.

In the heavy fighting here at the Seminary, Colonel Gates, of the 80th New York, felt his mount struck by bullets five times.[35] Colonel McFarland, of the 151st Pennsylvania, had his horse shot out from under him, then was himself shot through both legs. He was carried into the Seminary building, which served as a hospital for the wounded of both sides. Captain Owens assumed command of the 151st Pennsylvania.[36]

The Federals received no surcease from the determined Confederates. To the Union left, Perrin's brigade assaulted the breastworks. In the initial attack, however, only one Southern soldier—a color-bearer—reached the slight Federal entrenchments. But Perrin's right overlapped and eventually outflanked the Union left, and this proved to be invaluable to the grayclads. Cooper's battery, supporting Biddle, was closely pressed, but continued to fire steadily and effectively.[37] Perrin soon noted that he was supported but little on his left, where Scales' brigade had been nearly annihilated by Stewart's artillery fire, or on his right, where Gamble's dismounted carbineers, posted behind a stone wall on the ridge, had checked Lane's brigade in the Schultz Woods south of the Hagerstown road. This inability of the Confederate troops to rout the Federals to his left and right would prevent Perrin later from cutting off the Union retreat to Cemetery Hill, even after he had cracked the blue line in his front.

The troops which Perrin encountered in front were chiefly those of Biddle's reduced brigade, occupying Paul's breastworks in the grove in front of (that is, just to the west of) the Seminary building. When they came within range, the Southerners were greeted with a searing musketry fire. Biddle's terrific volleys were described by Perrin himself as "the most destructive fire I have ever been exposed to." The Southern brigade commander, however, skillfully regrouped his regiments and again pressed forward, and this time finally breached the weakened Union line just south of the Seminary building. Perrin's men then poured a heavy enfilading fire into the Federal line, despite a flank fire from some of Gamble's dismounted cavalrymen.[38] It was chiefly two of Perrin's regiments—the 1st South Carolina and the 14th South Carolina—that broke into the Union lines and made Biddle's position untenable. After an initial check, his 12th South Carolina and 13th South Carolina helped to drive Gamble's cavalrymen out from behind the stone wall to the Confederate right.[39] Perrin's lodgment within the National lines to the south of the Seminary caused Doubleday's final withdrawal.[40]

Here it was that Colonel Morrow of the 24th Michigan fell with a slight head wound while waving aloft his regimental flag in a last effort to rally and steady his men. Taken prisoner by the Confederates, Morrow later escaped by donning a green scarf (the Medical Corps badge) and posing as a surgeon—an unethical stunt which completely fooled the Southerners, including General Gordon.[41]

Meanwhile, over on the Union right, Cutler's brigade, aided by the 6th Wisconsin of the Iron Brigade and by the right section of Stewart's battery, was holding back Daniel, Ramseur, and O'Neal long enough for Paul's and Baxter's brigades to extricate themselves and retreat by way of the railroad fill at the eastern foot of Seminary Ridge.[42] Their previous escape earlier in the afternoon had been made possible by the splendid rear-guard action of the 16th Maine on Oak Ridge, described before.[43] Several of Stewart's guns, whose horses had been killed, were dragged off over Seminary Ridge by ropes manned by members of the 14th Brooklyn, which regiment had been supporting the battery.[44] Quite a number of Federal prisoners were taken on Seminary Ridge before Doubleday ordered his First Corps remnants to retreat through Gettysburg to Cemetery Hill.[45] Howard's belated order—dispatched at 4:10 p.m.—for the First Corps to pull back had never reached the commander of this unit.[46]

Doubleday had held the Confederates back for another half hour by his firm stand on Seminary Ridge.[47] But the end had now come for the die-hard Unionists. It was about 4:15 or 4:30 p.m. when the First Corps was finally impelled to yield the field west of the town to the enemy.[48] This Federal corps had been steadily and heavily engaged since early morning against overwhelming numbers of Southerners from Heth's, Rodes', and Pender's divisions. Its heroic stand, along with the assistance given by the Eleventh Corps, had kept the Confederates from seizing the strategic heights south of Gettysburg, and would thereby permit the scattered divisions of Meade's army to reach the field in time to bolster the two shattered corps which had been fighting Hill and Ewell and to hold tenaciously the vital Cemetery Ridge position on the following two days of desperate battle.

The Federal artillery batteries were the first organizations to leave Seminary Ridge. They got off successfully, except for one gun in Lieutenant Wilber's section of Reynolds' battery, which had four of its horses shot down, and which had to be abandoned when the Nationals saw that they did not have time to cut the dead animals out of the traces.[49] The Union infantry then moved down the eastern slope of the ridge. Some regiments were obliged to scurry quickly to escape capture, while others marched deliberately all the way to Cemetery Hill, stopping to fire well-directed volleys at the pursuing foe.[50]

The Federals were compelled to leave most of their wounded on the field in the hands of the Confederates. In many instances, the Southerners were too busy fighting and caring for their own wounded to give immediate attention to the wounded men in blue. Many cases of suffering and of horror were recorded. An eyewitness gave the following statement of what he saw on the field while a prisoner of the Confederates:

> Many received an additional wound while lying on the field, and relief did not come for several days and nights, nor until the maggots began to crawl and fatten in their festering wounds. . . . Last night the Colonel visited the scene of conflict and brought in some of the wounded who had lain there three days with no care except what the rebels bestowed, who gave them water and treated them well. They, however, stripped and robbed the bodies of the dead who still lie there so bloated as to be unrecognizable.[51]

In another case, more bizarre, Orderly Sergeant Henry Cliff, Company F, 76th New York, fell early in the action, and soon found himself helpless behind the Confederate lines. Being unable to move, and roasting in the blazing sun, he asked a nearby graycoat if he would carry him to the shade of a tree which was only a few yards away. "I shan't do it," replied the embittered Confederate. "Get some of your damned Yankee horde to help you. If you had been at home, where you belonged, instead of fighting for the damned nigger, you would not have needed help!" The sergeant remained on that spot for five days and nights, unattended, while the shade of the tree passed agonizingly close to him. He was finally picked up after the Army of Northern Virginia had retreated, his limb amputated, and his life saved.[52] This episode, while unusual, serves to indicate the extreme bitterness and rancor at times existing between the contending soldiery of both armies.

Doubleday had finally terminated his masterly fight against the outnumbering Confederate forces by ordering his depleted command to withdraw through the streets of the town of Gettysburg to Cemetery Hill, where Howard had maintained a small reserve of infantry and artillery. But whether the bulk of the Union soldiers of the First Corps, and the Eleventh, could extricate themselves from the presence of the closely-pursuing enemy and thread their way through the network of streets, alleys, houses, and yards, and reach the friendly heights south of the town in safety, was another question, the answer to which seemed likely to be in the negative.

CHAPTER 14

The Retreat

through the Town

WHILE A DESCRIPTION OF THE RETREAT OF THE UNION FIRST and Eleventh Corps soldiers through the streets of Gettysburg might seem a random and useless collection of isolated incidents put together at the whim of the author, the withdrawal *was* in reality chaotic, episodic, and filled with unconnected events. Therefore, if the reader finishes the chapter with a feeling of confusion, he is experiencing only the true flavor and spirit of what actually was a maelstrom of desperate, uncoordinated happenings in the retreat and pursuit.

In a previous chapter, the Union Eleventh Corps had been left retreating through the town from north to south a little earlier in the afternoon than when the First Corps commenced its withdrawal from Seminary Ridge. Most of the officers of the Eleventh Corps knew where the rallying point of Cemetery Hill was located, because, earlier in the afternoon, they had moved over this elevation while rushing out to the plain north of town to try to link up with Doubleday's right flank on Oak Ridge. But, on the other hand, very few officers of the First Corps knew exactly where the hill was situated, for they had bypassed it early in the morning when they cut diagonally across the fields from the Codori buildings to the Seminary. Therefore, this dearth of precise information would enhance the likelihood of failure in the already difficult task of extricating the remnants of the First Corps from the presence of the Confederates on Seminary Ridge and of making good their escape through the narrow streets of the town.

The southern portion of Doubleday's force on Seminary Ridge retreated via the Hagerstown road through the southern outskirts of Gettysburg, and most of them escaped the dread clutches of the relentlessly pursuing foe. The right section of the First Corps, however, was obliged to use the more northerly Chambersburg pike, which ran directly into the heart of the town. This latter route took them to the square, or diamond, where quite a number of Early's Confederate soldiers were waiting for them, having already finished with the Eleventh Corps refugees. Many Federals were captured, while those who escaped did so by climbing fences, and running through yards, houses, and shops.[1] Some Federal units retreated in good order all or most of the way; others were swept into confusion and near-rout, the flight in some cases being little better than *sauve qui peut*. Ramseur's and Hays' brigades were the principal pursuing Confederate forces, although it is probable that some men of Doles' and Avery's brigades also participated in the chase through town.[2]

Once the full-scale retreat into Gettysburg was under way, utter confusion reigned.[3] Some artillery pieces swept the streets with flying canister. Union forces rushing down one street would find Confederates charging them at right angles from a side street. All this furious action was taking place between approximately 4:15 and 4:45 p.m.[4] The exultant Confederates were shouting and yelping like madmen, their piercing "Rebel yell" rising above the din of battle. Some grayclads, setting up an ambuscade, allowed their exuberance to exceed their manners, and shouted, "Come in here, you Yankee sons of bitches!"[5] As the Nationals retreated up the streets, said one man in blue, "pale and frightened women came out and offered us coffee and food, and implored us not to abandon them."[6] The whole scene was one of complete and indescribable pandemonium.

Although some Federal guns occasionally halted, unlimbered, and fired several blasts at the onrushing enemy,[7] the Union forces nonetheless suffered heavy casualties in passing through Gettysburg to Cemetery Hill. Although the town experienced little damage, several men were downed by falling bricks as well as by overexertion in the terrific heat.[8] Some National soldiers, trapped and facing certain capture, threw their muskets down a well to keep them from falling into the hands of the foe.[9] Despite their best efforts to escape intact, at least 3,000 Union prisoners were taken in the streets of Gettysburg during this Federal withdrawal of the First and Eleventh Corps.[10] For example, the 45th New York, of Amsberg's brigade, was trapped in a dead-end alley, where fourteen officers and 164 men were captured.[11] The 6th Wisconsin, however, found time during their rapid retreat to halt and face their pursuers, "giving three cheers for the Old Flag and the 6th Wisconsin."

All the churches, as well as many of the homes in Gettysburg, were converted into temporary field hospitals for the wounded of both armies. One of the most tragic incidents of the first day's battle was the slaying of Chaplain Howell, of the 90th Pennsylvania, while he was coming out of one of these church-hospitals on Chambersburg Street. A Confederate soldier at the foot of the front church steps, seeing Howell wearing a straight dress sword, shouted up to him to unbuckle the sword and surrender. Howell protested that he was a chaplain—a noncombatant—and that the sword was proper, being just an ornament and part of his uniform, never to be used. But the insistent Southerner called again for the chaplain to drop his sword and capitulate. When Howell tried to explain once more his true pacific status, the defiant "Johnny Reb" quickly leveled his musket and shot him, Howell falling at the top of the steps, a dead man.[12] The only citizen of the town to be killed, however, was pretty, twenty-year-old Jennie Wade, who was struck down by a slug, which passed through two doors, while she was serenely baking bread in the kitchen of a house on Baltimore Street.[13]

General Schimmelfennig, commanding Schurz' Third Division, seeing himself about to be captured, dove under a woodpile to elude his pursuers. He quickly pulled the blocks of wood over him and all around him, and hid in this cramped position for two days and nights until the enemy departed.[14] In another house in Gettysburg, during the Union retreat on the first day, a shell cleared the supper table just as the brave members of the family had finished their meal, thus saving their having to wash the dishes! [15]

The wounded color-bearer of the 150th Pennsylvania, Frank Gutelius, stopped to rest for a moment at Power's stoneyard on the corner of High and Washington Streets. Here he was dispatched by a blood-thirsty Rebel, and the flag captured by Lieutenant Harvey of the 14th North Carolina. But Harvey was soon mortally wounded, his last words being to turn over this flag, with his compliments, to Governor Zebulon Vance of North Carolina. This was done. Vance, in turn, sent the flag to Jefferson Davis in Richmond, and it was found among the Confederate president's luggage when he was caught fleeing southward after Appomattox.[16]

Some soldiers, however, simply refused to be measured for a coffin. Private Little of the 88th Pennsylvania, shot through the body, was pronounced to be in a dying condition. He would be fortunate, the physician said, to last two more hours. "On hearing this the wounded man flared up in unrighteous indignation, and swore by many strange oaths that he would not die just yet, but would outlive the surgeon, which prediction, notwithstanding his horrible wound, he lived to verify."[17] Many of the wounded of both armies—especially of the Union army—lying in churches and homes in the town, received scant medical attention. After a time they presented a ghastly appearance. "Their lacerated limbs were frightfully swollen and, turning black, had begun to decompose; the blood flowing from gaping wounds had glued some of the sufferers to the floor."[18] It all presented a grisly picture to behold.

Even the youngest soldiers among the Confederate pursuers were having a field day. George Greer, "a chubby boy of sixteen" belonging to a Georgia regiment, brought in over fifty demoralized Federal prisoners, whom he presented proudly to his superiors.[19] Another youthful Southern officer, noting that Gordon's brigade had suffered few casualties as it was moving toward the outskirts of the town, asked General Gordon, who was mounted on a magnificent steed, "General, where are your dead men?" Gordon shouted back to the boyish subaltern, "I haven't any, Sir; the Almighty has covered my men with His shield and buckler!"[20]

An altercation, bordering on the humorous as well as on the grim side, occurred when a huge Federal prisoner of Irish descent was brought behind the lines of Jones' artillery battalion. A Confederate gunner—also an Irishman—began to heckle the Union soldier on his bad fortune. Soon, they found out that one was a wearer of the green, while the other was an Orangeman. One bandied word led to another. Then, in the midst of the great battle, with other soldiers looking on, these two men suddenly squared off against each other, barefisted, in a regular Bowery brawl. It was soon noted by a Confederate officer, however, that the Union man's right fist was bloody and gory, and carried stumps of two fingers which had been blown off the hand during the day's battle. When apprised of this fact, the Confederate Irishman immediately dropped his fists and, in a friendly fashion, shook hands with his worthy adversary.[21]

In an Eleventh Corps regiment, a Union soldier named Schwarz suddenly encountered a familiar face in the person of a Confederate prisoner who had just been brought in. The captured man turned out to be the Federal's brother. The two had not seen each other since one had left Germany many years before. "They embraced right there and then";[22] the Brothers' War had ended for the man in gray.

But Youth would have to share the day with Age. Colonel Wheelock of the 97th New York took refuge during the retreat in a house in town. A Southern lieutenant entered the dwelling, with pistol drawn. He called upon the Colonel to surrender his sword. This the proud old man refused to do. The Confederate officer then called in a number of his infantrymen, and said to the Colonel, while drawing out his watch, "You are an old gray-headed man, and I dislike to kill you, but if you don't give up that sword in five minutes, I shall order these men to blow your brains out." After the five minutes had expired, the doughty Colonel still refused to comply. As the Confederate lieutenant was about to order his men to open fire on the brave old martinet before him, a sudden tumult in the street distracted the attention of the Southerners for a few moments. This gave the Colonel time to slip his sword to a girl in the house, who secreted it away under a mattress. The Rebel officer, furious upon learning that the sword had suddenly vanished, stalked out of the house in a huff, leaving his men to bring in the Colonel as a prisoner. The latter escaped, however, and made his way back to the Union lines, though minus his sword.[23]

Despite the herculean efforts of the Confederates to cut off the retreating Nationals, the majority of the Federal First and Eleventh Corps, despite heavy casualties in men shot down and especially in prisoners, was able to make its way through the town of Gettysburg to Cemetery Hill. When the panting Federals began to arrive there, they found the brigade of Orland Smith, of Steinwehr's division, in reserve, ready to contest any enemy assault, and supported by a number of frowning guns of the artillery. General Lee, witnessing the final Union retreat through the town, had issued a discretionary order to Ewell to carry Cemetery and Culp's Hills, "if practicable"; but Ewell had hesitated to attempt this.[24] The usually combative Hill—sick at the time—stated that the Unionists had fought with unusual determination and tenacity,[25] and that his own soldiers were disorganized and exhausted.[26] And, as Glenn Tucker has said, "Lee himself might have ridden more speedily to Gettysburg and assumed a more vigorous control of the action on his arrival." [27] The sun, a burnished copper disk wanly penetrating the smoke and haze of battle, was sinking lower toward the western horizon, and the men in gray were quite confused and intermingled in their victorious pursuit through the streets of Gettysburg.

Perhaps the new and vital Federal position could be held now, until reinforcements would arrive from the south. After all, Lee had no fresh troops in large numbers readily available at the moment, and the other Confederate soldiers who had fought so hard throughout the hot day were not only jaded, but many units were fearfully cut up, having suffered staggering losses, and would not be overly eager to try a frontal assault on Cemetery Hill. If the Nationals, therefore, could retain their new position, then Doubleday's superb tactical handling of the First Corps, the magnificent staying powers of his troops, and the help rendered by the Eleventh Corps, would be, despite their enormous casualties, of inestimable significance, not only to the whole battle but perhaps to the entire war itself. And Doubleday was now about to receive the assistance of one of the Army of the Potomac's most accomplished and splendid generals, whose mere presence would act as a tonic to the battered Federals now reeling backward in retreat to Cemetery Hill.

CHAPTER 15

The Federals Rally

on Cemetery Hill

EVENTS FOLLOWED ONE ANOTHER QUICKLY AFTER THE REM-
nants of the Federal First and Eleventh Corps neared Cemetery Hill.
During the retreat through Gettysburg, Howard, the Union commander of the field, sent an aide to Slocum, Howard's senior, in
command of the Right Wing of the Army of the Potomac, requesting
that Slocum come forward and assume command. However, being
unfamiliar with the field and with the events of the battle which had
transpired, Slocum declined to come up, saying that Meade did not
wish to bring on a general engagement.[1]

The retreating Nationals of the First and Eleventh Corps encountered a small but much needed reinforcement as they toiled up the
northern slope to the crest of Cemetery Hill. Although Howard earlier
had sent Coster's brigade of Steinwehr's division to succor Schurz in
his withdrawal, he had retained on Cemetery Hill as a reserve the brigade of Orland Smith and Wiedrich's battery of six three-inch rifles.
They were a most welcome sight indeed to the battered Unionists who
had been striving for hours north and west of the town. These fresh
units would form the nucleus about which Doubleday's and Schurz'
fragments would be rallied.

At approximately 5:00 p.m., the bulk of the forces remaining from
the two Union corps were being posted on Cemetery Hill.[2] The danger of a successful Confederate assault on the elevation was greatest in
the period just after the Federal remnants had reached the crest of the
eminence.[3] However, the confusion existing among the Southerners

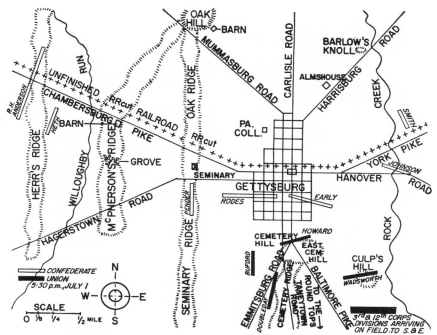

was a deterring factor. They simply could not reorganize swiftly enough to launch an all-out, sustained attack on Cemetery Hill before the Federal Third and Twelfth Corps would arrive on the ground. (This is a most significant point to be kept in mind!) Besides, the caliber of the tenacious Union fighting west and north of Gettysburg was thought by a number of Confederates to have been the highest encountered during the entire course of the war.[4] And this includes, too, the brave but hopeless combat fought by the Eleventh Corps. A number of writers on the battle have stated that this corps failed to stand up and fight manfully. Nothing could be further from the truth, as an examination of the losses will show. Actually, throughout the day, some 18,000 Federal effectives had been pitted against approximately 28,000 Confederates,[5] and had finally yielded only to sheer weight of numbers. The Confederate generals were hesitant to renew the attack against the staunch blue defenders, especially when the latter were being posted on such an easily defended height as Cemetery Hill.

It must be remembered, too, that it was the Confederates who were doing the attacking during the course of the day. They had, to a large degree, worn themselves out in these assaults. The day was a terrifically hot and humid one,[6] and many of the Southern units had given forth as much as human flesh would endure. Perhaps the Confederate leaders would have agreed with Pyrrhus' exclamation after his first triumph over the Romans: "One more such victory and I am undone!" Lee, who had witnessed the retreat of the Nationals, himself stated that the "weakened and exhausted" divisions of Hill and Ewell were unfit for further attack that day on "the strong position which the enemy had assumed." [7] Having watched (from a position on Seminary Ridge) the withdrawal of the Federals, Lee established his army headquarters in some tents in an apple orchard between the Seminary building and the Chambersburg pike.[8]

After the First and Eleventh Corps had fallen back to Cemetery Hill, the intrepid Buford formed the remains of his cavalry division near the Emmitsburg road, west of Cemetery Ridge, ready to assail on the right flank any Confederate attack on Cemetery Hill.[9] As General Hancock asserted, "The splendid spectacle of that gallant cavalry as it stood there, unshaken and undaunted, was one of the most inspiring sights of my military experience." [10]

As his depleted units were climbing the northern slope of Cemetery Hill, Doubleday reported to Howard at the cemetery gate. Howard instructed him to post his First Corps on the left, in the Citizens' Evergreen Cemetery, "while he assembled the Eleventh Corps on the right" of the Baltimore pike, on what is now called East Cemetery Hill—the highest part of the elevation.[11]

These events set the stage for the advent of Hancock, who was to play a most dramatic and vital role at the eleventh hour in the proceedings of the First Day. The background of Meade's effective, though somewhat unusual, action in determining to send Hancock to Gettysburg must now be noted. From his army headquarters at Taneytown, Maryland, Meade dispatched the following message at noon on July 1st to General-in-Chief Halleck in Washington:

> The news proves my advance has answered its purpose. I shall not advance any, but prepare to receive an attack in case Lee makes one. A battlefield is being selected to the rear, on which the army can be rapidly concentrated, on Pipe Creek, between Middleburg and Manchester, covering my depot at Westminister.
>
> If I am not attacked, and I can from reliable intelligence have reason to believe I can attack with reasonable degree of success, I will do so; but at present, having relieved the pressure on the Susquehanna, I

am now looking to the protection of Washington, and fighting my army to the best advantage.[12]

In the same message—which was not gotten off promptly, even though marked "Noon"—in a postscript added at 1:00 p.m., Meade added a line which indicated that he had just received additional intelligence from the fighting front: "The enemy are advancing in force on Gettysburg, and I expect the battle will begin today." [13]

Meade had no sooner sent off the message to Halleck when, at approximately 1:00 p.m., or very shortly thereafter, he received the calamitous news of the death of Reynolds, his most trusted subordinate. Meade's drawn countenance instantly manifested shock and sorrow, as observed by a courier, Major William Riddle.[14] But his reaction and decisions were instant. At 1:10 p.m., Meade directed Hancock, commanding the Union Second Corps, to proceed to Gettysburg and assume command of all the troops there. The orders to Hancock—issued through Meade's chief of staff, Major General Daniel Butterfield—further stated: "If you think the ground and position there a better one to fight a battle under existing circumstances, you will so advise the general [Meade], and he will order all the troops up." [15]

This was a severe responsibility which Meade placed upon Hancock's broad shoulders: rushing to a battlefield, the terrain of which Hancock did not know; assuming command of a battle, if it still continued, of whose course he was ignorant up to the time he would arrive on the field; determining whether the Army of the Potomac should be ordered to concentrate there and risk a general battle, the outcome of which might well determine the issue of the entire war—all this in spite of the fact that Hancock was junior in rank to such generals as Howard, Slocum, and Sickles, who were either at Gettysburg or nearby. Possibly Meade himself should have ridden forward from Taneytown to the field to see the exact state of affairs. At any rate, the trust which the army commander placed in Hancock is noteworthy; the decision which the latter would make as to risking a major engagement at Gettysburg would be one of the most momentous ones made by a subordinate commander during the Civil War. Charged with this great responsibility, Hancock, escorted by his personal staff, started at once for Gettysburg, the general reclining for a time in an ambulance so that he could study maps of the area about the town.[16]

At about 4:30 p.m., just as the first of the refugees of the Eleventh and First Corps had reached Cemetery Hill in their retreat, Hancock arrived on the field.[17] He encountered Howard in front of the cemetery gate, and there immediately ensued a terse and unfortunate debate, initiated by Howard, as to which of the two generals was in command of the field. Howard did not doubt the veracity of Hancock's statement that Meade had appointed him (Hancock) to the command of all forces on the field; but Howard stated that this order could not be complied with since he (Howard) was Hancock's senior, and that Meade must have made the appointment under the delusion that Hancock was the senior major general of the two. The debate was soon resolved, however, in the interest of the serious Union situation, with both generals plunging into the trying task of rallying and posting the remnants which were arriving on the hill, each thinking that he was in command of the field. Therefore, despite this controversy, which showed the petty side of Howard, Hancock and Howard worked side by side with a firm spirit of mutual cooperation.[18]

It was the timely arrival, dramatic personal appearance, and mien of the magnificent-looking Hancock, however, which did more than anything else to rally and raise the morale of the severely mauled Federal troops.[19] He was a needed tonic, and he grasped the situation instantly. Truly, he deserved the sobriquet of "The Superb" which McClellan had given him. The blue soldiers probably thought that Hancock was the harbinger of reinforcements, possibly his own Second Corps. Hancock saw to it that the infantrymen were deployed in excellent defensive positions and that the many artillery pieces were well dug in, protected by lunettes. In all, about forty-three cannon were soon in position, ready to belch out a hail of destruction at any adventurous graycoats who exposed themselves.[20] At about the time of Hancock's arrival, Major General Gouverneur K. Warren, chief engineer of the Army of the Potomac, had also reached the field. He at once proceeded to render valuable assistance in preparing defensive positions for the Federal infantry and artillery.[21] Wadsworth's division was wisely ordered to occupy Culp's Hill, which guarded the Union right flank.[22]

Meantime, at 5:00 p.m., Slocum, from a point "near Gettysburg," sent the following scarcely comforting message to Meade at Taneytown: "A portion of our troops have fallen back from Gettysburg. Matters do not appear well. My Second Division has gone up to the town, and the First on the right [that is, east] of the town. I hope the work for the day is nearly over." [23] At about the same time, or perhaps near 5:15 p.m., Hancock, who had sized up the whole situation admirably, dispatched a communiqué to the army commander in which he stated that he would hold the lines at Gettysburg until dark so as to enable Meade to decide whether or not to fight there. Hancock said further that, although the position could be turned, it was nonetheless a good defensive one on which to wage a major battle.[24] The view expressed by Hancock in his last statement was echoed by Howard in a note to Meade later that evening.[25]

The problem facing the victorious Confederates was a thorny one. Even after they managed to regroup, it would be too late in the evening to mount a sustained, all-out attack.[26] Small numbers of Southerners did, however, attempt a feeble and ineffective minor sortie which sought in vain to turn the right of the Federal position on East Cemetery Hill.[27] In order to carry Cemetery Hill, the Confederates would have had to launch an almost immediate, coordinated offensive—one which would have called for the cooperation of a number of brigades and divisions. It was far easier to pose the problem than to solve it. It had taken the Confederates some six hours to launch an attack in concert all along their line earlier in the day. After the disruption of their organizations in the heavy fighting of the day, and especially during the pursuit through the streets of the town, it was impossible for the Southern leaders to duplicate this feat again at approximately 5:00 p.m. Besides Lee and Hill, Ewell, too, reported that his troops were too exhausted for further heavy fighting.[28]

Meanwhile, timely Union reinforcements were coming forward. The 7th Indiana, of Cutler's brigade—which regiment had been absent on wagon train duty during the day—arrived on the field in the evening and took position on Culp's Hill with the remnants of Wadsworth's division. This regiment, being the only fresh, unengaged unit present, was directed to form the picket line for the division.[29] Also, skirmishers from the Eleventh Corps occupied the second floors of houses along the southern edge of town. Their fire discouraged Confederate reconnaissance units which were trying to investigate the Union position.[30] It was probably the fire from these Federals which was responsible for Ewell's receiving a minié ball in his wooden leg.[31]

Additional fresh National forces were surging to the fore. The report that "Extra Billy" Smith sent to Early to the effect that Federal troops were approaching along the York pike was more than a rumor. Units of Brigadier General Thomas Ruger's First Division of the Twelfth Corps—including also the 5th and 20th Connecticut regiments—as well as Brigadier General John W. Geary's Second Division, had reached a point one and one-half miles east of Gettysburg, near the York pike, by about 5:00 p.m.[32] This move tied down a sizeable Confederate force, which was required to watch these Federals, and thereby reduced the strength of any column contemplating attack against Cemetery Hill. Therefore, the difference of one hour in the time of retreat of the First and Eleventh Corps to Cemetery Hill was of momentous consequence! A Confederate attack on Cemetery Hill at 3:00 or even 4:00 p.m. would likely have been successful—with a resultant defeat in detail likely for Meade's scattered divisions arriving by several roads at the Cemetery Hill apex—while a Southern assault (could they have mounted one) at 5:00, 5:30, or 6:00 p.m. would probably have been doomed to failure.

As mentioned above, the Federal Twelfth Corps, commanded by Brigadier General Alpheus S. Williams,[33] reached the field at approximately 5:00 p.m.[34] Slocum himself rode up to the cemetery gate at about 6:30 p.m.[35] and, being the senior of Howard and Hancock, assumed command of the entire field for the Army of the Potomac until the advent of Meade, hours later. Brigadier General George J. Stannard's Third Brigade, Third Division, First Corps, arrived on the field at dusk to augment the gathering Union clans.[36] Between 5:30 and 6:00 p.m., Sickles' Third Corps reached the battlefield.[37] The Third Corps' arrival, in conjunction with that of the Twelfth Corps, assured the safety and impenetrability of the Federal position. Then, at nightfall, Hancock's own Second Corps came onto the field in the vicinity of the Round Tops.[38]

As the weary, blood-stained soldiers of the battered First and Eleventh Corps saw the arrival of these welcome reinforcements—meaning that the whole Army of the Potomac was marching to their relief—they gave vent to their jubilant feelings. "The night," wrote one participant, "was made hideous by our yells of joy because of their opportune arrival." [39]

And Hancock himself was not idle. At 5:25 p.m., he dispatched from Cemetery Hill the following message to Meade at Taneytown: "The battle is now quiet. I think we will be all right until night . . . when . . . it can be told better what had best be done. I think we can retire; if not, we can fight here, as the ground appears not unfavorable with good troops." [40] Meantime, at 6:00 p.m. (before the arrival of Hancock's 5:25 note) Meade was replying to Hancock's previous dispatch. "It seems to me," declared Meade, "that we have so concentrated that a battle at Gettysburg is now forced on us, and that if we can get up our people and attack with our whole force tomorrow we ought to defeat the force the enemy has." [41] At the same time, Meade sent Halleck a report on the day's action at Gettysburg, so far as he knew it, and the movements of his various units. The message went on to say that "A.P. Hill and Ewell are certainly concentrating; Longstreet's whereabouts I do not know. If he is not up tomorrow, I hope with the force I have concentrated to defeat Hill and Ewell. At any rate, I see no other course than to hazard a general battle." [42] Halleck's reply to Meade—sent from Washington at 9:15 p.m.—read as follows: "Your tactical arrangements for battle seem good . . . but in a strategic view are you not too far east, and may not Lee attempt to turn your left and cut you off from Frederick? Please give your full attention to this suggestion." [43] As so often before, Halleck had failed utterly to grasp the strategic picture, and Meade wisely ignored his suggestion.

During the night of July 1–2, the majority of the units of both armies arrived on or near the field. The men, knowing that a titanic battle was in the offing, nevertheless slumbered peacefully, many of them for the last time on this earth. A number of companies were singing hymns.[44] On the field north and west of town, where the fighting had been heavy during the day, the lanterns of Confederate ambulances and surgeons bobbed about among the heaps of dead and wounded—men in blue and men in gray—scattered widely and thickly about amidst the fields, streams, and woods.

Hancock left Gettysburg at dusk and arrived at army headquarters at Taneytown to report in person to Meade.[45] The two generals discussed the situation for a time, and then the careworn commander of the Union army mounted and rode toward Gettysburg, to keep a rendezvous with destiny. While en route, at about 11:00 p.m or shortly thereafter, Meade stopped for a little while at the headquarters of Brigadier General John Gibbon, commanding a division of the Second Corps. Meade told Gibbon that the entire Army of the Potomac would concentrate at Gettysburg and wage battle there if the Confederates attacked.[46] The commanding general then rode on toward the field.

A full moon was casting beams of silvery light on the tombstones of the Cemetery as Meade and his staff arrived at the cemetery gate at 1:00 a.m. on the morning of July 2, 1863.[47] There, under the tall pines surrounding the cemetery, he met and conferred with Slocum, Howard, Sickles, Warren, and other officers.[48] The Union generals saw before them a tall, spare, scholarly-looking man, gaunt and hollow-eyed from the anxiety, responsibility, and lack of sleep.[49] Meade queried the various officers as to whether the Cemetery Ridge position was a suitable one on which to fight a major battle. The generals replied in the affirmative. "I am glad to hear you say so, gentlemen," Meade declared. "I have already ordered the other corps to concentrate here and it is too late to change." [50] Then, accompanied by an entourage of high-ranking officers, the Union commander toured the lines and examined the battlefield beneath the brilliant moonlight.[51] He would stand firm on the morrow, and compel Lee to wage combat on his (Meade's) terms.

The fighting on the First Day at Gettysburg was over. If technically a Confederate victory, the gray legions had suffered irreparable losses in units which Lee would call upon to play leading roles in the combats on the 2nd and 3rd. The Southerners, too, had been prevented from occupying the vital road-hub position of Cemetery Hill before Meade's far-flung forces could arrive and concentrate on the Cemetery Ridge site. The clash on the first day had been one of the most fierce and sanguinary of the war, as the casualty figures will reveal. The two great blue and gray hosts were coiling like cobras for a mighty shock of arms on July 2 and 3, 1863—a combat that would shake the continent and the civilized world, so momentous were the issues involved.

For the men in the ranks, however, only sleep was essential. As Abner Doubleday—one of the true heroes of the First Day's Battle of Gettysburg—accurately recorded, "We lay on our arms that night among the tombs of the Cemetery, so suggestive of the shortness of life and the nothingness of fame; but the men were little disposed to moralize on themes like these and were much too exhausted to think of anything but much needed rest." [52]

CHAPTER 16

The Price in Blood*

IN ANY COMPILATION AND ASSESSMENT OF THE BATTLE CASUAL-
ties of July 1, 1863, one begins with the official reports of both armies,
even though later information reveals that these figures should be re-
vised. Many of those men reported missing in the Union and Confederate armies, it was subsequently learned, were either wounded or
killed; and one-fourth of the missing, on an average, should be added
to the killed or wounded. However, to save confusion, and to adopt
a consistent standard throughout, the figures will be taken from the
official reports made out in each army shortly after the battle at Gettysburg.

In general, the Union figures are more reliable than the Confederate.
The Southern losses were generally understated, due in part to the
following order of May 14, 1863, issued by General Lee: "The practice which prevails in the army of including in the list of casualties
those cases of slight injuries which do not incapacitate the recipients
for duty is calculated to mislead our friends and encourage our enemies by giving false impressions as to the extent of our losses . . . . It is
therefore ordered that in the future the reports of the wounded shall

* The material in this chapter is based on the following sources and
works: 43 *O.R.*, pp. 173–187; Vanderslice, *Gettysburg*, pp. 104–132; Fox,
New York at Gettysburg, I, 91, pp. 108–109, 176–187; Nicholson, *Pennsylvania at Gettysburg*, I, pp. 33–38, 172–173; II, 1055ff.; William F. Fox,
Regimental Losses in the American Civil War, 1861–1865 . . . passim.

include only those whose injuries, in the opinion of medical officers, render them unfit for duty." "That these instructions were observed," writes William F. Fox, "is evident from some of the Confederate official reports at Gettysburg in which wounded men were omitted because they were expected to return to duty in 'a week or ten days.' One report states that 'the wounded includes only those disabled indefinitely.' Now, this same class—the slightly wounded—was included in the casualty lists of the Unioin army, and embraced, as a general thing, fully 15 per cent of the losses . . . . Some of the Confederate brigade returns did not include their missing."

Another problem is that pointed out by John M. Vanderslice: ". . . in considering the losses of Archer's, Davis', Pettigrew's, Scales', and Lane's brigades, it must be remembered that they participated in Longstreet's assault, July 3, and that their reported losses include those for both days, as do those of O'Neal's and Daniel's include the losses in their fight at Culp's Hill on the 3d." However, a rough breakdown of the losses which these specified Confederate brigades suffered on July 1st will be attempted. Further, as Vanderslice notes, the Confederates "report a loss at Gettysburg of captured or missing of 5150, while the record of prisoners of war in the office of the Adjutant-General at Washington bears the names of 12,227 captured at Gettysburg from July 1 to 5. Again, for Iverson's brigade, there is a [Confederate] report of 308 captured or missing, while Robinson's division [allegedly] captured over 1000 of that brigade in one charge." In the tabular compilations which follow—taken down to the regimental level—the numbers engaged in each regiment, as well as the casualties suffered, will be given where available.

McPHERSON RIDGE AND SEMINARY RIDGE

UNION LOSSES

Meredith's Brigade

Regiment	Killed & Wounded	Missing	Total Loss	Engaged
2nd Wisconsin	182	51	233	302
6th Wisconsin	146	22	168	....
7th Wisconsin	126	52	178	....
19th Indiana	160	50	210	338
24th Michigan	272	91	363	496
Total	886	266	1152	....

Cutler's Brigade

Regiment	Killed & Wounded	Missing	Total Loss	Engaged
56th Pennsylvania	74	56	130	252
76th New York	164	70	234	369
14th Brooklyn	118	99	217	344
95th New York	69	46	115	261
147th New York	204	92	296	380
Total	629	363	992	1606

Stone's Brigade

Regiment	Killed & Wounded	Missing	Total Loss	Engaged
143rd Pennsylvania	162	91	253	465
149th Pennsylvania	225	111	336	450
150th Pennsylvania	187	77	264	397
Total	574	279	853	1312

Biddle's Brigade

Regiment	Killed & Wounded	Missing	Total Loss	Engaged
20th New York	146	24	170	287
121st Pennsylvania	118	61	179	306
142nd Pennsylvania	141	70	211	362
151st Pennsylvania	237	100	337	467
Total	642	255	897	1422

Artillery Brigade

Battery	Killed & Wounded
Hall's Maine	18
Stevens' Maine	23
Reynolds' New York	17
Cooper's Pennsylvania	11
Stewart's U.S.	36
Total	105

Gamble's Cavalry Brigade

Regiment	Killed & Wounded	Missing
8th Illinois	6	1
12th Illinois	14	6
3rd Indiana	27	5
8th New York	24	16
Calef's U.S. Battery	12	....
Total	83	28

CONFEDERATE LOSSES

Davis' Brigade

Regiment	Killed & Wounded
2nd Mississippi	232
42nd Mississippi	265
55th North Carolina	198
Total	695

The brigade report gives no figure for the missing, although a large portion of the first two regiments above was captured. A part of the other losses was incurred on July 3rd.

Brockenbrough's Brigade

Regiment	Killed & Wounded
40th Virginia	42
47th Virginia	48
55th Virginia	34
22nd Virginia Battalion	24
Total	148

Archer's Brigade

Regiment	Killed & Wounded	Missing	Total Loss
13th Alabama	42	......	......
5th Alabama Battalion	26	......	......
1st Tennessee (Provis. Army)	42	......	......
7th Tennessee	23	......	......
14th Tennessee	27	......	......
Total	160	517	677

Many of the missing of Archer's brigade were captured by the Federals on July 1st, the rest being lost on the 3rd.

Pettigrew's Brigade

Regiment	Killed & Wounded
11th North Carolina	209
26th North Carolina	588
47th North Carolina	161
52nd North Carolina	147
Total	1105

This brigade lost, perhaps, some 500 men from this figure on July 3rd.

Scales' Brigade

Regiment	Killed & Wounded
13th North Carolina	126
16th North Carolina	66
22nd North Carolina	89
34th North Carolina	64
38th North Carolina	79
Total	424

The missing (110) of this brigade, and perhaps some 100 of the other casualties were lost on July 3rd.

Perrin's Brigade

Regiment	Killed & Wounded
1st South Carolina	95
1st South Carolina Rifles	11
12th South Carolina	132
13th South Carolina	130
14th South Carolina	209
Total	577

Lane's Brigade

General Lane reported his total loss for the three days of battle at Gettysburg as being 660. The brigade was only lightly engaged on the first day, its losses then being probably 120.

Daniel's Brigade

Regiment	Killed & Wounded
32nd North Carolina	142
43rd North Carolina	147
45th North Carolina	219
53rd North Carolina	117
2nd North Carolina Battalion	153
Total	778

The missing of this brigade aggregated 116. On the first day's battle, the brigade loss totaled approximately 750.

The Confederate artillery battalions of McIntosh, Pegram, and Garnett reported a total loss of 84 killed and wounded, and 16 missing.

John M. Vanderslice states that "the total Federal losses [on McPherson Ridge and Seminary Ridge] in the brigades of Cutler, Meredith, Stone, and

145

Biddle, constituting the divisions of Wadsworth and . . . Rowley, and including those of the corps artillery and Gamble's cavalry, were 2880 killed and wounded and 1191 missing, while those of the eight Confederate brigades opposing them were, according to their imperfect reports, 3971 killed and wounded, and 317 missing."

OAK RIDGE

UNION LOSSES

Baxter's Brigade

Regiment	Killed & Wounded	Missing	Total Loss	Engaged
11th Pennsylvania	70	62	132	292
88th Pennsylvania	59	51	110	296
90th Pennsylvania	50	44	94	208
83rd New York	24	58	82	215
97th New York	48	78	126	255
12th Massachusetts	57	59	116	....
Total	308	352	660	....

Paul's Brigade

Regiment	Killed & Wounded	Missing	Total Loss	Engaged
13th Massachusetts	84	101	185	....
94th New York	70	175	245	445
104th New York	102	92	194	309
107th Pennsylvania	67	98	165	255
16th Maine	68	164	232	298
Total	391	630	1021	....

CONFEDERATE LOSSES

O'Neal's Brigade

Regiment	Killed & Wounded
3rd Alabama	91
6th Alabama	131
12th Alabama	83
26th Alabama	130
Total	435

The missing of this brigade totaled 193. A part of O'Neal's loss occurred at Culp's Hill on the morning of the 3rd, although it was probably a much smaller loss than the brigade suffered on the first day's combat.

Iverson's Brigade

Regiment	Killed & Wounded
5th North Carolina	143
12th North Carolina	56
20th North Carolina	122
23rd North Carolina	134
Total	455

The missing of this brigade aggregated 308. But these figures are undoubtedly very inaccurate, since Iverson at one time gave his loss in killed and wounded as 500, and since it is a well established fact that Iverson lost hundreds in prisoners alone.

Ramseur's Brigade

Regiment	Killed & Wounded	Missing	Total Loss
2nd North Carolina	31	1	32
4th North Carolina	32	24	56
14th North Carolina	42	2	44
30th North Carolina	40	5	45
Total	145	32	177

John M. Vanderslice states that "the total losses of the brigades of Baxter and Paul, Robinson's division, First Corps, on Oak Ridge were 707 killed and wounded and 982 missing, and those of the [Confederate] troops opposing them were 955 killed and wounded and at least 1400 missing."

The total casualties of the First Corps on July 1 were 3587 killed and wounded, and 2173 missing, while those of the Confederates facing it were 4926 killed and wounded and 1717 missing.

THE PLAIN NORTH OF GETTYSBURG

UNION LOSSES

Krzyzanowski's Brigade

Regiment	Killed & Wounded	Missing	Total Loss	Engaged
119th New York	81	59	140	300
82nd Ohio	102	89	191	....
26th Wisconsin	155	62	217	....
75th Pennsylvania	108	3	111	258
Total	446	213	659	....

Amsberg's Brigade

Regiment	Killed & Wounded	Missing	Total Loss	Engaged
82nd Illinois	23	89	112	------
45th New York	46	178	224	447
157th New York	193	114	307	431
61st Ohio	42	12	54	------
74th Pennsylvania	50	60	110	381
Total	354	473	807	------

Gilsa's Brigade

Regiment	Killed & Wounded	Missing	Total Loss	Engaged
54th New York	54	48	102	216
153rd Pennsylvania	165	46	211	569
Total	219	94	313	785

Ames' Brigade

Regiment	Killed & Wounded	Missing	Total Loss	Engaged
17th Connecticut	101	96	197	386
25th Ohio	109	75	184	------
75th Ohio	90	96	186	------
107th Ohio	134	77	211	------
Total	434	344	778	------

Coster's Brigade

Regiment	Killed & Wounded	Missing	Total Loss	Engaged
27th Pennsylvania	34	77	111	324
134th New York	193	59	252	488
154th New York	22	178	200	274
Total	249	314	563	1086

Corps Artillery

Battery	Killed & Wounded	Missing
Wheeler's New York	8	3
Dilger's Ohio	13	..
Heckman's Ohio	13	2
Wilkeson's U.S.	13	4
Total	47	9

CONFEDERATE LOSSES

Doles' Brigade

Regiment	Killed & Wounded	Missing	Total Loss
4th Georgia	38	7	45
12th Georgia	39	10	49
21st Georgia	12	7	19
44th Georgia	9	58	67
5th Alabama (O'Neal's Brig.)	209	....	209
Total	307	82	389

Gordon's Brigade

Regiment	Killed & Wounded	Missing	Total Loss
13th Georgia	103	....	103
26th Georgia	6	5	11
31st Georgia	43	....	43
38th Georgia	63	29	92
60th Georgia	33	5	38
61st Georgia	93	....	93
Total	341	39	380

The casualties on the first day, according to John M. Vanderslice, of Hays' Confederate brigade totaled 63, while those for Avery's brigade aggregated 145.

"The total losses," asserts Vanderslice, "of the Eleventh Corps on this day, in less than two hours, were 1768 killed and wounded and 1427 missing. Those of the [Confederates], as reported, were 856 killed and wounded and 121 missing."

According to Vanderslice, the losses on July 1st in the two Federal Corps were 5,355 killed and wounded, and 3,600 missing—a total loss of 8,955. The aggregate Confederate losses on this day amounted to 5,882 killed and wounded, and 1,838 missing—total losses of 7,720. The Confederate figure must, however, be considered as a minimum one, owing to their unsatisfactory returns, as noted above.

In any evaluation of the casualty figures of both sides on July 1, 1863, one is immediately struck by the fact that the Confederates, even though eventually victorious, lost more men shot down—that is, killed and wounded—than did the Nationals. And, of course, a high percentage of the 3,600 Union missing were captured by the Southerners in the hasty Federal retreat through the streets of Gettysburg.

The severity of the fighting on the First Day's Battle cannot be overemphasized. The Union First Corps took into action 8,200 men, and lost 5,760—a loss of 70 per cent of the effectives engaged! Of the total of 9,197 men in the Eleventh Corps, General Howard states that "hardly 6,000" were engaged. This corps lost 3,195—a percentage loss of 53 per cent. According to Captain Joseph G. Rosengarten, an authority on the battle, the Iron Brigade lost 61 per cent of its men engaged; Biddle's brigade, 69 per cent; Stone's brigade, 66 per cent; while losses in Cutler's, Baxter's, and Paul's brigades were comparable. The total loss in the Army of the Potomac in the three days at Gettysburg was 27 per cent, while that of the First Corps on the first day, as noted above, was 70 per cent, and that of the Eleventh Corps, 53 per cent. These casualties were fearfully high, but it must be remembered that Meade on the second had 15,000 more men than Lee; and as on the first day, so too on the second and third, the Confederates did the attacking. "The Confederate Army," declares Rosengarten, "fought to win the first day, but the Union Army fought to win the next day and the next day, and the final victory."

On the Confederate side on the first day, percentage losses were generally not so heavy as those suffered by the outnumbered Federals, who were determined to hold their ground and buy valuable time regardless of casualties. Nonetheless, Confederate losses in units which Lee would feel impelled to call upon for further decisive fighting on the second and third were so serious as to impair their effectiveness in the subsequent combat.

Two of Rodes' brigades, O'Neal's and Daniel's, which were heavily engaged on the first day, were also committed by Lee to the heavy fighting at Culp's Hill on the morning of the third. But their efficiency had been impaired by the heavy losses they had incurred on July 1st: O'Neal had lost 500 out of 1794 engaged on the first, a loss of some 28 percent; while Daniel had lost 750 out of 2,300 engaged on the first, a loss of 33 percent. In the great Confederate infantry charge on the afternoon of July 3rd, Pettigrew's division (Heth had been injured on the 1st) played a major role. All four of the brigades of this division had been engaged on July 1st, and three had suffered on that day serious casualties: Archer had lost 677 out of 1800 engaged on the first, a loss of 37 percent; Davis had lost 695 out of 2000 engaged on the first, a loss of 35 percent; Brockenbrough had lost but 148 out of 1700 engaged on the first, a loss of 9 percent; and Marshall (Pettigrew's own brigade) had lost 500 out of 2000 engaged on the first, a loss of 25 percent. Two brigades of Pender's division, Lowrance's (Scales had been wounded) and Lane's, were also a part of the attacking Confederate column on the afternoon of July 3rd. On the first day, Lane had lost 120 men out of 1355 engaged, a loss of 9 percent; while Lowrance (Scales) had lost 324 out of 1250 engaged, a loss of 26 percent.

Captain Joseph G. Rosengarten contends that, on the first day, "on the Confederate side, in Hill's Corps, Heth says he took in 7,000 and lost 2,850 [41% casualties], and Pender lost 1,690 out of 4,260 engaged [40% casualties] .... Rodes' Division, out of 6,207, lost 2,853 [46% casualties], and Early's, 1,188 out of 5,477 [22% casualties]." Truly, as Vanderslice intones, the struggle of the Union First Corps and the Confederates arrayed against it on July 1, 1863, "is unsurpassed for bravery and endurance." "From the dawn of July 1st," remarks Rosengarten, "when Buford's cavalry first met the advance of Hill's Corps, until nightfall, when the Army of the Potomac was concentrated at and near Gettysburg, there was sturdy fighting, stout resistance against a largely superior force, and an all-important position and time to concentrate on it gained .... The battle of Gettysburg was a varying series of successive engagements, with alternate gains and losses, but the final result was that crowning success which was largely due to the good fight on the first day against heavy odds .... Thus ... was gained the practical fruits of the first day's battle, in the rapid concentration of Meade's Army on the position [to the south] of Gettysburg, where General Meade turned his offensive defense into a final repulse and defeat of Lee's Army. It was the first day that prepared the way for this result, and dearly purchased as it was, the price was none too great to pay for the infinite advantage .... To the events of the first day is largely due the final issue of the battle of Gettysburg, and therefore it deserves a special record...."

CHAPTER 17

Conclusion

"THE FIRST DAY'S BATTLE," ASSERTS AN AUTHORITY ON GETTYS-burg, Captain Joseph G. Rosengarten, "was . . . indeed 'the soldier's battle,' for it was the fixed determination of the soldiers to hold the ground that counted far more than any skillful maneuvers of military art or the best tactical methods." [1] Yet, while this statement may well be true, in part at least, it does not mean that strategic and tactical leadership, especially on the part of the generals, was not of vital significance. If Napoleon's maxim, "In war, *men* are nothing, a *man* is everything," goes too far in elevating the role of the commander at the expense of the men in the ranks, it nonetheless does indicate the necessity of an army's possessing leaders of competence. The First Day's Battle of Gettysburg, July 1, 1863, demonstrates in a manner that is crystal clear the magnificent fighting qualities of both the Union and Confederate soldiers in action, as well as the pivotal roles played by their commanders in shaping the fate of the combat.

In the preliminary maneuvering of the two armies on the several days prior to July 1st, Lee seems to have had the edge over Meade. The gray chieftain, even though largely in ignorance of the precise whereabouts of the Federal army, still managed to keep his various divisions fairly well in hand—certainly better concentrated than were the scattered blue units. Meade allowed his forces to get too far apart, some units not being within supporting distance of others. Lee came within an ace, on July 1, of achieving what he had planned when the Nationals were encountered: "I shall throw an overwhelming force on their advance, crush it, follow up the success, drive one corps back on another, and by successive repulses and surprises, *before they can concentrate*, create a panic and virtually destroy the army." [2] It took, on the first day at Gettysburg, surpassing courage on the part of the Union troops, and inspired leadership by several of the Federal generals to prevent Lee's design from being realized.

When the command of the Army of the Potomac was suddenly thrust upon Meade, his reaction to this heavy responsibility was sound though cautious. There was a paucity of information as to the locations of the enemy, and Meade had to feel his way northward. His selection and appointment of Reynolds to command the advance of the Left Wing, and the dispatching of Buford's cavalry to Gettysburg, were wise and soldierly decisions. On the other hand, if Lee had not wanted to bring on a general engagement while Longstreet was west of the South Mountains, the Southern leader should have kept a tighter rein on Hill and other subordinate commanders. Discretionary orders could easily be abused, as Jeb Stuart demonstrated in his ill-advised, wide-sweeping circuit of the Union army. Hill certainly erred, as evidenced by Lee's later painful surprise, in permitting Heth to march on Gettysburg for forage and shoes. Hill should have urged Heth to be more circumspect in developing the situation in the event that Federal troops were present there in numbers.

There can be only praise for Buford's and Reynolds' actions on the morning of July 1st. The former staunchly battled against heavy odds, seeing that he must make every possible effort to contain the Confederates until Reynolds could reinforce him with infantry. And Reynolds instantly perceived the need to hold the Southerners west and north of Gettysburg—regardless of the cost to his own and Howard's Eleventh Corps—long enough to give Meade time to concentrate his far-flung legions on the commanding Cemetery heights south of town. Upon the gallant Reynolds' death, Doubleday continued what the former was trying to accomplish, and, throughout the long hot day of fighting, did an outstanding tactical job in handling the First Corps so as to fulfill Reynolds' intentions. Each of Doubleday's division and brigade commanders—except possibly Rowley—performed creditably in this most trying situation.

On the Confederate side, in the initial clash, there was a certain looseness of command. Heth was too slow to commit his reserve brigades, once he had seen that Archer and Davis were in trouble. And these two brigade leaders were careless in the handling of their units, with the result that both brigades were severely punished by Wadsworth. When Rodes arrived at Oak Hill with his large division, he too failed to distinguish himself in his early maneuvers. Daniel was allowed to get off to the south, unsupported, in an endeavor to cross the railroad grading. O'Neal and Iverson—both of whom, especially the latter, demonstrated poor judgment and inept brigade leadership—were permitted to attack Robinson's position on Oak Ridge in a piecemeal fashion. Their bloody repulse was almost inevitable under the circumstances.

Meantime, Howard had arrived and taken over from Doubleday the command of the entire field. His appreciation of the importance of the Cemetery heights and his posting of a reserve on Cemetery Hill were as sagacious as his hasty inspection and premature condemnation of the First Corps were reprehensible. While Howard's prompt effort to bolster the right flank of Doubleday with Schurz' Eleventh Corps was understandable and commendable, his (and especially Schurz') permitting Barlow to press rashly northward from the Almshouse line with the First Division without reconnaissance was most unfortunate. Nor does the fact add luster to their military record at Gettysburg that Howard and Schurz knew of and failed to counter effectively the close approach of Early's division by way of the Harrisburg road —an approach which led directly to the Union right flank and rear. Otherwise, the performance of the rest of the Eleventh Corps division and brigade commanders was competent, though not brilliant.

Only in mid-afternoon did the Confederates begin to hit their stride. Early's timely arrival on Schurz's right flank, his rapid appreciation of the situation, and his energetic and skillful attack all entitle him to the unalloyed encomiums he has received. His brigade leaders handled their units well, as did Doles, whose brigade from Rodes' division assisted Early in routing the Eleventh Corps. And while the Union artillery batteries were well served throughout the first day's battle, special laurels must be given to the Confederate artillery battalions of Jones and Carter, which played leading roles in helping the Southern infantry finally to throw back Schurz and Doubleday.

The Union First Corps was forced from McPherson Ridge chiefly by the able action of Pettigrew's brigade, and from Oak Ridge and Seminary Ridge by the adept attacks of Ramseur and Perrin, respectively. Nonetheless the masterful Doubleday, and Schurz, had purchased enough time by their tenacious fighting to render secure the vital Cemetery heights south of Gettysburg; for, by the time they were compelled to fall back to Cemetery Hill—5:00 p.m.—sufficient Union reinforcements were nearby to thwart any likely new Confederate on-slaught. Hancock's action in rallying the First and Eleventh Corps fugi-tives and his discerning statements sent to Meade were as superb as Howard's challenge to his authority was petty.

Finally, Lee would have done better, if he desired a definite attack on Cemetery and Culp's Hills, to have given Ewell specific orders, in-stead of discretionary ones, as to when and how he wished Early to assault these positions. Ewell—a new corps commander—proved that he was by no means up to stepping into Jackson's shoes and filling them, though he was perhaps correct in not launching an attack on these eminences, as the Unionists, by 5 o'clock, were well on their way toward rendering the elevations impregnable. And wise indeed was Meade's decision to order a rapid concentration of his army at Gettys-burg after the reception of intelligence from Hancock and others as to the transpiration of events and the suitability of terrain at that bloody locale.

Although the conduct of certain generals on both sides might be ar-gued and challenged, there is no denying the superior fighting that oc-curred on July 1, 1863, or the desperate nature of the combat that day at Gettysburg. Confederate General E. P. Alexander declares that "the fighting done by the Federal brigades was of the best type."[3] A more recent authority, Edwin B. Coddington, asserts of the First Day's battle, "The Army of the Potomac had again displayed its resil-iency under extreme adversity. The men of the First and Eleventh Corps and Buford's cavalry, though defeated, were able to regroup and turn once more to face the foe. They had forced the enemy to pay such a heavy price for his victory that he hesitated until it was too late to renew the contest."[4]

And what Colonel Roy Stone said of his Bucktails might well be applied to the soldiers in blue and in gray who were engaged on the first: "They all fought as if each man felt that upon his own arm hung the fate of . . . the nation."

In the Valhalla of American military endeavor, there is no brighter or more imperishable niche than that which is reserved for the un-heralded soldiers of both sides who strove heroically and with extreme devotion for the cause they believed just in the crucial First Day's Battle of Gettysburg. Their conduct was indeed sublime.

Notes

PREFACE

1. Jesse Bowman Young, *The Battle of Gettysburg: A Comprehensive Narrative* (New York: Harper & Bros., 1913), p. 190.
2. Glenn Tucker, *High Tide at Gettysburg: The Campaign in Pennsylvania* (Indianapolis: Bobbs-Merrill Co., 1958), pp. 123, 171.
3. Cecil Battine, *The Crisis of the Confederacy: A History of Gettysburg and the Wilderness* (London: Longmans, Green & Co., 1905), p. viii.

CHAPTER 1

1. James K. P. Scott, *The Story of the Battles of Gettysburg* (Harrisburg: Telegraph Press, 1927), pp. 24–25.
2. Robert Underwood Johnson and Clarence Clough Buel (eds.), *Battles and Leaders of the Civil War* (New York: The Century Co., 1887), III, p. 289; cited hereinafter as *B. & L.*
3. *Ibid.*
4. William F. Fox, *New York at Gettysburg* (Albany: J. B. Lyon Co., 1900), I, p. 162.
5. *Ibid.*, p. 116.
6. *The War of the Rebellion: A Compilation of the Official Records of the Union and Confederate Armies* (Washington: Government Printing Office, 1889), Series I, Serial No. 44, p. 443; cited hereinafter as *O.R.*, all references being to Series I.
7. This is now the Pennsylvania Railroad section of the Penn-Central.

8. 44 *O.R.*, pp. 464–66.

9. *Ibid.*, pp. 307, 316.

10. William Miller Owen, *In Camp and Battle with the Washington Artillery of New Orleans* (Boston: Ticknor & Co., 1885), p. 242.

11. 45 *O.R.*, pp. 942–43.

12. *Southern Historical Society Papers*, XXVI, p. 121; cited hereinafter as *S.H.S.P.* (Italics mine in the text.)

13. William Calvin Oates, *The War Between the Union and the Confederacy and its Lost Opportunities* (New York: Neale Publishing Co., 1906), p. 201.

14. *S.H.S.P.*, XXVI, p. 121.

15. A.J.L. Fremantle, *Three Months in the Southern States, April–June, 1863* (New York: J. Bradburn, 1864), p. 239.

16. *Ibid.*, p. 240.

17. Thomas Chamberlin, *History of the One Hundred and Fiftieth Regiment Pennsylvania Volunteers, Second Regiment, Bucktail Brigade* (Philadelphia: J. B. Lippincott Co., 1895), pp. 107–109; William W. Strong, *History of the 121st Regiment Pennsylvania Volunteers* (Philadelphia: Burk & McFetridge Co., 1893), p. 42; Charles E. Davis, *Three Years in the Army: The Story of the Thirteenth Massachusetts Volunteers from July 16, 1861, to August 1, 1864* (Boston: Estes & Lauriat, 1894), pp. 221–23.

18. 43 *O.R.*, p. 60.

19. Abner Doubleday, *Chancellorsville and Gettysburg* (New York: C. Scribner's Sons, 1882), pp. 113–14, 116; R. K. Beecham, *Gettysburg, The Pivotal Battle of the Civil War* (Chicago: A. C. McClurg & Co., 1911), p. 44.

20. Doubleday, *Chancellorsville and Gettysburg*, p. 116.

21. 43 *O.R.*, p. 61.

22. 45 *O.R.*, p. 374.

23. David B. Steinman, *The Builders of the Bridge: The Story of John Roebling and His Son* (New York: Harcourt, Brace & Co., 1945), p. 258.

24. 43 *O.R.*, p. 61.

25. *Ibid.*, p. 114.

26. *Ibid.*, p. 61.

27. *Ibid.*, p. 114.

28. J. W. Forney (comp.), *Report of the Joint Committee on the Conduct of the War* (Washington: Government Printing Office, 1865), I, pp. 329–30; cited hereinafter as *C.C.W.*

29. Doubleday, *Chancellorsville and Gettysburg*, p. 115.

30. William Swinton, *Campaigns of the Army of the Potomac: A Critical History of Operations in Virginia, Maryland and Pennsylvania from the Commencement to the Close of the War, 1861–1865* (New York: Charles B. Richardson, 1866), p. 325.

31. *B. & L.*, III, p. 244.

32. 44 *O.R.*, p. 307; James Longstreet, *From Manassas to Appomattox: Memoirs of the Civil War in America* (Philadelphia: J. B. Lippincott Co., 1896), p. 347; John Bell Hood, *Advance and Retreat* (New Orleans: Hood Orphan Memorial Fund, 1880), p. 55; Randolph H. McKim, *A Soldier's Recollections* (New York: Longmans, Green & Co., 1910), pp. 337–62.

33. A. L. Long, *Memoirs of Robert E. Lee; His Military and Personal History, Embracing a Large Amount of Information Hitherto Unpublished* (New York: J. M. Stoddart & Co., 1886), p. 274.

34. George Cary Eggleston, *A Rebel's Recollections* (New York: Hurd & Houghton, 1875), pp. 145–46.

35. Walter H. Taylor, *Four Years with General Lee* (New York: D. Appleton & Co., 1878), p. 92.

36. *Ibid.*; Owen, *Washington Artillery*, p. 242; Jacob Hoke, *The Great Invasion of 1863; or, General Lee in Pennsylvania* (Dayton: W. J. Shuey, 1887), pp. 205–206.

37. J. H. Stine, *History of the Army of the Potomac* (Washington: Gibson Bros., 1893), p. 450.

38. *S.H.S.P.*, IV, p. 156; Taylor, *Four Years with General Lee*, p. 187.

39. Matthew Forney Steele, *American Campaigns* (Washington: U. S. Infantry Assoc. 1935), I, p. 362.

40. H. J. Eckenrode and Bryan Conrad, *James Longstreet, Lee's War Horse,* (Chapel Hill: University of North Carolina Press, 1936), p. 180.

41. 44 *O.R.*, 307, 316; Longstreet, *Manassas to Appomattox*, p. 347.

42. Eckenrode and Conrad, *James Longstreet*, p. 179.

43. Fox, *New York at Gettysburg*, III, pp. 1000–1001.

44. Long, *Memoirs of Robert E. Lee*, p. 275.

45. 45 *O.R.*, p. 943.

46. 44 *O.R.*, p. 321.

47. *Ibid.*, p. 317; A. K. McClure (ed.), *Annals of the War, Written by Leading Participants, North and South* (Philadelphia: Times Publishing Co., 1879), p. 419.

48. Oliver Lyman Spaulding, *The United States Army in War and Peace* (New York: G. P. Putnam's Sons, 1937), p. 300.

49. 44 *O.R.*, p. 317.

50. 43 *O.R.*, pp. 143–44; Fox, *New York at Gettysburg*, I, p. 116; George A. Bruce, *The Twentieth Regiment of Massachusetts Volunteer Infantry, 1861–1865* (Boston: Houghton, Mifflin & Co., 1906), p. 265; William H. Powell, *The Fifth Army Corps, Army of the Potomac: A Record of Operations During the Civil War in the United States of America, 1861–1865* (New York: G. P. Putnam's Sons, 1896), p. 499.

51. 44 *O.R.*, pp. 307, 317.

52. *Ibid.*, p. 317.

53. Cecil Battine, *The Crisis of the Confederacy: A History of Gettysburg and the Wilderness* (London: Longmans, Green & Co., 1905), p. 155; Scott, *Story of the Battles at Gettysburg,* pp. 100–101.

54. 44 *O.R.*, p. 317.

55. E. P. Alexander, *Military Memoirs of a Confederate: A Critical Narrative* (New York: C. Scribner's Sons, 1907), p. 380; 44 *O.R.*, pp. 606–607.

56. Hood, *Advance and Retreat,* p. 55.

57. Beecham, *Gettysburg,* p. 49.

58. 43 *O.R.*, p. 67.

59. *Ibid.*

60. George Meade, *The Life and Letters of General George Gordon Meade* (New York: C. Scribner's Sons, 1913), II, pp. 13–14.

61. Fox, *New York at Gettysburg,* I, p. 117.

62. 43 *O.R.*, p. 114; Powell, *Fifth Corps,* p. 506; Scott, *Story of the Battles at Gettysburg,* pp. 75, 85; Jesse Bowman Young, *The Battle of Gettysburg: A Comprehensive Narrative* (New York: Harper & Bros., 1913), pp. 160–61.

63. Alexander, *Military Memoirs,* p. 382.

64. Owen, *Washington Artillery,* p. 242; Davis, *Thirteenth Massachusetts,* p. 223: Chamberlin, *One Hundred Fiftieth Pennsylvania,* p. 109; David Craft, *History of the One Hundred Forty-First Regiment Pennsylvania Volunteers, 1862–1865* (Towanda, Pa.: Reporter-Journal Printing Co., 1885), p. 112.

65. 45 *O.R.*, pp. 414, 417.

66. 43 *O.R.*, p. 68.

67. Spaulding, *United States Army,* p. 300.

68. 45 *O.R.*, pp. 414–17.

69. *Ibid.*, p. 420.

70. *Ibid.*, pp. 414–15.

71. Fox, *New York at Gettysburg,* I, p. 9.

72. Jennings Cropper Wise, *The Long Arm of Lee, or the History of the Artillery of the Army of Northern Virginia* (Lynchburg, Va.: J. P. Bell Co., 1915), II, pp. 615.

73. 44 *O.R.*, p. 607.

74. *Ibid.*, p. 358.

75. *Ibid.*, pp. 317, 358, 607, 613.

76. Longstreet, *Manassas to Appomattox,* p. 348.

77. John D. Vautier, *History of the 88th Pennsylvania Volunteers in the War for the Union, 1861–1865* (Philadelphia: J. B. Lippincott Co., 1894), p. 116.

78. 43 *O.R.*, pp. 66–67; W. W. Blackford, *War Years with Jeb Stuart* (New York: C. Scribner's Sons, 1946), pp. 226–27; Louis N. Boudrye, *Historic Records of the Fifth New York Cavalry* (Albany: S. R. Gray, 1865), p. 645; William Anthony, *Anthony's History of the Battle of Hanover, York County, Pennsylvania, Tuesday, June 30, 1863, Compiled from the Writings of George R. Prowell and Others* (Hanover, Pa.: William Anthony, 1945), *passim*.

79. Doubleday, *Chancellorsville and Gettysburg*, p. 121.

80. Richard Eddy, *History of the Sixtieth New York State Volunteers* (Philadelphia: Richard Eddy, 1864), *passim*.

81. Swinton, *Army of the Potomac*, p. 327; Hillman A. Hall, et al, *History of the Sixth New York Cavalry, Second Ira Harris Guard, Second Brigade, First Division, Cavalry Corps, Army of the Potomac, 1861–1865* (Worcester, Mass.: The Blanchard Press, 1908), p. 133; John M. Vanderslice, *Gettysburg Then and Now* (New York: G. W. Dillingham Co., 1899), p. 52; Stine, *Army of the Potomac*, p. 452.

82. Fox, *New York at Gettysburg*, III, p. 1145; Newel Cheney, *History of the Ninth Regiment New York Volunteer Cavalry* (Jamestown, N.Y.: Poland Center, 1901), p. 102.

83. Hall, *Sixth New York Cavalry*, p. 133; Cheney, *Ninth New York Cavalry*, p. 102.

84. Cheney, *Ninth New York Cavalry*, p. 102.

85. Abner Hard, *History of the Eighth Cavalry Regiment Illinois Volunteers during the Great Rebellion* (Aurora, Ill., 1868), p. 256.

86. Stine, *Army of the Potomac*, p. 450.

87. Hall, *Sixth New York Cavalry*, p. 134; Fox, *New York at Gettysburg*, I, p. 7.

88. Samuel P. Bates, *The Battle of Gettysburg* (Philadelphia: T. H. Davis & Co., 1875), p. 54.

89. 44 *O.R.*, pp. 317, 607, 637; *S.H.S.P.*, IV, p. 157; Stine, *Army of the Potomac*, p. 452; Young, *Battle of Gettysburg*, pp. 161–62.

90. Alexander, *Military Memoirs*, p. 380; Fox, *New York at Gettysburg*, I, p. 7.

91. Wayland Fuller Dunaway, *Reminiscences of a Rebel* (New York: Neale Publishing Co., 1913), p. 84.

92. Charles Marshall, *An Aide-de-Camp of Lee* (Boston: Little, Brown & Co., 1927), p. 250.

93. Steele, *American Campaigns*, p. 364.

94. Beecham, *Gettysburg*, p. 44.

95. Alexander, *Military Memoirs*, p. 382.

96. 45 *O.R.*, p. 415; Davis, *Thirteenth Massachusetts*, pp. 223–24.

97. Davis, *Thirteenth Massachusetts*, p. 224.

98. 45 *O.R.*, p. 415.

99. 43 *O.R.*, p. 69.

100. Battine, *Crisis of the Confederacy*, p. 183.

101. 44 *O.R.*, p. 444.

102. Jubal A. Early, *Autobiographical Sketch and Narrative of the War Between the States* (Philadelphia: J. B. Lippincott Co., 1912), p. 264.

103. Barron Deaderick, *Strategy in the Civil War* (Harrisburg: Military Service Publishing Co., 1946), p. 89.

104. *S.H.S.P.*, IV, p. 157; Stine, *Army of the Potomac*, p. 451; Young, *Battle of Gettysburg*, p. 162.

105. Wise, *The Long Arm of Lee*, II, p. 615.

106. Alexander, *Military Memoirs*, p. 381.

107. 45 *O.R.*, p. 448.

108. *Ibid.*, p. 434.

109. 43 *O.R.*, p. 924.

110. Fox, *New York at Gettysburg*, I, p. 9.

111. *B. & L.*. III, p. 273.

112. Wise, *The Long Arm of Lee*, II, p. 615.

113. Longstreet, *Manassas to Appomattox*, p. 350.

114. Bates, *Battle of Gettysburg*, p. 56.

115. 44 *O.R.*, p. 444.

116. Fox, *New York at Gettysburg*, I, p. 163; Longstreet, *Manassas to Appomattox*, p. 349.

117. 43 *O.R.*, p. 144; Fox, *New York at Gettysburg*, I, p. 117; Young, *Battle of Gettysburg*, pp. 156–57; Longstreet, *Manassas to Appomattox*, pp. 349–50.

118. 45 *O.R.*, pp. 416, 418.

119. *C.C.W.* (1865), I, p. 330.

120. Doubleday, *Chancellorsville and Gettysburg*, p. 122.

121. *Ibid.*

CHAPTER 2

1. Now U.S. Route 30–the Lincoln Highway.

2. This is the Lincoln Highway east of Gettysburg–U.S. 30.

3. Samuel Adams Drake, *The Battle of Gettysburg* (Boston: Lee & Shepard, 1892), p. 11.

4. *Ibid.*

5. Swinton, *Army of the Potomac*, p. 329.

6. Comte de Paris, *History of the Civil War in America* (Philadelphia: Porter & Coates, 1883), III, p. 540.

7. Swinton, *Army of the Potomac*, p. 334.

8. Also known as Reynolds' Woods, or Reynolds' Grove.

9. Scott, *Battles at Gettysburg*, p. 135.

10. Doubleday, *Chancellorsville and Gettysburg*, p. 136.

11. Scott, *Battles at Gettysburg*, pp. 163–64.

12. *Ibid.*, 133.

13. 44 *O.R.*, p. 492; "Map of the Battlefield of Gettysburg, July 1st, 2nd, 3rd, 1803. Published by authority of the Hon. the Secretary of War, Office of the Chief of Engineers, U.S. Army (1876), First Day's Battle, Position of Troops, Compiled by John B. Bachelder"; cited hereinafter as Bachelder's Map.

14. This was the first national military cemetery in the United States. It was dedicated on November 19, 1863, by President Abraham Lincoln, who on this occasion delivered his immortal Gettysburg Address.

15. Young, *Battle of Gettysburg*, p. 178.

CHAPTER 3

1. 43 *O.R.*, p. 482; Craft, *One Hundred Forty-First Pennsylvania*, p. 115; Battine, *Crisis of the Confederacy*, p. 185; Vanderslice, *Gettysburg*, p. 67; Paris, *History of the Civil War*, III, p. 539; Davis, *Thirteenth Massachusetts*, p. 225; Vautier, *88th Pennsylvania*, p. 105.

2. Bruce, *Twentieth Massachusetts*, pp. 269–70.

3. C. V. Tevis, *The History of the Fighting Fourteenth* (New York: Brooklyn Eagle Press, 1911), p. 81. This history of the Fourteenth Brooklyn regiment, known also as the Eighty-Fourth New York Volunteers, will be cited hereinafter as *Fourteenth Brooklyn*.

4. Fox, *New York at Gettysburg*, I, p. 29.

5. Longstreet, *From Manassas to Appomattox*, p. 351.

6. Scott, *Battles at Gettysburg*, p. 125.

7. *Ibid.*, p. 130.

8. *Ibid.*, p. 101. See also 44 *O.R.*, p. 552.

9. Scott, *Battles at Gettysburg*, 101–102; 44 *O.R.*, p. 468.

10. 43 *O.R.*, p. 70.

11. *Ibid.*

12. 45 *O.R.*, pp. 458–59.

13. Paris, *History of the Civil War*, III, pp. 549–50.

14. 45 *O.R.*, pp. 460–61. Thomas L. Livermore, *Numbers and Losses in the Civil War in America, 1861–65* (Boston: Houghton, Mifflin Co., 1901), pp. 102–103, estimates that 88,289 Union soldiers were engaged at the Battle of Gettysburg, as compared with 75,000 Confederates.

15. 43 *O.R.*, p. 927.

16. Bachelder's Map; 43 *O.R.*, p. 934.

17. Paris, *History of the Civil War*, III, p. 545.

18. *B. & L.*, III, p. 275; Scott, *Battles at Gettysburg*, pp. 133, 136; Paris, *History of the Civil War*, III, p. 545; Hall, *Sixth New York Cavalry*, p. 137; Young, *Battle of Gettysburg*, p. 165; Francis Marshal, *The Battle of Gettysburg, The Crest-Wave of the American Civil War*. (New York: The Nagle Publishing Co., 1914), p. 110; Bates, *Battle of Gettysburg*, p. 55; Battine, *Crisis of the Confederacy*, p. 184; Fox, *New York at Gettysburg*, I, p. 10; Vautier, *88th Pennsylvania*, p. 117; William Roscoe Livermore, *The Story of the Civil War* (New York: G. P. Putnam's Sons, 1913), II, p. 416; R. L. Ashhurst, *Remarks on Certain Questions Relating to the First Day's Fight at Gettysburg* (Philadelphia, 1897), p. 6.

19. 43 *O.R.*, p. 934.

20. The Calef Battery government tablet, on the Gettysburg battle-fields; 43 *O.R.*, p. 1031.

21. Douglas Southall Freeman, *R. E. Lee: A Biography* (New York: Charles Scribner's Sons, 1934), III, p. 78.

22. Fox, *New York at Gettysburg*, I, 19; 43 *O.R.*, pp. 938–39.

23. 44 *O.R.*, p. 607; Alexander, *Military Memoirs of a Confederate*, p. 381; Wise, *Long Arm of Lee*, II, p. 616; Vanderslice, *Gettysburg*, p. 67; Longstreet, *From Manassas to Appomattox*, p. 353; John Richards Boyle, *Soldiers True: The Story of the One Hundred and Eleventh Regiment Pennsylvania Veteran Volunteers and of Its Campaigns in the War for the Union, 1861–1865* (New York: Eaton & Mains, 1903), p. 115.

24. 44 *O.R.*, p. 607; Wise, *Long Arm of Lee*, II, p. 616.

25. W. C. Storrick, *Gettysburg: The Place, The Battle, The Outcome* (Harrisburg: J. Horace McFarland Co. 1932), p. 19.

26. Scott, *Battles at Gettysburg*, p. 154; John P. Nicholson, (ed.), *Pennsylvania at Gettysburg* (Harrisburg: William Stanley Ray, 1914), I, p. 28.

27. General Davis was the nephew of the President of the Confederate States of America, Jefferson Davis.

28. Freeman, *R. E. Lee*, III, p. 78; 44 *O.R.*, pp. 637–38.

29. Battine, *Crisis of the Confederacy*, p. 167.

30. Vautier, *88th Pennsylvania*, p. 117.

31. Doubleday, *Chancellorsville and Gettysburg*, pp. 124–25.

32. O. B. Curtis, *History of the Twenty-Fourth Michigan of the Iron Brigade, Known as the Detroit and Wayne County Regiment* (Detroit: Winn & Hammond, 1891), p. 155.

33. *Ibid.*

34. 43 *O.R.*, p. 265; Longstreet, *From Manassas to Appomattox*, p. 353; Scott, *Battles at Gettysburg*, p. 155; Paris, *History of the Civil War*, III, pp. 547–48.

35. *B. & L.*, III, p. 287; 43 *O.R.*, p. 701.

36. Chamberlin, *One Hundred and Fiftieth Pennsylvania*, p. 110.

37. Vautier, *88th Pennsylvania*, p. 105.

38. Chamberlin, *One Hundred and Fiftieth Pennsylvania*, p. 110.

39. Paris, *History of the Civil War*, III, pp. 546, 551; 43 *O.R.*, pp. 934, 938–39.

40. Bachelder's Map.

41. *Ibid.*

42. Fox, *New York at Gettysburg*, I, pp. 9–10.

43. Vanderslice, *Gettysburg*, p. 67; the 8th Illinois monument, on the Gettysburg battlefield; marker near Chambersburg pike bridge over Marsh Creek.

44. Cheney, *Ninth New York Cavalry*, p. 106; Young, *Battle of Gettysburg*, p. 166; Fox, *New York at Gettysburg*, I, pp. 9–10; Hall, *Sixth New York Cavalry*, p. 137; Vautier, 88th Pennsylvania, p. 117.

45. Vanderslice, *Gettysburg*, p. 68.

46. 44 *O.R.*, pp. 317, 632.

47. *Ibid.*

48. The infantrymen of both armies were generally armed with .58 caliber, single-shot, muzzle-loading, rifled muskets. Only the Union cavalrymen were equipped with the carbines, which had a shorter effective range than the muskets. (see Edwin B. Coddington, *The Gettysburg Campaign: A Study in Command* (New York: Charles Scribner's Sons, 1968), pp. 252–58.)

49. Nicholson, *Pennsylvania at Gettysburg*, II, p. 885.

50. *B. & L.*, III, p. 275; Cheney, *Ninth New York Cavalry*, pp. 107–108.

51. Hall, *Sixth New York Cavalry*, p. 137; Fox, *New York at Gettysburg*, I, p. 10.

52. Vautier, *88th Pennsylvania*, p. 117; *B. & L.*, III, pp. 274.

53. *S.H.S.P.*, IV, p. 158.

54. Vanderslice, *Gettysburg*, p. 68; Wise, *Long Arm of Lee*, II, p. 616; Paris, *History of the Civil War*, III, p. 546; Beecham, *Gettysburg*, p. 61; 43 *O.R.*, p. 927.

55. Paris, *History of the Civil War*, III, p. 546.

56. Fox, *New York at Gettysburg*, III, p. 1145; 43 *O.R.*, p. 934.

57. Vanderslice, *Gettysburg*, p. 71; 43 *O.R.*, p. 927.

58. Scott, *Battles at Gettysburg*, p. 135.

59. Wise, *Long Arm of Lee*, II, pp. 616–17; Bachelder's Map; p. 44 *O.R.*, p. 610.

60. The Brander battery government tablet, on the Gettysburg battlefield.

61. The McGraw battery government tablet, on the Gettysburg battlefield.

62. The Zimmerman battery government tablet, on the Gettysburg battlefield.

63. The Crenshaw battery government tablet, on the Gettysburg battlefield.

64. The Marye battery government tablet, on the Gettysburg battlefield.

65. Bachelder's Map; Wise, *Long Arm of Lee*, II, pp. 616–17; 44 *O.R.*, p. 610.

66. The Wallace battery government tablet, on the Gettysburg battlefield.

67. The Hurt battery government tablet, on the Gettysburg battlefield.

68. The Rice battery government tablet, on the Gettysburg battlefield.

69. The Johnson battery government tablet, on the Gettysburg battlefield.

70. *S.H.S.P.*, IV, p. 158; Stine, *Army of the Potomac*, p. 451.

71. The Marye battery government tablet, on the Gettysburg battlefield; Scott, *Battles at Gettysburg*, pp. 123, 133; Fox *New York at Gettysburg*, I, p. 10; Storrick, *Gettysburg*, p. 19; Bruce, *Twentieth Massachusetts*, p. 271; Doubleday, *Chancellorsville and Gettysburg*, p. 126.

72. Battine, *Crisis of the Confederacy*, p. 186; Bates, *Battle of Gettysburg*, p. 58; Alexander, *Military Memoirs of a Confederate*, p. 381; Boyle, *One Hundred and Eleventh Pennsylvania*, p. 115; Powell, *Fifth Corps*, p. 507; Swinton, *Army of the Potomac*, p. 328; Doubleday, *Chancellorsville and Gettysburg*, p. 126.

73. Vautier, *88th Pennsylvania*, p. 118; 43 *O.R.*, p. 927.

74. Paris, *History of the Civil War*, III, p. 546; Cheney, *Ninth New York Cavalry*, p. 108; 43 *O.R.*, p. 1030.

75. Vautier, *88th Pennsylvania*, p. 121.

76. Young, *Battle of Gettysburg*, p. 169; Storrick, *Gettysburg*, p. 117.

77. Fox, *New York at Gettysburg*, I, p. 10.

78. *B. & L.*, III, p. 276.

79. Paris, *History of the Civil War*, III, p. 546; 43 *O.R.*, p. 927.

80. Young, *Gettysburg*, pp. 162–63.

81. 44 *O.R.*, p. 444.

82. Fremantle, *Three Months in the Southern States*, p. 254; Battine, *Crisis of the Confederacy*, p. 191; Paris, *History of the Civil War*, III, p. 547.

83. 43 *O.R.*, p. 927.

84. 45 *O.R.*, p. 470.

85. *Ibid.*

86. 43 *O.R.*, p. 927.

87. *Ibid.*, p. 924.

88. 44 *O.R.*, p. 348; Longstreet, *From Manassas to Appomattox*, p. 352.

89. Long, *Memoirs of Robert E. Lee*, p. 275.

90. Longstreet, *From Manassas to Appomattox*, p. 352; Taylor, *Four Years with General Lee*, pp. 92–93.

91. *S.H.S.P.*, XLIII, p. 56.

CHAPTER 4

1. *C.C.W.* (1865), I, p. 305; 43 *O.R.*, p. 244.

2. Paris, *History of the Civil War*, III, p. 550; Stine, *Army of the Potomac*, p. 454; Edward J. Nichols, *Toward Gettysburg: A Biography of General John F. Reynolds* (University Park, Pa.: Pennsylvania State University Press, 1958), p. 255. The able study by Nichols is now the standard treatment of Reynolds.

3. Stine, *Army of the Potomac*, p. 453.

4. Paris, *History of the Civil War*, III, p. 547.

5. *Ibid.*

6. Vanderslice, *Gettysburg*, p. 72; Battine, *Crisis of the Confederacy*, p. 187; Swinton, *Army of the Potomac*, p. 328; Paris, *History of the Civil War*, III, p. 550. After studying thoroughly the many accounts of the battle as regards the times of different events, one is struck immediately by the wide variance of estimates made by officers present. Obviously, a great many watches were wrong at Gettysburg.

7. Hall, *Sixth New York Cavalry*, p. 139; Theodore B. Gates, *The Ulster Guard (20th N.Y. State Militia) and the War of the Rebellion* (New York: B. H. Tyrrel, 1879), p. 424.

8. John Watts DePeyster, *Decisive Conflicts of the Late Civil War* (New York: C. H. Ludwig, 1867), p. 153.

9. Stine, *Army of the Potomac*, p. 454; Stephen M. Weld, *War Diary and Letters of Stephen Minot Weld, 1861–1865* (Cambridge, Mass.: Riverside Press, 1912), p. 230; Meade, *Life and Letters of Meade*, II, pp. 36, 222, 230, 232.

10. Doubleday, *Chancellorsville and Gettysburg*, pp. 126–27.

11. 43 *O.R.*, p. 401.

12. Nicholson, *Pennsylvania at Gettysburg*, I, p. 28; Beecham, *Gettysburg*, p. 60; Bates, *Battle of Gettysburg*, p. 82; Marshall, *Battle of Gettysburg*, p. 114; Carl Schurz, *The Reminiscences of Carl Schurz* (New York: The McClure Co., 1908), III, p. 6; 43 *O.R.*, p. 251.

13. Fox, *New York at Gettysburg*, III, p. 990.

14. Bates, *Battle of Gettysburg*, p. 60.

15. Beecham, *Gettysburg*, p. 61; 43 *O.R.*, pp. 244, 281.

16. A.P. Smith, *History of the Seventy-Sixth Regiment New York Volunteers* (Cortland, N.Y.: Truair, Smith, & Miles, 1867), p. 236.

17. Fox, *New York at Gettysburg*, III, p. 990.

18. Gates, *Ulster Guard*, p. 425; Smith, *Seventy-Sixth New York*, p. 237.

19. Scott, *Battles at Gettysburg*, p. 139; Vanderslice, *Gettysburg*, p. 72; Paris, *History of the Civil War*, III, p. 551; 43 *O.R.*, pp. 244, 265.

20. Fox, *New York at Gettysburg*, III, p. 1145. This line is now indicated by Reynolds Avenue on the Gettysburg battlefield. See also 43 *O.R.*, pp. 927, 934.

21. Scott, *Battles at Gettysburg*, p. 140; 43 *O.R.*, pp. 265–66.

22. Scott, *Battles at Gettysburg*, p. 156.

23. 43 *O.R.*, p. 244.

24. Doubleday, *Chancellorsville and Gettysburg*, p. 128; 43 *O.R.*, p. 282.

25. Vautier, *88th Pennsylvania*, p. 118; Bachelder's Map.

26. Fox, *New York at Gettysburg*, II, p. 733.

27. *C.C.W.* (1865), I, p. 306; Doubleday, *Chancellorsville and Gettysburg*, p. 130; Bates, *Battle of Gettysburg*, p. 62; 43 *O.R.*, p. 244.

28. Doubleday, *Chancellorsville and Gettysburg*, p. 130.

29. *Ibid.*

30. Stine, *Army of the Potomac*, p. 457; Nichols, *Toward Gettysburg*, pp. 205, 252–53.

31. Bates, *Battle of Gettysburg*, p. 63.

32. Doubleday, *Chancellorsville and Gettysburg*, p. 131; Nichols, *Toward Gettysburg*, pp. 205, 206, 253–54.

33. 43 *O.R.*, p. 266; Hall, *Sixth New York Cavalry*, p. 141; Battine, *Crisis of the Confederacy*, p. 189; Storrick, *Gettysburg*, p. 20; Marshal, *Battle of Gettysburg*, p. 114; Paris, *History of the Civil War*, III, p. 553; First Corps government tablet, on the Gettysburg battlefield.

34. Stine, *Army of the Potomac*, p. 457.

35. 43 *O.R.*, p. 245. Doubleday is not widely known for being the able Union First Corps commander at Gettysburg, but rather for being the man who drew up the rules, positioned men, and laid out the first modern baseball diamond in 1839 at Cooperstown, N.Y., and who reputedly fired the first shot by the Federals at Fort Sumter in reply to Confederate fire.

36. Paris, *History of the Civil War*, III, p. 553.

37. Nicholson, *Pennsylvania at Gettysburg*, I, p. 27.

38. Stine, *Army of the Potomac*, p. 455.

39. Swinton, *Army of the Potomac*, p. 330; Stine, *Army of the Potomac*, p. 455; J.R. Sypher, *History of the Pennsylvania Reserve Corps* (Lancaster, Pa.: E. Barr & Co., 1865), p. 451; 43 *O.R.*, pp. 245, 266; Regis de Trobriand, *Four Years with the Army of the Potomac* (Boston: Ticknor & Co., 1889), p. 488.

40. Doubleday, *Chancellorsville and Gettysburg*, 134; 43 *O.R.*, pp. 246–47.

CHAPTER 5

1. *C.C.W.* (1865), I, p. 413.
2. The 7th Indiana of Cutler's brigade was absent on wagon train guard duty and did not rejoin the brigade until evening (Scott, *Battles at Gettysburg*, p. 145; Nicholson, *Pennsylvania at Gettysburg*, I, p. 343; Stine, *Army of the Potomac*, p. 461; 43 *O.R.*, pp. 281–82.)
3. Battine, *Crisis of the Confederacy*, p. 188; Fox, *New York at Gettysburg*, III, p. 990; 43 *O.R.*, p. 265.
4. 43 *O.R.*, pp. 279, 345, 939; Hall, *Sixth New York Cavalry*, p. 139.
5. Nicholson, *Pennsylvania at Gettysburg*, I, p. 343; Vanderslice, *Gettysburg*, p. 72.
6. Fox, *New York at Gettysburg*, III, pp. 991, 1003; Scott, *Battles at Gettysburg*, pp. 146–48.
7. Fox, *New York at Gettysburg*, III, p. 1001.
8. 44 *O.R.*, p. 649.
9. The Davis brigade government tablet, on the Gettysburg battlefield.
10. 44 *O.R.*, p. 649.
11. Doubleday, *Chancellorsville and Gettysburg*, pp. 128–29.
12. Fox, *New York at Gettysburg*, II, p. 616.
13. Bachelder's Map; Vanderslice, *Gettysburg*, p. 76.
14. Vautier, *88th Pennsylvania*, pp. 120–121; 44 *O.R.*, p. 649; 43 *O.R.*, pp. 266, 281–82.
15. Nicholson, *Pennsylvania at Gettysburg*, I, pp. 27, 344; Bates, *Battle of Gettysburg*, p. 61; Vanderslice, *Gettysburg*, p. 75.
16. Vanderslice, *Gettysburg*, p. 75.
17. Smith, *Seventy-Sixth New York*, p. 238.
18. Fox, *New York at Gettysburg*, II, p. 616; but see 43 *O.R.*, p. 282.
19. 44 *O.R.*, p. 649; Fox, *New York at Gettysburg*, III, pp. 1001, 1005, 1006.
20. Vanderslice, *Gettysburg*, p. 76; Fox, *New York at Gettysburg*, I, p. 12; 43 *O.R.*, p. 266.
21. Scott, *Battles at Gettysburg*, p. 148; Vautier, *88th Pennsylvania*, p. 120; Stine, *Army of the Potomac*, p. 462; Fox, *New York at Gettysburg*, II, p. 616.
22. Doubleday, *Chancellorsville and Gettysburg*, p. 129; 43 *O.R.*, pp. 266, 282.
23. Scott, *Battles at Gettysburg*, p. 147; 43 *O.R.*, p. 359.
24. Stine, *Army of the Potomac*, pp. 461–62; 43 *O.R.*, p. 359.
25. Vautier, *88th Pennsylvania*, p. 121; 43 *O.R.*, p. 360.
26. Stine, *Army of the Potomac*, p. 464.
27. Wise, *Long Arm of Lee*, II, p. 617; 43 *O.R.*, p. 359.

28. Fox, *New York at Gettysburg*, III, p. 994; Vautier, *88th Pennsylvania*, p. 121; 43 *O.R.*, p. 359.

29. Fox, *New York at Gettysburg*, III, p. 994.

30. Stine, *Army of the Potomac*, p. 462; Nicholson, *Pennsylvania at Gettysburg*, I, p. 344; 43 *O.R.*, p. 282.

31. Smith, *Seventy-Sixth New York*, pp. 241–42.

32. *Ibid.*

33. *Ibid.*, p. 242.

34. Fox, *New York at Gettysburg*, III, p. 991.

35. *Ibid.* See also 43 *O.R.*, p. 245.

36. Fox, *New York at Gettysburg*, III, p. 992.

37. *Ibid.*, p. 1003.

38. *Ibid.*, p. 992.

39. *Ibid.*

40. Scott, *Battles at Gettysburg*, p. 149; Fox, *New York at Gettysburg*, III, p. 995.

41. Fox, *New York at Gettysburg*, III, p. 1003; but see 43 *O.R.*, pp. 245, 282.

42. Stine, *Army of the Potomac*, p. 462; 43 *O.R.*, p. 282.

43. Fox, *New York at Gettysburg*, III, p. 993.

44. Paris, *History of the Civil War*, III, p. 555; 44 *O.R.*, p. 649.

45. C.V. Tevis, *History of the Fighting Fourteenth [Brooklyn]* (New York: Brooklyn Eagle Press, 1911), p. 83; Rufus R. Dawes, *Service with the Sixth Wisconsin Volunteers* (Marietta, Ohio: E.R. Alderman & Sons, 1890), p. 165; 43 *O.R.*, p. 246.

46. *Fourteenth Brooklyn*, pp. 83, 85.

47. Bachelder's Map; Stine, *Army of the Potomac*, p. 465; 43 *O.R.*, p. 287; Scott, *Battles at Gettysburg*, p. 149; Vanderslice, *Gettysburg*, pp. 76–79.

48. Dawes, *Sixth Wisconsin*, p. 168.

49. *Fourteenth Brooklyn*, p. 84.

50. Fox, *New York at Gettysburg*, II, p. 736.

51. Stine, *Army of the Potomac*, p. 466.

52. Dawes, *Sixth Wisconsin*, p. 168; Vautier, *88th Pennsylvania*, p. 121.

53. Stine, *Army of the Potomac*, pp. 465–68; Fox, *New York at Gettysburg*, I, p. 13; 43 *O.R.*, p. 266.

54. Stine, *Army of the Potomac*, pp. 467–68.

55. Battine, *Crisis of the Confederacy*, p. 189.

56. *B. & L.*, III, p. 277; Wise, *Long Arm of Lee*, II, p. 617.

57. Doubleday, *Chancellorsville and Gettysburg*, p. 133; Paris, *History of the Civil War*, III, p. 555; Fox, *New York at Gettysburg*, III, p. 996.

58. 43 *O.R.*, p. 282; Nicholson, *Pennsylvania at Gettysburg*, I, p. 344;

Fox, *New York at Gettysburg*, I, p. 14; Stine, *Army of the Potomac*, p. 469; Doubleday, *Chancellorsville and Gettysburg*, p. 133.

59. Doubleday, *Chancellorsville and Gettysburg*, p. 133; see 43 *O.R.*, p. 246.

60. Battine, *Crisis of the Confederacy*, p. 189.

61. Storrick, *Gettysburg*, p. 21; 44 *O.R.*, p. 649.

62. Doubleday, *Chancellorsville and Gettysburg*, p. 134; 44 *O.R.*, p. 649.

63. Nicholson, *Pennsylvania at Gettysburg*, I, p. 491.

CHAPTER 6

1. Beecham, *Gettysburg*, p. 62; 43 *O.R.*, pp. 265–66.

2. Doubleday, *Chancellorsville and Gettysburg*, p. 128; 43 *O.R.*, p. 244.

3. Beecham, *Gettysburg*, p. 64; Doubleday, *Chancellorsville and Gettysburg*, p. 132.

4. Doubleday, *Chancellorsville and Gettysburg*, p. 132.

5. 43 *O.R.*, p. 273.

6. The Archer Brigade government tablet, on the Gettysburg battlefield.

7. Doubleday, *Chancellorsville and Gettysburg*, p. 130; 43 *O.R.*, p. 244.

8. Curtis, *Twenty-Fourth Michigan*, p. 156.

9. Stine, *Army of the Potomac*, p. 454; Curtis, *Twenty-Fourth Michigan*, p. 156.

10. Vanderslice, *Gettysburg*, p. 75; Bachelder's Map; 43 *O.R.*, p. 245. It must be remembered that the 6th Wisconsin of this brigade was in reserve at the Seminary before assisting in the fight against Davis at the railroad cut, described previously.

11. Bachelder's Map; Vanderslice, *Gettysburg*, p. 75.

12. Beecham, *Gettysburg*, p. 65.

13. 44 *O.R.*, p. 646; Vautier, *88th Pennsylvania*, p. 119.

14. Doubleday, *Chancellorsville and Gettysburg*, p. 131; Curtis, *Twenty-Fourth Michigan*, pp. 59–60.

15. Doubleday, *Chancellorsville and Gettysburg*, p. 132; Beecham, *Gettysburg*, p. 65.

16. Stine, *Army of the Potomac*, p. 458.

17. *Ibid.*; 44 *O.R.*, p. 646.

18. 43 *O.R.*, pp. 265–67; 44 *O.R.*, pp. 607, 638.

19. Curtis, *Twenty-Fourth Michigan*, pp. 157, 166; 44 *O.R.*, p. 646.

20. Curtis, *Twenty-Fourth Michigan*, p. 157.

21. Nicholson, *Pennsylvania at Gettysburg*, I, pp. 77, 490; 44 *O.R.*, 646;

Fox, *New York at Gettysburg*, I, p. 14; Longstreet, *From Manassas to Appomattox*, p. 354; 43 *O.R.*, p. 266.

22. Stine, *Army of the Potomac*, pp. 458–59.

23. Beecham, *Gettysburg*, p. 66.

24. 44 *O.R.*, p. 646; *Confederate Veteran*, VIII, pp. 535–37.

25. Stine, *Army of the Potomac*, pp. 458–59; 43 *O.R.*, p. 245.

26. Beecham, *Gettysburg*, pp. 66–67.

27. *Ibid.*

28. Stine, *Army of the Potomac*, pp. 458–59; Beecham, *Gettysburg*, pp. 66–67.

29. 44 *O.R.*, p. 646; *Confederate Veteran*, VIII, pp. 535–37.

30. *B. & L.*, III, p. 284; Doubleday, *Chancellorsville and Gettysburg*, p. 132.

31. 44 *O.R.*, p. 639.

32. 43 *O.R.*, p. 243; Doubleday, *Chancellorsville and Gettysburg*, p. 133; 44 *O.R.*, p. 646.

33. Beecham, *Gettysburg*, p. 69.

34. Doubleday, *Chancellorsville and Gettysburg*, p. 133; Stine, *Army of the Potomac*, pp. 460–61; 43 *O.R.*, p. 245.

35. Beecham, *Gettysburg*, pp. 68–69.

36. Vanderslice, *Gettysburg*, p. 76; Scott, *Battles at Gettysburg*, p. 203; Stine, *Army of the Potomac*, p. 461; 43 *O.R.*, p. 245.

37. Curtis, *Twenty-Fourth Michigan*, pp. 157–58.

38. Doubleday, *Chancellorsville and Gettysburg*, p. 133; Beecham, *Gettysburg*, p. 70.

39. 44 *O.R.*, p. 674; Battine, *Crisis of the Confederacy*, p. 191; Fox, *New York at Gettysburg*, L, p. 14.

40. The Hurt Battery government tablet, on the Gettysburg battlefield; 44 *O.R.*, p. 674.

41. Wise, *Long Arm of Lee*, II, pp. 618–19.

42. Fremantle, *Three Months in the Southern States*, p. 256.

43. Doubleday, *Chancellorsville and Gettysburg*, p. 134.

CHAPTER 7

1. Paris, *History of the Civil War*, III, p. 555; Fox, *New York at Gettysburg*, I, p. 14; Doubleday, *Chancellorsville and Gettysburg*, p. 135; Scott, *Battles at Gettysburg*, p. 160; Strong, *121st Pennsylvania*, p. 44; 43 *O.R.*, p. 312.

2. Paris, *History of the Civil War*, III, pp. 555–56; but see 43 *O.R.*, pp. 151, 291.

3. Doubleday, *Chancellorsville and Gettysburg*, p. 135; 43 *O.R.*, p. 354.

4. The Reynolds Battery government tablet, on the Gettysburg battlefield.

5. The Stevens Battery government tablet, on the Gettysburg battlefield.

6. The Cooper Battery government tablet, on the Gettysburg battlefield.

7. The Stewart Battery government tablet, on the Gettysburg battlefield.

8. Chamberlin, *One Hundred and Fiftieth Pennsylvania*, p. 111; 43 *O.R.*, pp. 247, 312.

9. The Stone Brigade government tablet, on the Gettysburg battlefield; 43 *O.R.*, p. 334.

10. Chamberlin, *One Hundred and Fiftieth Pennsylvania*, p. 111.

11. *Ibid.*, p. 112.

12. 43 *O.R.*, pp. 315, 329; the Stone Brigade government tablet.

13. 43 *O.R.*, pp. 315, 329; The Biddle Brigade government tablet, on the Gettysburg battlefield.

14. Gates, *Ulster Guard*, p. 432.

15. *Ibid.;* Scott, *Battles at Gettysburg*, p. 160.

16. Vanderslice, *Gettysburg*, p. 79; Fox, *New York at Gettysburg*, II, pp. 768–69; 43 *O.R.*, p. 315.

17. Bachelder's Map; Vanderslice, *Gettysburg*, p. 80; Stine, *Army of the Potomac*, 43 *O.R.*, p. 470; p. 315.

18. Vanderslice, *Gettysburg*, p. 80; 43 *O.R.*, pp. 355, 364.

19. Ashhurst, *First Day's Fight at Gettysburg*, p. 10; 43 *O.R.*, pp. 927, 934.

20. Gates, *Ulster Guard*, pp. 432–33. See also Coddington, *The Gettysburg Campaign*, pp. 307–308, p. 706; and Allan Nevins (ed.), *A Diary of Battle: The Personal Journals of Colonel Charles S. Wainwright, 1861–1865* (New York: Harcourt, Brace & World, 1962), p. 237.

21. Ashhurst, *First Day's Fight at Gettysburg*, p. 10.

22. Strong, *121st Pennsylvania*, p. 45.

23. Paris, *History of the Civil War*, III, p. 556.

24. Gates, *Ulster Guard*, p. 440.

25. Doubleday, *Chancellorsville and Gettysburg*, p. 135; 43 *O.R.*, p. 356.

26. Fox, *New York at Gettysburg*, III, p. 1256; *B. & L.*, III, p. 278; Vautier, *88th Pennsylvania*, p. 124; 43 *O.R.*, p. 356.

27. Fox, *New York at Gettysburg*, III, pp. 1256, 1258; 43 *O.R.*, p. 356.

28. Fox, *New York at Gettysburg*, III, p. 1257.

29. Vautier, *88th Pennsylvania*, p. 124; 43 *O.R.*, pp. 355–56.

30. So-called, owing to the unique insignia of a buck's tail on the left side of these soldiers' kepis.

31. *C.C.W.*, (1865), I, p. 307; Swinton, *Army of the Potomac*, p. 332; Doubleday, *Chancellorsville and Gettysburg*, p. 136.

32. Vautier, *88th Pennsylvania*, p. 124.

33. Doubleday, *Chancellorsville and Gettysburg*, p. 132; 43 *O.R.*, pp. 247, 289.

34. Bachelder's Map; Stine, *Army of the Potomac*, p. 474; Chamberlin, *One Hundred and Fiftieth Pennsylvania*, p. 114; 43 *O.R.*, p. 329.

35. Ashhurst, *First Day's Fight at Gettysburg*, pp. 12–13.

36. Chamberlin, *One Hundred and Fiftieth Pennsylvania*, p. 112; 43 *O.R.*, p. 329.

37. 43 *O.R.*, p. 329; Chamberlin, *One Hundred and Fiftieth Pennsylvania*, p. 112.

38. Vautier, *88th Pennsylvania*, pp. 130–31.

39. *Ibid.*; 43 *O.R.*, p. 329.

40. *Ibid.*; Vautier, *88th Pennsylvania*, pp. 130–31.

41. Storrick, *Gettysburg*, p. 22; Young, *Battle of Gettysburg*, p. 186; Marshal, *Battle of Gettysburg*, p. 115.

42. Chamberlin, *One Hundred and Fiftieth Pennsylvania*, p. 114.

43. *B. & L.*, III, pp. 276n, 284; 43 *O.R.*, p. 927; Curtis, *Twenty-Fourth Michigan*, p. 183; Chamberlin, *One Hundred and Fiftieth Pennsylvania*, pp. 113–14; Boyle, *One Hundred and Eleventh Pennsylvania*, p. 116; Vanderslice, *Gettysburg*, p. 99. It is claimed by one writer (Cheney, *Ninth New York Cavalry*, pp. 111–12) that John Burns secured his musket and cartridges from a wounded trooper of the 9th New York Cavalry near Pennsylvania College, about 11:00 a.m. Burns' wounds were said to have been dressed by Assistant Surgeon Collar of the 24th Michigan (Curtis, *Twenty-Fourth Michigan*, p. 183). But see Glenn Tucker, *High Tide at Gettysburg: The Campaign in Pennsylvania* (Indianapolis: Bobbs-Merrill Co., 1958), p. 120.

44. William Henry Locke, *The Story of the [Eleventh Pennsylvania Infantry] Regiment* (Philadelphia: J.B. Lippincott & Co., 1872), p. 226.

45. Isaac Hall, *History of the Ninety-Seventh New York Volunteers* (Utica: Press of L.C. Childs & Son, 1890), p. 134.

46. Vautier, *88th Pennsylvania*, p. 114; Davis, *Thirteenth Massachusetts*, p. 226; Doubleday, *Chancellorsville and Gettysburg*, p. 135; Fox, *New York at Gettysburg*, II, p. 752; Young, *Battle of Gettysburg*, pp. 185–86; Paris, *History of the Civil War*, III, p. 555; Storrick, *Gettysburg*, p. 21; George A. Hussey, *History of the Ninth Regiment, N.Y.S.M.-N.G.S.N.Y.*

(Eighty-Third N.Y. Volunteers) (New York: Regimental Veterans Association, 1889), p. 268; 43 *O.R.*, p. 307.

47. Davis, *Thirteenth Massachusetts*, p. 226; Scott, *Battles at Gettysburg*, p. 161; 43 *O.R.*, p. 247.

48. Davis, *Thirteenth Massachusetts*, p. 226.

49. Fox, *New York at Gettysburg*, I, p. 125; 43 *O.R.*, pp. 292, 308.

50. Alexander, *Military Memoirs of a Confederate*, p. 383; Beecham, *Gettysburg*, p. 51; Vautier, *88th Pennsylvania*, p. 123; Storrick, *Gettysburg*, p. 22; Vanderslice, *Gettysburg*, pp. 80, 83; 44 *O.R.*, p. 566.

51. Vautier, *88th Pennsylvania*, p. 122; 44 *O.R.*, p. 562.

52. 44 *O.R.*, p. 581; Vautier, *88th Pennsylvania*, p. 122.

53. Marshall, *Battle of Gettysburg*, p. 118.

54. The Carter Battery government tablet, on the Gettysburg battlefield.

55. The Fry Battery government tablet, on the Gettysburg battlefield.

56. The Page Battery government tablet, on the Gettysburg battlefield.

57. The Reese Battery government tablet, on the Gettysburg battlefield; 44 *O.R.*, pp. 602–603.

58. Swinton, *Army of the Potomac*, p. 332.

59. Marshal, *Battle of Gettysburg*, p. 118; see also 43 *O.R.*, pp. 247–48.

CHAPTER 8

1. Beecham, *Gettysburg*, p. 60; Fox, *New York at Gettysburg*, I, 102; 43 *O.R.*, p. 151.

2. Chapman Biddle, *The First Day of the Battle of Gettysburg* (Philadelphia: J.B. Lippincott & Co., 1880), p. 24; Battine, *Crisis of the Confederacy*, p. 192.

3. *Philadelphia Weekly Times*, May 31, 1879; 43 *O.R.*, p. 701.

4. *B. & L.*, III, p. 287; Storrick, *Gettysburg*, p. 23; 43 *O.R.*, p. 702.

5. 43 *O.R.*, p. 247; Vautier, *88th Pennsylvania*, p. 124; Boyle, *One Hundred and Eleventh Pennsylvania*, p. 115; Scott, *Battles at Gettysburg*, p. 158; Wise, *The Long Arm of Lee*, II, p. 618; Paris, *History of the Civil War*, III, p. 557; *B. & L.*, III, p. 278.

6. *B. & L.*, III, p. 287; 43 *O.R.*, p. 702.

7. 43 *O.R.*, pp. 247, 701; Marshal, *Battle of Gettysburg*, p. 116; Storrick, *Gettysburg*, p. 23.

8. Scott, *Battles at Gettysburg*, p. 158; Marshal, *Battle of Gettysburg*, p. 116. See also 43 *O.R.*, pp. 258, 261, 366.

9. Bates, *Battle of Gettysburg*, p. 70.

10. Oliver O. Howard, "Campaign of Gettysburg," *Atlantic Monthly*

(July, 1876), p. 54; *B. & L.*, III, p. 287; Schurz, *Reminiscences*, III, p. 5; 43 *O.R.*, p. 702.

11. Schurz, *Reminiscences*, III, p. 4; 43 *O.R.*, p. 727.

12. Fox, *New York at Gettysburg*, I, pp. 15, 378.

13. *Ibid.*, p. 378; 43 *O.R.*, p. 727.

14. Fox, *New York at Gettysburg*, I, p. 378.

15. *Ibid.;* 43 *O.R.*, p. 727.

16. Fox, *New York at Gettysburg*, I, pp. 15, 378.

17. *Ibid.;* 43 *O.R.*, p. 754.

18. John S. Applegate, *Reminiscences and Letters of George Arrowsmith of New Jersey* (Red Bank, N.J.: J.H. Cook, 1893), p. 212. Arrowsmith was Lieutenant Colonel of the 157th New York at Gettysburg.

19. The Dilger battery government tablet, on the Gettysburg battlefield; 43 *O.R.*, p. 754.

20. 43 *O.R.*, p. 754; the Dilger tablet.

21. Fox, *New York at Gettysburg*, I, p. 378; 44 *O.R.*, pp. 553, 581.

22. Fox, *New York at Gettysburg*, I, p. 379; 44 *O.R.*, pp. 552–54.

23. Fox, *New York at Gettysburg*, I, picture opposite p. 16; p. 379.

24. *Ibid.*, p. 379.

25. Boyle, *One Hundred and Eleventh Pennsylvania*, p. 115; Young, *Battle of Gettysburg*, p. 192; Battine, *Crisis of the Confederacy*, pp. 192–93; Powell, *Fifth Corps*, p. 507; Swinton, *Army of the Potomac*, p. 333; Scott, *Battles at Gettysburg*, p. 186; Doubleday, *Chancellorsville and Gettysburg*, p. 138; *B. & L.*, III, pp. 285, 288; Vautier, *88th Pennsylvania*, p. 125; Schurz, *Reminiscences*, III, p. 7.

26. Paris, *History of the Civil War*, III, p. 558; Vautier, *88th Pennsylvania*, p. 125.

27. Nicholson, *Pennsylvania at Gettysburg*, I, p. 438; 43 *O.R.*, p. 727.

28. 43 *O.R.*, pp. 721, 727; Doubleday, *Chancellorsville and Gettysburg*, p. 138; Fox, *New York at Gettysburg*, I, p. 15.

29. Fox, *New York at Gettysburg*, III, p. 1245.

30. *B. & L.*, III, p. 288; Fox, *New York at Gettysburg*, I, p. 26.

31. Beecham, *Gettysburg*, p. 75; Bates, *Battle of Gettysburg*, p. 75.

32. Schurz, *Reminiscences*, III, p. 8; *B. & L.*, III, p. 278.

33. Biddle, *The First Day*, p. 39; 43 *O.R.*, pp. 702, 727.

34. The Wiedrich battery government tablet, on the Gettysburg battlefield.

35. The Wheeler battery government tablet, on the Gettysburg battlefield.

36. The Dilger battery government tablet, on the Gettysburg battlefield.

37. The Heckman battery government tablet, on the Gettysburg battle-field.

38. The Wilkeson battery government tablet, on the Gettysburg battle-field; 43 *O.R.*, p. 747.

39. Vautier, *88th Pennsylvania*, p. 125; 43 *O.R.*, p. 748.

40. The Wilkeson battery government tablet, on the Gettysburg battle-field; 43 *O.R.*, p. 748.

41. Paris, *History of the Civil War*, III, p. 559; 43 *O.R.*, pp. 702, 727.

42. Vautier, *88th Pennsylvania*, p. 126.

43. Livermore, *Story of the Civil War*, II, p. 424.

44. Schurz, *Reminiscences*, III, p. 9; 43 *O.R.*, pp. 727–28.

45. Vautier, *88th Pennsylvania*, p. 126; 43 *O.R.*, p. 728.

46. 43 *O.R.*, pp. 727–28.

47. Scott, *Battles at Gettysburg*, p. 187; 44 *O.R.*, pp. 553–54.

48. Bachelder's Map; Vanderslice, *Gettysburg*, p. 88; the Gilsa brigade government tablet, on the Gettysburg battlefield.

49. Nicholson, *Pennsylvania at Gettysburg*, I, 438; 43 *O.R.*, p. 728.

50. Bachelder's Map; Vanderslice, *Gettysburg*, p. 88; Fox, *New York at Gettysburg*, I, p. 430.

51. The Ames brigade government tablet, on the Gettysburg battle-field; 43 *O.R.*, p. 712.

52. Bachelder's Map; Vanderslice, *Gettysburg*, p. 91.

53. The 25th and 75th Ohio monument, on the Gettysburg battlefield.

54. Bachelder's Map; Vanderslice, *Gettysburg*, p. 88.

55. Doubleday, *Chancellorsville and Gettysburg*, p. 138; 43 *O.R.*, p. 939.

56. Nicholson, *Pennsylvania at Gettysburg*, II, p. 885; 43 *O.R.*, p. 939.

57. Doubleday, *Chancellorsville and Gettysburg*, p. 142; Vautier, *88th Pennsylvania*, p. 126; Paris, *History of the Civil War*, III, p. 564.

58. Vautier, *88th Pennsylvania*, pp. 126–27; 43 *O.R.*, p. 748.

59. Paris, *History of the Civil War*, III, p. 564; Vautier, *88th Pennsylvania*, pp. 126–27.

60. Livermore, *Story of the Civil War*, II, pp. 420–21; 43 *O.R.*, pp. 727–28.

61. Bruce, *Twentieth Massachusetts*, p. 272; Scott, *Battles at Gettysburg*, p. 92; Nicholson, *Pennsylvania at Gettysburg*, I, p. 27; 43 *O.R.*, p. 728.

62. Marshall, *Battle of Gettysburg*, p. 120.

63. Bachelder's Map; Vanderslice, *Gettysburg*, p. 88.

64. Doubleday, *Chancellorsville and Gettysburg*, p. 141; Paris, *History of the Civil War*, III, p. 559; 43 *O.R.*, p. 702.

65. Vanderslice, *Gettysburg*, pp. 88, 132.

66. 43 *O.R.*, p. 727.

67. Doubleday, *Chancellorsville and Gettysburg*, p. 142.

68. *Ibid.*

69. *Confederate Veteran*, V, p. 614.

CHAPTER 9

1. Robert Stiles, *Four Years Under Marse Robert* (New York: Neale Publishing Co., 1904), p. 209; Wise, *Long Arm of Lee*, II, p. 620; Vanderslice, *Gettysburg*, p. 91; Scott, *Battles at Gettysburg*, p. 185; Taylor, *Four Years with General Lee*, p. 94; 44 *O.R.*, p. 492.

2. Livermore, *Story of the Civil War*, II, p. 425; 40 *O.R.*, p. 846.

3. Fox, *New York at Gettysburg*, I, p. 19; 43 *O.R.*, pp. 927, 939.

4. 44 *O.R.*, pp. 468, 582; Bachelder's Map; Vautier, *88th Pennsylvania*, p. 138; Vanderslice, *Gettysburg*, p. 91; Paris, *History of the Civil War*, III, p. 564.

5. 44 *O.R.*, p. 492.

6. *Ibid.*, p. 479; Vautier, *88th Pennsylvania*, p. 138; Bachelder's Map.

7. Bachelder's Map; Vanderslice, *Gettysburg*, p. 92.

8. Bachelder's Map; 44 *O.R.*, p. 468.

9. Carrington's battery, soon after arriving on the field with Jones' other batteries, was ordered to cross Rock Creek in the rear of Gordon's Brigade, and to support him in his advance on the Federal line. Consequently, this battery was little engaged during the afternoon, the brunt of the artillery support falling on the other three batteries (The Carrington battery government tablet, on the Gettysburg battlefield). See also 44 *O.R.*, p. 495.

10. The Garber battery government tablet, on the Gettysburg battlefield; Bachelder's Map.

11. The Green battery government tablet, on the Gettysburg battlefield; Bachelder's Map; Vautier, *88th Pennsylvania*, p. 128.

12. The Tanner battery government tablet, on the Gettysburg battlefield; Bachleder's Map; Vautier, *88th Pennsylvania*, p. 128.

13. Stiles, *Four Years Under Marse Robert*, p. 210.

14. 43 *O.R.*, p. 729.

15. Bruce, *Twentieth Massachusetts*, p. 272; Doubelday, *Chancellorsville and Gettysburg*, p. 141; Battine, *Crisis of the Confederacy*, p. 196; 44 *O.R.*, p. 468.

16. 44 *O.R.*, p. 495; Wise, *Long Arm of Lee*, II, p. 621; Vanderslice, *Gettysburg*, p. 91; Fox, *New York at Gettysburg*, I, p. 20; Paris, *History of the Civil War*, III, p. 564.

17. The Garber and Green government tablets, on the Gettysburg battlefield; 44 *O.R.*, p. 495.

18. The Wilkeson battery government tablet, on the Gettysburg battle-field.

19. *Ibid.*

20. The Garber, Green, Tanner, and Carrington government tablets, on the Gettysburg battlefield.

21. 44 *O.R.*, p. 495.

22. *Ibid.*, p. 458.

23. *Ibid.*, p. 497.

24. *Ibid.*, p. 495.

25. Stiles, *Four Years under Marse Robert*, pp. 150–51.

26. 44 *O.R.*, p. 582.

27. *Ibid.*, p. 492.

28. Livermore, *Story of the Civil War*, II, p. 424.

29. *Ibid.*

30. Scott, *Battles at Gettysburg*, p. 190.

31. 44 *O.R.*, p. 582.

32. Stine, *Army of the Potomac*, p. 479; 44 *O.R.*, pp. 468–69, 492–93.

33. Vautier, *88th Pennsylvania*, pp. 138–39.

34. The Gordon brigade government tablet, on the Gettysburg battle-field.

35. Boyle, *One Hundred and Eleventh Pennsylvania*, p. 116.

36. Marshal, *Battle of Gettysburg*, p. 123.

37. Battine, *Crisis of the Confederacy*, p. 197.

38. Fox, *New York at Gettysburg*, I, p. 21; 43 *O.R.*, p. 729.

39. Vautier, *88th Pennsylvania*, p. 140; 44 *O.R.*, p. 492.

40. 44 *O.R.*, p. 492; Fox, *New York at Gettysburg*, I, p. 20.

41. John B. Gordon, *Reminiscences of the Civil War* (New York, 1903), p. 151.

42. Stiles, *Four Years under Marse Robert*, p. 211.

43. 82nd Ohio monument, on the Gettysburg battlefield; Fox, *New York at Gettysburg*, I, p. 379.

44. Gordon, *Reminiscences*, p. 151; 44 *O.R.*, p. 492.

45. Stine, *Army of the Potomac*, p. 479; 43 *O.R.*, p. 729.

46. Boyle, *One Hundred and Eleventh Pennsylvania*, p. 116.

47. 43 *O.R.*, p. 712.

48. Frank Moore, *The Rebellion Record; A Diary of American Events, with Documents, Narratives, Illustrative Incidents, Poetry, etc.* (New York: G.P. Putnam, 1862–71), X, p. 181; 43 *O.R.*, p. 729.

49. Fox, *New York at Gettysburg*, I, p. 379.

50. 43 *O.R.*, p. 712; Livermore, *Story of the Civil War*, II, p. 424.

51. Marshal, *Battle of Gettysburg*, p. 123; 43 *O.R.*, p. 729.

52. Paris, *History of the Civil War*, III, p. 565.

53. Scott, *Battles at Gettysburg*, p. 214.

54. 44 *O.R.*, p. 495.

55. Stine, *Army of the Potomac*, p. 479; Paris, *History of the Civil War*, III, p. 565; 44 *O.R.*, pp. 468–69.

56. Paris, *History of the Civil War*, III, p. 565.

57. 44 *O.R.*, 469; Scott, *Battles at Gettysburg*, p. 214.

58. Vanderslice, *Gettysburg*, p. 92.

59. The old Buschbeck brigade, of Chancellorsville fame.

60. 43 *O.R.*, p. 729; Fox, *New York at Gettysburg*, III, p. 1051.

61. Fox, *New York at Gettysburg*, II, p. 918; 43 *O.R.*, p. 748.

62. Bachelder's Map; Fox, *New York at Gettysburg*, III, p. 1051.

63. Fox, *New York at Gettysburg*, III, p. 1051.

64. *Ibid.*

65. *Ibid.*, I, p. 22. See also 43 *O.R.*, p. 729.

66. Fox, New York at Gettysburg, I, p. 22.

67. *Ibid.*, III, p. 1055.

68. Vautier, *88th Pennsylvania*, p. 143; 43 *O.R.*, p. 748.

69. The Heckman battery government tablet, on the Gettysburg battlefield.

70. 44 *O.R.*, p. 484; Scott, *Battles at Gettysburg*, pp. 214–15.

71. Fox, *New York at Gettysburg*, III, p. 1054.

72. *Ibid.*, p. 1055.

73. Vautier, *88th Pennsylvania*, p. 141.

74. 44 *O.R.*, p. 480.

75. *Ibid.*, p. 555.

76. Doubleday, *Chancellorsville and Gettysburg*, p. 142; 43 *O.R.*, p. 729.

77. 44 *O.R.*, pp. 317, 445, 468, 554, 638–39.

78. Stine, *Army of the Potomac*, p. 479.

79. Fox, *New York at Gettysburg*, III, pp. 1057, 1060–61.

80. *Ibid.*, II, p. 808.

81. Paris, *History of the Civil War*, III, p. 564.

82. Scott, *Battles at Gettysburg*, p. 216; 43 *O.R.*, p. 754.

83. Vanderslice, *Gettysburg*, p. 91; 43 *O.R.*, pp. 729–30.

84. Schurz, *Reminiscences*, III, p. 12; Fox, *New York at Gettysburg*, I, p. 134.

85. Schurz, *Reminiscences*, III, p. 10; 43 *O.R.*, p. 704.

86. Fox, *New York at Gettysburg*, I, p. 21. On July 5, two days after the third day's battle, this piece was recovered by the Federals, the Confederates evidently not desiring to try to use it in its unserviceable condition.

87. Vautier, *88th Pennsylvania*, p. 141; 44 *O.R.*, p. 582.

88. The Schurz division government tablet, on the Gettysburg battlefield; 43 *O.R.*, p. 729.

89. Bates, *Battle of Gettysburg*, p. 78; 43 *O.R.*, p. 730.

90. Young, *Battle of Gettysburg*, p. 200.

CHAPTER 10

1. Vautier, *88th Pennsylvania*, p. 114; Davis, *Thirteenth Massachusetts*, p. 226; Doubleday, *Chancellorsville and Gettysburg*, p. 135; Fox, *New York at Gettysburg*, II, p. 752; Hussey, *Eighty-Third New York*, p. 268; 43 *O.R.*, p. 307.

2. Fox, *New York at Gettysburg*, II, p. 752; Vautier, *88th Pennsylvania*, p. 105; 43 *O.R.*, pp. 289, 307.

3. The Baxter brigade government tablet, on the Gettysburg battlefield.

4. Vautier, *88th Pennsylvania*, p. 123; 43 *O.R.*, p. 249.

5. Hussey, *Eighty-Third New York*, p. 269; 43 *O.R.*, p. 307.

6. Nicholson, *Pennsylvania at Gettysburg*, I, p. 178.

7. 43 *O.R.*, p. 307.

8. Hussey, *Eighty-Third New York*, p. 270. Doubleday states, however, that Robinson himself moved out to Oak Ridge with Paul's brigade, not Baxter's (Doubleday, *Chancellorsville and Gettysburg*, pp. 144–45; Doubleday's testimony, *C.C.W.* (1865), I, p. 307).

9. Locke, *Story of the Regiment*, p. 229; Hussey, *Eighty-Third New York*, p. 270; Vautier, *88th Pennsylvania*, p. 105; 43 *O.R.*, p. 248.

10. Nicholson, *Pennsylvania at Gettysburg*, I, p. 27; *B. & L.*, III, p. 279; Paris, *History of the Civil War*, III, p. 559; Bates, *Battle of Gettysburg*, p. 70.

11. 44 *O.R.*, p. 596.

12. The Carter battery government tablet, on the Gettysburg battlefield.

13. The Fry battery government tablet, on the Gettysburg battlefield.

14. The Page battery government tablet, on the Gettysburg battlefield.

15. The Reese battery government tablet, on the Gettysburg battlefield; 44 *O.R.*, pp. 602–603.

16. Vautier, *88th Pennsylvania*, pp. 127–28; 44 *O.R.*, pp. 602–603.

17. 44 *O.R.*, pp. 602–603; Vautier, *88th Pennsylvania*, pp. 127–28.

18. 44 *O.R.*, p. 603.

19. Nicholson, *Pennsylvania at Gettysburg*, II, p. 907.

20. The Carter battery government tablet, on the Gettysburg battlefield; 44 *O.R.*, p. 602.

21. The Fry battery government tablet, on the Gettysburg battlefield.

22. The Page battery government tablet, on the Gettysburg battlefield; 44 *O.R.*, p. 602.

23. The Reese battery government tablet, on the Gettysburg battlefield.
24. *S.H.S.P.*, IV, p. 158.
25. 44 *O.R.*, p. 552.
26. *Ibid.*, p. 566; Bachelder's Map; Vautier, *88th Pennsylvania*, p. 122.
27. The Doles brigade government tablet, on the Gettysburg battlefield.
28. 44 *O.R.*, p. 552.
29. Nicholson, *Pennsylvania at Gettysburg*, I, p. 345; Fox, *New York at Gettysburg*, I, p. 16; 43 *O.R.*, pp. 282–83.
30. 43 *O.R.*, p. 552; 44 *O.R.*, pp. 317, 352.
31. Benjamin F. Cook, *History of the Twelfth Massachusetts Volunteers, Webster Regiment* (Boston: Twelfth Regiment Association, 1882), p. 100; Vautier, *88th Pennsylvania*, p. 106; Hussey, *Eighty-Third New York*, p. 270; 43 *O.R.*, p. 248.
32. Bachelder's Map; Vanderslice, *Gettysburg*, p. 84.
33. Nicholson, *Pennsylvania at Gettysburg*, I, p. 491.
34. 44 *O.R.*, p. 553.
35. Bachelder's Map; Vanderslice, *Gettysburg*, p. 84; 44 *O.R.*, p. 592.
36. 44 *O.R.*, p. 587.
37. *Ibid.*, p. 553.
38. *Ibid.*
39. The O'Neal brigade government tablet, on the Gettysburg battlefield.
40. 44 *O.R.*, pp. 444, 553, 592.
41. *Ibid.*, p. 444.
42. Fox, *New York at Gettysburg*, I, p. 21; Vautier, *88th Pennsylvania*, p. 135; 43 *O.R.*, p. 754.
43. 44 *O.R.*, p. 579; Vautier, *88th Pennsylvania*, p. 135.
44. Paris, *History of the Civil War*, III, p. 562; 43 *O.R.*, p. 307.
45. 44 *O.R.*, p. 553.
46. Scott, *Battles at Gettysburg*, p. 173; 44 *O.R.*, pp. 553–54, 592–93.
47. Paris, *History of the Civil War*, III, p. 562; 43 *O.R.*, pp. 289, 307.
48. Stine, *Army of the Potomac*, p. 472; Vautier, *88th Pennsylvania*, p. 135; Hussey, *Eighty-Third New York*, p. 270; Nicholson, *Pennsylvania at Gettysburg*, I, p. 491; Bachelder's Map.
49. Scott, *Battles at Gettysburg*, p. 169; Bachelder's Map.
50. Bachelder's Map; Scott, *Battles at Gettysburg*, p. 169.
51. 44 *O.R.*, p. 602.
52. Wise, *The Long Arm of Lee*, II, p. 619; Paris, *History of the Civil War*, III, p. 561; 44 *O.R.*, pp. 602–603.
53. Doubleday, *Chancellorsville and Gettysburg*, p. 139; 43 *O.R.*, pp. 248, 315.

54. Scott, *Battles at Gettysburg*, p. 170.

55. Vanderslice, *Gettysburg*, p. 83; Bachelder's Map.

56. 44 *O.R.*, p. 587.

57. Scott, *Battles at Gettysburg*, p. 174.

58. Nicholson, *Pennsylvania at Gettysburg*, II, pp. 492, 908.

59. Hall, *Ninety-Seventh New York*, p. 135.

60. Scott, *Battles at Gettysburg*, p. 169.

61. *Ibid.*, p. 175; 44 *O.R.*, pp. 554, 579.

62. Stine, *Army of the Potomac*, p. 472; Fox, *New York at Gettysburg*, II, p. 763; Vanderslice, *Gettysburg*, p. 83; Ashhurst, *The First Day's Fight at Gettysburg*, p. 10; Paris, *History of the Civil War*, III, p. 563; 43 *O.R.*, p. 282.

63. Hussey, *Eighty-Third New York*, p. 270; Doubleday, *Chancellorsville and Gettysburg*, p. 143; Vanderslice, *Gettysburg*, p. 83; Stine, *Army of the Potomac*, p. 472.

64. Vautier, *88th Pennsylvania*, p. 135; Fox, *New York at Gettysburg*, II, p. 678; Stine, *Army of the Potomac*, p. 472.

65. 44 *O.R.*, p. 579.

66. Vautier, *88th Pennsylvania*, p. 135.

67. 44 *O.R.*, p. 444.

68. Vautier, *88th Pennsylvania*, pp. 106, 135; 44 *O.R.*, pp. 579–80.

69. Vautier, *88th Pennsylvania*, pp. 106–107.

70. Fox, *New York at Gettysburg*, I, p. 17; 43 *O.R.*, p. 307.

71. Hall, *Ninety-Seventh New York*, p. 138.

72. Hussey, *Eighty-Third New York*, p. 271; Fox, *New York at Gettysburg*, II, p. 678; Hall, *Ninety-Seventh New York*, p. 136; 44 *O.R.*, p. 579; 43 *O.R.*, pp. 289, 307.

73. Vautier, *88th Pennsylvania*, p. 136; 43 *O.R.*, pp. 289, 307.

74. Vautier, *88th Pennsylvania*, p. 135; 44 *O.R.*, p. 579.

75. Nicholson, *Pennsylvania at Gettysburg*, I, p. 481; Vanderslice, *Gettysburg*, pp. 83–84.

76. Vautier, *88th Pennsylvania*, p. 107.

77. Fox, *New York at Gettysburg*, II, p. 743; Vanderslice, *Gettysburg*, pp. 83–84.

78. Vautier, *88th Pennsylvania*, p. 135.

79. 44 *O.R.*, pp. 444, 554; Stine, *Army of the Potomac*, p. 473; Doubleday, *Chancellorsville and Gettysburg*, p. 143; Hussey, *Eighty-Third New York*, p. 271.

80. Paris, *History of the Civil War*, III, p. 563.

81. 44 *O.R.*, p. 445.

82. Vanderslice, *Gettysburg*, p. 84.

83. Fox, *New York at Gettysburg*, II, p. 753.

84. Stine, *Army of the Potomac*, p. 473; the Paul brigade government tablet, on the Gettysburg battlefield; 43 *O.R.*, p. 289.

85. Vautier, *88th Pennsylvania*, p. 136; Bachelder's Map; Fox, *New York at Gettysburg*, II, p. 753.

86. The Paul brigade government tablet, on the Gettysburg battlefield.

87. Cook, *Twelfth Massachusetts*, p. 101; Scott, *Battles at Gettysburg*, pp. 209–210; 43 *O.R.*, p. 307.

88. Fox, *New York at Gettysburg*, II, p. 756. (Italics mine in the text.)

89. *Ibid.*, p. 753.

90. Vanderslice, *Gettysburg*, p. 84.

91. Stine, *Army of the Potomac*, p. 483; 43 *O.R.*, p. 290.

92. Stine, *Army of the Potomac*, p. 484; Fox, *New York at Gettysburg*, I, p. 125.

93. Fox, *New York at Gettysburg*, II, pp. 724, 756; Stine, *Army of the Potomac*, p. 484; 43 *O.R.*, p. 290.

94. Fox, *New York at Gettysburg*, II, p. 724; the Baxter brigade government tablet, on the Gettysburg battlefield.

95. Fox, *New York at Gettysburg*, II, p. 757.

96. *Ibid.*

97. Nicholson, *Pennsylvania at Gettysburg*, I, p. 565.

98. The Ramseur brigade government tablet, on the Gettysburg battlefield.

99. Bachelder's Map; Vanderslice, *Gettysburg*, p. 84.

100. 44 *O.R.*, p. 554.

101. 43 *O.R.*, p. 249.

102. Fox, *New York at Gettysburg*, I, p. 17.

103. 43 *O.R.*, pp. 295, 299.

104. Fox, *New York at Gettysburg*, II, p. 723.

105. Davis, *Thirteenth Massachusetts*, p. 227; Vautier, *88th Pennsylvania*, p. 144.

106. The Ramseur brigade government tablet, on the Gettysburg battlefield; 44 *O.R.*, p. 587.

107. Nicholson, *Pennsylvania at Gettysburg*, I, p. 566.

108. Doubleday, *Chancellorsville and Gettysburg*, p. 145; Scott, *Battles at Gettysburg*, p. 212; Vautier, *88th Pennsylvania*, p. 144; 43 *O.R.*, p. 307.

109. Vautier, *88th Pennsylvania*, p. 108.

110. Smith, *Seventy-Sixth New York*, p. 241.

111. Fox, *New York at Gettysburg*, II, p. 757.

112. Hall, *Ninety-Seventh New York*, p. 141.

113. A.R. Small, *The Sixteenth Maine Regiment in the War of the Rebellion, 1861–1865* (Portland, Me.: B. Thurston & Co., 1886), p. 119.

114. *Ibid.*

115. 44 *O.R.*, p. 587; Paris, *History of the Civil War*, III, pp. 566–67.

116. Scott, *Battles at Gettysburg*, pp. 212–13; 44 *O.R.*, pp. 566–67.

117. Vautier, *88th Pennsylvania*, p. 143; 44 *O.R.*, p. 587.

118. 43 *O.R.*, p. 290; Davis, *Thirteenth Massachusetts*, p. 227.

119. Small, *Sixteenth Maine*, p. 118; Vanderslice, *Gettysburg*, pp. 92, 124; Scott, *Battles at Gettysburg*, pp. 217–18; Stine, *Army of the Potomac*, p. 484.

120. Fox, *New York at Gettysburg*, II, p. 743.

121. *Ibid.*

122. Vautier, *88th Pennsylvania*, p. 108.

123. Fox, *New York at Gettysburg*, II, p. 751.

124. Smith, *Seventy-Sixth New York*, p. 240; 43 *O.R.*, pp. 282–83.

125. 43 *O.R.*, pp. 282–83; Smith, *Seventy-Sixth New York*, p. 240.

CHAPTER 11

1. Vautier, *88th Pennsylvania*, p. 127; Bachelder's Map; 44 *O.R.*, pp. 610, 652, 674–75.

2. Vanderslice, *Gettysburg*, p. 87.

3. 44 *O.R.*, p. 444.

4. The Daniel brigade government tablet, on the Gettysburg battlefield; Vautier, *88th Pennsylvania*, p. 131; Nicholson, *Pennsylvania at Gettysburg*, II, p. 745; Young, *Battle of Gettysburg*, pp. 377–78.

5. 44 *O.R.*, p. 566.

6. Stine, *Army of the Potomac*, p. 474; Scott, *Battles at Gettysburg*, p. 175.

7. 44 *O.R.*, p. 566; the Daniel brigade government tablet, on the Gettysburg battlefield; Vautier, *88th Pennsylvania*, p. 131; Nicholson, *Pennsylvania at Gettysburg*, II, p. 745.

8. 43 *O.R.*, p. 282.

9. Chamberlin, *One Hundred and Fiftieth Pennsylvania*, p. 115; 43 *O.R.*, pp. 341–42.

10. 44 *O.R.*, pp. 567, 649.

11. *Ibid.*, p. 567.

12. *Ibid.*, pp. 566–67.

13. *Ibid.*, p. 567.

14. Scott, *Battles at Gettysburg*, p. 199; Stine, *Army of the Potomac*, pp. 474–75; 43 *O.R.*, pp. 329–30.

15. Nicholson, *Pennsylvania at Gettysburg*, II, p. 908; 43 *O.R.*, pp. 329–30.

16. 43 *O.R.*, p. 330; Nicholson, *Pennsylvania at Gettysburg*, II, p. 745.

17. Doubleday, *Chancellorsville and Gettysburg*, p. 144.

18. 44 *O.R.*, p. 567.

19. Vautier, *88th Pennsylvania*, p. 131; Doubleday, *Chancellorsville and Gettysburg*, p. 144; 44 *O.R.*, pp. 566–67.

20. Scott, *Battles at Gettysburg*, p. 200; Vautier, *88th Pennsylvania*, p. 131; 43 *O.R.*, pp. 329–30.

21. Chamberlin, *One Hundred and Fiftieth Pennsylvania*, p. 116; 43 *O.R.*, pp. 341–42.

22. Chamberlin, *One Hundred and Fiftieth Pennsylvania*, p. 117; 43 *O.R.*, p. 330.

23. Stine, *Army of the Potomac*, p. 475.

24. 43 *O.R.*, p. 332; Doubleday, *Chancellorsville and Gettysburg*, p. 145; Chamberlin, *One Hundred and Fiftieth Pennsylvania*, p. 117; Vautier, *88th Pennsylvania*, p. 133; Stine, *Army of the Potomac*, pp. 475–76; Scott, *Battles at Gettysburg*, pp. 201–202; Nicholson, *Pennsylvania at Gettysburg*, II, p. 746.

25. Vautier, *88th Pennsylvania*, p. 131; 43 *O.R.*, pp. 330, 341–43.

26. Vautier, *88th Pennsylvania*, p. 132.

27. Chamberlin, *One Hundred and Fiftieth Pennsylvania*, p. 117.

28. *Ibid.*, p. 119; 44 *O.R.*, pp. 566–67.

29. Chamberlin, *One Hundred and Fiftieth Pennsylvania*, p. 119; 43 *O.R.*, p. 333.

30. Nicholson, *Pennsylvania at Gettysburg*, II, p. 746; Fox, *New York at Gettysburg*, I, p. 126; 43 *O.R.*, p. 250.

31. 44 *O.R.*, p. 567.

32. Vanderslice, *Gettysburg*, p. 99; 43 *O.R.*, p. 330; Stine, *Army of the Potomac*, p. 477.

33. Stine, *Army of the Potomac*, p. 477; the Calef battery government tablet, on the Gettysburg battlefield; 43 *O.R.*, p. 330.

34. Vautier, *88th Pennsylvania*, p. 132.

35. 44 *O.R.*, p. 572.

36. Doubleday, *Chancellorsville and Gettysburg*, p. 145; 43 *O.R.*, p. 250.

37. Marshal, *Battle of Gettysburg*, p. 123; see also Tucker, *High Tide at Gettysburg*, p. 166.

38. 45 *O.R.*, pp. 463–65.

CHAPTER 12

1. Gates, *Ulster Guard*, pp. 433–34; Doubleday, *Chancellorsville and Gettysburg*, p. 139; Stine, *Army of the Potomac*, p. 478; Fox, *New York at Gettysburg*, II, p. 643; 43 *O.R.*, p. 317.

2. The Calef battery government tablet, on the Gettysburg battlefield; 43 *O.R.*, p. 1032.

3. Nicholson, *Pennsylvania at Gettysburg*, II, p. 908; 43 *O.R.*, pp. 364–65.

4. Doubleday, *Chancellorsville and Gettysburg*, pp. 139–40; 43 *O.R.*, p. 247.

5. Nicholson, *Pennsylvania at Gettysburg*, II, p. 769; Stine, *Army of the Potomac*, p. 478; Bates, *Battle of Gettysburg*, p. 73; 43 *O.R.*, p. 327.

6. Stine, *Army of the Potomac*, p. 478; 43 *O.R.*, p. 250. See also Glenn Tucker, "Hancock at Gettysburg," pp. 5–6, a paper presented at the Fourth Annual Civil War Study Group program at Gettysburg College, Aug. 1, 1961.

7. Vautier, *88th Pennsylvania*, p. 125.

8. 44 *O.R.*, pp. 637, 642.

9. The Brockenbrough brigade government tablet, on the Gettysburg battlefield; 44 *O.R.*, pp. 637, 642. But see Bates, *Battle of Gettysburg*, p. 70.

10. Vanderslice, *Gettysburg*, p. 80.

11. The Pettigrew brigade government tablet, on the Gettysburg battlefield.

12. 44 *O.R.*, p. 643.

13. Strong, *121st Pennsylvania*, p. 108.

14. *Ibid.*, p. 112; 44 *O.R.*, p. 639.

15. 43 *O.R.*, p. 571; Vautier, *88th Pennsylvania*, p. 128.

16. Curtis, *Twenty-Fourth Michigan*, p. 160.

17. Vautier, *88th Pennsylvania*, p. 130.

18. Fox, *New York at Gettysburg*, I, pp. 18–19; 44 *O.R.*, p. 643.

19. 44 *O.R.*, p. 643; Strong, *121st Pennsylvania*, p. 113.

20. Ashhurst, *First Day's Fight at Gettysburg*, p. 15; 44 *O.R.*, p. 645.

21. Nicholson, *Pennsylvania at Gettysburg*, II, p. 769; Vautier, *88th Pennsylvania*, p. 130; 43 *O.R.*, p. 328.

22. Scott, *Battles at Gettysburg*, p. 229; Young, *Battle of Gettysburg*, p. 389; 43 *O.R.*, p. 328.

23. Vanderslice, *Gettysburg*, p. 115.

24. Scott, *Battles at Gettysburg*, p. 205; 44 *O.R.*, p. 645.

25. Nicholson, *Pennsylvania at Gettysburg*, II, p. 769.

26. Vanderslice, *Gettysburg*, p. 116; 44 *O.R.*, p. 639.

27. Dunaway, *Reminiscences of a Rebel*, p. 85; Scott, *Battles at Gettysburg*, pp. 198–99; Vanderslice, *Gettysburg*, p. 92; 44 *O.R.*, p. 638.

28. Chamberlin, *One Hundred and Fiftieth Pennsylvania*, pp. 119–20; 43 *O.R.*, pp. 332–33.

29. Scott, *Battles at Gettysburg*, p. 204.

30. Paris, *History of the Civil War*, III, p. 563; 44 *O.R.*, p. 638.

31. Chamberlin, *One Hundred and Fiftieth Pennsylvania*, pp. 120–21.

32. *Ibid.*, p. 121.

33. *Ibid.*, pp. 120, 122–23; 43 *O.R.*, pp. 331, 347.

34. Scott, *Battles at Gettysburg*, p. 205.

35. *Ibid.*, p. 206.

36. 44 *O.R.*, p. 643.

37. Scott, *Battles at Gettysburg*, p. 207; 44 *O.R.*, p. 638.

38. Curtis, *Twenty-Fourth Michigan*, pp. 162–63.

39. *Ibid.*, pp. 163–65.

40. Vautier, *88th Pennsylvania*, p. 130; 44 *O.R.*, p. 638.

41. Scott, *Battles at Gettysburg*, p. 228; 44 *O.R.*, p. 567.

42. Dunaway, *Reminiscences of a Rebel*, p. 86.

43. Strong, *121st Pennsylvania*, p. 113; 44 *O.R.*, p. 643.

44. Vautier, *88th Pennsylvania*, p. 129.

45. Alexander, *Military Memoirs of a Confederate*, p. 384.

46. Vanderslice, *Gettysburg*, p. 95; Strong, *121st Pennsylvania*, pp. 46, 121; 44 *O.R.*, p. 643.

47. Strong, *121st Pennsylvania*, p. 46.

48. Vanderslice, *Gettysburg*, p. 120.

49. Gates, *Ulster Guard*, p. 442.

50. Strong, *121st Pennsylvania*, p. 48; Chamberlin, *One Hundred and Fiftieth Pennsylvania*, p. 123; 43 *O.R.*, p. 315.

51. Vautier, *88th Pennsylvania*, p. 133; 43 *O.R.*, p. 330.

52. Chamberlin, *One Hundred and Fiftieth Pennsylvania*, p. 124.

53. Horatio N. Warren, *Two Reunions of the 142d Regiment, Pa. Vols.* (Buffalo: The Courier Co., 1890), p. 10.

54. Boyle, *One Hundred and Eleventh Pennsylvania*, p. 116; Nicholson, *Pennsylvania at Gettysburg*, II, p. 702; Stine, *Army of the Potomac*, p. 476.

CHAPTER 13

1. *B. & L.*, III, p. 285; Doubleday, *Chancellorsville and Gettysburg*, p. 146; Stine, *Army of the Potomac*, p. 480; 43 *O.R.*, p. 703.

2. Stine, *Army of the Potomac*, p. 480; Scott, *Battles at Gettysburg*, pp. 164, 232; Marshal, *Battle of Gettysburg*, p. 125.

3. Vanderslice, *Gettysburg*, p. 96; 44 *O.R.*, p. 665; Bachelder's Map.

4. 44 *O.R.*, p. 665.

5. The Lane brigade government tablet, on the Gettysburg battlefield; 44 *O.R.*, p. 667.

6. Nicholson, *Pennsylvania at Gettysburg*, I, p. 493; the Perrin brigade government tablet, on the Gettysburg battlefield. See also 43 *O.R.*, p. 250.

7. Doubleday, *Chancellorsville and Gettysburg*, p. 147; 44 *O.R.*, p. 665.

8. Vanderslice, *Gettysburg*, p. 95; Bachelder's Map.

9. The Perrin brigade government tablet, on the Gettysburg battle-field; 44 *O.R.*, p. 661.

10. Vanderslice, *Gettysburg*, p. 96; Bachelder's Map.

11. Bachelder's Map.

12. The Scales brigade government tablet, on the Gettysburg battlefield.

13. The Davis brigade government tablet, on the Gettysburg battlefield; 44 *O.R.*, p. 649.

14. Bachelder's Map; 44 *O.R.*, p. 668.

15. Chamberlin, *One Hundred and Fiftieth Pennsylvania*, pp. 124–25.

16. *Ibid.*, p. 125.

17. Vautier, *88th Pennsylvania*, p. 130; 43 *O.R.*, p. 250.

18. Stine, Army of the Potomac, p. 480; Paris, *History of the Civil War*, III, p. 567.

19. Stine, *Army of the Potomac*, p. 480; 44 *O.R.*, p. 670.

20. Longstreet, *From Manassas to Appomattox*, p. 355; 44 *O.R.*, p. 607.

21. 44 *O.R.*, pp. 657, 665; Vanderslice, *Gettysburg*, pp. 96, 123; Stine, *Army of the Potomac*, p. 481; *B. & L.*, III, p. 285; Fox, *New York at Gettysburg*, I, p. 380.

22. Stine, *Army of the Potomac*, p. 481; Abner Perrin to Governor M.L. Bonham, letter of Jul. 29, 1863, *Mississippi Valley Historical Review* (Mar. 1938), pp. 520 ff; Paris, *History of the Civil War*, III, p. 568.

23. Stine, *Army of the Potomac*, p. 480.

24. Beecham, *Gettysburg*, pp. 76–77.

25. Scott, *Battles at Gettysburg*, p. 232; 43 *O.R.*, p. 356.

26. Vautier, *88th Pennsylvania*, p. 145; Bates, *Battle of Gettysburg*, p. 79; Doubleday, *Chancellorsville and Gettysburg*, p. 140; Beecham, *Gettysburg*, pp. 79–80; 43 *O.R.*, pp. 251, 356–57.

27. Beecham, *Gettysburg*, p. 79.

28. Doubleday, *Chancellorsville and Gettysburg*, p. 147; 43 *O.R.*, p. 250.

29. 43 *O.R.*, p. 307.

30. *Ibid.*

31. 44 *O.R.*, pp. 658, 670; the Stewart battery government tablet, on the Gettysburg battlefield; Vautier, *88th Pennsylvania*, pp. 146–47; Stine, *Army of the Potomac*, pp. 486–87; Vanderslice, *Gettysburg*, pp. 99–100; Scott, *Battles at Gettysburg*, pp. 232–38; Bates, *Battle of Gettysburg*, p. 79; Fox, *New York at Gettysburg*, I, p. 23; Nicholson, *Pennsylvania at Gettysburg*, II, pp. 908–909.

32. *Fourteenth Brooklyn*, p. 85.

33. Nicholson, *Pennsylvania at Gettysburg*, II, p. 483; *C.C.W.* (1863), I, p. 308; 43 *O.R.*, p. 251.

34. Gordon, *Reminiscences of the Civil War*, p. 114.

35. Gates, *Ulster Guard*, p. 443.

36. Nicholson, *Pennsylvania at Gettysburg*, II, p. 770; 43 *O.R.*, p. 328.

37. Nicholson, *Pennsylvania at Gettysburg*, II, p. 909; 44 *O.R.*, pp. 661–62.

38. 44 *O.R.*, pp. 661–62; Doubleday, *Chancellorsville and Gettysburg*, pp. 147–48; Scott, *Battles at Gettysburg*, pp. 234–37; Fox, *New York at Gettysburg*, III, p. 1145.

39. Vautier, *88th Pennsylvania*, p. 146; Strong, *121st Pennsylvania*, p. 110; Scott, *Battles at Gettysburg*, pp. 237–38; Doubleday, *Chancellorsville and Gettysburg*, pp. 148–49; 44 *O.R.*, p. 662.

40. Ashhurst, *First Day's Fight at Gettysburg*, p. 8.

41. Curtis, *Twenty-Fourth Michigan*, pp. 163, 188–89, 191; 43 *O.R.*, pp. 269, 272.

42. Scott, *Battles at Gettysburg*, p. 238; 43 *O.R.*, pp. 283, 307.

43. 43 *O.R.*, pp. 250–51.

44. *Fourteenth Brooklyn*, p. 86.

45. Strong, *121st Pennsylvania*, p. 121.

46. 43 *O.R.*, p. 704.

47. Gates, *Ulster Guard*, pp. 442–43; 43 *O.R.*, pp. 250–51.

48. Nicholson, *Pennsylvania at Gettysburg*, I, p. 493; 43 *O.R.*, pp. 250, 315, 335–36, 365.

49. Doubleday, *Chancellorsville and Gettysburg*, p. 149; Fox, *New York at Gettysburg*, III, p. 1257; 43 *O.R.*, p. 357.

50. Beecham, *Gettysburg*, pp. 93–94; Strong, *121st Pennsylvania*, p. 49; Doubleday, *Chancellorsville and Gettysburg*, p. 150; 43 *O.R.*, p. 253.

51. Curtis, *Twenty-Fourth Michigan*, pp. 182, 184.

52. Smith, *Seventy-Sixth New York*, p. 144.

CHAPTER 14

1. Chamberlin, *One Hundred and Fiftieth Pennsylvania*, p. 126; Beecham, *Gettysburg*, p. 96; 44 *O.R.*, pp. 469, 555.

2. 44 *O.R.*, p. 607.

3. 43 *O.R.*, pp. 251, 704.

4. *B. & L.*, III, p. 281; Wise, *The Long Arm of Lee*, II, p. 623; Fox, *New York at Gettysburg*, I, p. 25; Schurz, *Reminiscences*, III, p. 10; 43 *O.R.*, pp. 250, 315, 335–36, 365.

5. Davis, *Thirteenth Massachusetts*, p. 228.

6. Doubleday, *Chancellorsville and Gettysburg*, p. 149; Smith, *Seventy-Sixth New York*, p. 242; 43 *O.R.*, p. 251.

7. Fremantle, *Three Months in the Southern States*, p. 255.

8. Vautier, *88th Pennsylvania*, p. 149.

9. Fox, *New York at Gettysburg*, I, p. 380; the 45th New York regiment monument, on the Gettysburg battlefield.

10. 44 *O.R.*, pp. 317, 445; Fox, *New York at Gettysburg*, I, p. 25.

11. Fox, *New York at Gettysburg*, I, p. 25; 43 *O.R.*, p. 735.

12. Boyle, *One Hundred and Eleventh Pennsylvania*, p. 117; Fox, *New York at Gettysburg*, I, p. 24.

13. Boyle, *One Hundred and Eleventh Pennsylvania*, p. 117.

14. Fox, *New York at Gettysburg*, I, p. 25; 43 *O.R.*, p. 730.

15. Boyle, *One Hundred and Eleventh Pennsylvania*, p. 117.

16. 44 *O.R.*, p. 555; Vanderslice, *Gettysburg*, p. 100; Scott, *Battles at Gettysburg*, p. 345.

17. Vautier, *88th Pennsylvania*, p. 109.

18. *Ibid.*

19. Stiles, *Four Years Under Marse Robert*, p. 212.

20. *Ibid.*, p. 211.

21. *Ibid.*, pp. 213–14.

22. Fox, *New York at Gettysburg*, I, pp. 380–81.

23. Doubleday, *Chancellorsville and Gettysburg*, p. 154; 43 *O.R.*, pp. 308, 310.

24. 44 *O.R.*, p. 318; Walter H. Taylor, *Four Years with General Lee* (New York: D. Appleton & Co., 1878), p. 190; *S.H.S.P.*, XXX, p. 145, XLIII, p. 57. See also Douglas Southall Freeman, *R.E. Lee, A Biography* (New York: Charles Scribner's Sons, 1935), III, pp. 72, 75–80; and Douglas Southall Freeman, *Lee's Lieutenants, A Study in Command* (New York: Charles Scribner's Sons, 1944), III, ch. 6.

25. Fremantle, *Three Months in the Southern States*, p. 254; 44 *O.R.*, p. 607.

26. 44 *O.R.*, p. 607.

27. Tucker, *High Tide at Gettysburg*, p. 391.

CHAPTER 15

1. *B. & L.*, III, p. 288; 43 *O.R.*, p. 696.

2. Ashhurst, *First Day's Fight at Gettysburg*, pp. 17–19; Fox, *New York at Gettysburg*, II, p. 754; Chamberlin, *One Hundred and Fiftieth Pennsylvania*, p. 129; Gates, *Ulster Guard*, p. 444; Beecham, *Gettysburg*, p. 96; 43 *O.R.*, p. 704; *B. & L.*, III, p. 288; Scott, *Battles at Gettysburg*, p. 221.

3. Ashhurst, *First Day's Fight at Gettysburg*, p. 20.

4. Fremantle, *Three Months in the Southern States*, p. 254; Marshal, *Battle of Gettysburg*, p. 125; 44 *O.R.*, pp. 492, 545, 607, 661.

5. Storrick, *Gettysburg*, p. 24; Ashhurst, *First Day's Fight at Gettysburg*, pp. 6–7; Schurz, *Reminiscences*, III, p. 9; Curtis, *Twenty-Fourth*

Michigan, p. 166; Marshal, *Battle of Gettysburg*, p. 130; Boyle, *One Hundred and Eleventh Pennsylvania*, p. 116; Longstreet, *From Manassas to Appomattox*, p. 357; Paris, *History of the Civil War*, III, p. 570; Fox, *New York at Gettysburg*, I, p. 16; *B. & L.*, III, p. 289; Nicholson, *Pennsylvania at Gettysburg*, I, p. 481; 43 *O.R.*, p. 704.

6. Tucker, *High Tide at Gettysburg*, p. 408.

7. 44 *O.R.*, p. 317.

8. The Lee headquarters marker, on the Gettysburg battlefield; Storrick, *Gettysburg*, p. 25.

9. 43 *O.R.*, pp. 250–52, 927; Young, *Battle of Gettysburg*, p. 201; Swinton, *Army of the Potomac*, p. 335.

10. Vanderslice, *Gettysburg*, p. 103; 43 *O.R.*, p. 368.

11. Doubleday, *Chancelorsville and Gettysburg*, p. 150; 43 *O.R.*, p. 252.

12. 43 *O.R.*, pp. 70–71.

13. *Ibid.*

14. A.B. Underwood, *Three Years' Service in the Thirty-Third Massachusetts Infantry Regiment, 1862–1865* (Boston: A. Williams & Co., 1881), p. 115.

15. 45 *O.R.*, p. 461.

16. Clarence E. Macartney, *Highways and Byways of the Civil War* (Pittsburgh: Gibson Press, 1938), p. 40; Bruce, *Twentieth Massachusetts*, p. 269; Boyle, *One Hundred and Eleventh Pennsylvania*, p. 117; Fox, *New York at Gettysburg*, I, p. 28.

17. Doubleday, *Chancellorsville and Gettysburg*, p. 150; 43 *O.R.*, p. 368; Vanderslice, *Gettysburg*, pp. 102–103; Nicholson, *Pennsylvania at Gettysburg*, I, p. 493; O.O. Howard, "The Campaign of Gettysburg," *Atlantic Monthly* (July, 1876), p. 58; Swinton, *Army of the Potomac*, p. 334.

18. *B. & L.*, III, p. 285; Doubleday, *Chancellorsville and Gettysburg*, p. 151; 43 *O.R.*, pp. 366, 696; Schurz, *Reminiscences*, III, p. 14.

19. Paris, *History of the Civil War*, III, p. 571; Swinton, *Army of the Potomac*, p. 335.

20. Vautier, *88th Pennsylvania*, p. 151; see 43 *O.R.*, pp. 357, 748.

21. *C.C.W.* (1865), I, p. 377; Young, *Battle of Gettysburg*, p. 209.

22. Steele, *American Campaigns*, p. 368; 43 *O.R.*, p. 266.

23. 45 *O.R.*, p. 466.

24. Francis A. Walker, *History of the Second Army Corps* (New York: Charles Scribner's Sons, 1886), p. 267; *B. & L.*, III, p. 287; Meade, *Life and Letters of Meade*, II, p. 38; Paris, *History of the Civil War*, III, p. 579; 43 *O.R.*, p. 366.

25. 45 *O.R.*, p. 1067.

26. Fremantle, *Three Months in the Southern States*, p. 255; 44 *O.R.*, pp. 318, 445.

27. 43 *O.R.*, pp. 704, 751; *B. & L.*, III, pp. 287–88.

28. 44 *O.R.*, pp. 317–18, 445, 607.

29. *B. & L.*, III, p. 283; Fox, *New York at Gettysburg*, I, p. 26; 43 *O.R.*, p. 283.

30. 43 *O.R.*, pp. 231, 283, 730.

31. Gordon, *Reminiscences of the Civil War*, p. 157.

32. Ashhurst, *First Day's Fight at Gettysburg*, pp. 23–26; 45 *O.R.*, p. 466.

33. Major General Henry W. Slocum, the regular commander of the Twelfth Corps was, at this time, in command of the entire Right Wing of the Army of the Potomac.

34. 43 *O.R.*, p. 825; 45 *O.R.*, p. 466; Beecham, *Gettysburg*, pp. 151–52; Scott, *Battles at Gettysburg*, p. 223; Paris, *History of the Civil War*, III, pp. 578–79; Fox, *New York at Gettysburg*, I, p. 30; Sypher, *Pennsylvania Reserves*, pp. 453–54; Alexander, *Military Memoirs*, p. 389; Swinton, *Army of the Potomac*, p. 336; Vanderslice, *Gettysburg*, p. 103.

35. Paris, *History of the Civil War*, III, p. 579; *B. & L.*, III, p. 289; Sypher, *Pennsylvania Reserves*, pp. 453–54; Vanderslice, *Gettysburg*, p. 103; Boyle, *One Hundred and Eleventh Pennsylvania*, p. 117.

36. Davis, *Thirteenth Massachusetts*, p. 229; 43 *O.R.*, p. 348.

37. 43 *O.R.*, p. 530; Fox, *New York at Gettysburg*, I, p. 31; *B. & L.*, III, p. 289; Strong, *121st Pennsylvania*, p. 122; Scott, *Battles at Gettysburg*, pp. 81, 223–24; Vanderslice, *Gettysburg*, p. 103; Paris, *History of the Civil War*, III, p. 577; Battine, *Crisis of the Confederacy*, p. 202; Powell, *Fifth Corps*, p. 511; Alexander, *Military Memoirs*, p. 389; Swinton, *Army of the Potomac*, p. 337.

38. Bruce, *Twentieth Massachusetts*, p. 270; Alexander, *Military Memoirs*, p. 389; Battine, *Crisis of the Confederacy*, p. 203; 43 *O.R.*, p. 369.

39. Warren, *142nd Pennsylvania*, p. 23.

40. *B. & L.*, III, p. 292; 43 *O.R.*, p. 366.

41. 45 *O.R.*, p. 466.

42. 43 *O.R.*, pp. 71–72.

43. *Ibid.*, p. 71.

44. Strong, *121st Pennsylvania*, p. 114.

45. Paris, *History of the Civil War*, III, p. 579; Fox, *New York at Gettysburg*, I, p. 29; Scott, *Battles at Gettysburg*, p. 226; 43 *O.R.*, p. 369.

46. Frank A. Haskell, *The Battle of Gettysburg*, (Madison: Wisconsin Historical Association, 1908), p. 19.

47. Meade, *Life and Letters of Meade*, II, p. 62; Paris, *History of the Civil War*, III, p. 581; Powell, *Fifth Corps*, p. 512; Battine, *Crisis of the Confederacy*, p. 209; Doubleday, *Chancellorsville and Gettysburg*, p. 156; James Ford Rhodes, *History of the United States From the Compromise of*

1850 (New York: Harper & Bros., 1899), IV, p. 283; 43 *O.R.*, p. 705; Oliver Otis Howard, *Autobiography of Oliver Otis Howard* (New York: Baber & Taylor Co., 1908), I, p. 423.

48. Meade, *Life and Letters of Meade*, II, p. 62.

49. Schurz, *Reminiscences*, III, p. 20; Doubleday, *Chancellorsville and Gettysburg*, p. 156.

50. Howard's *Autobiography*, I, p. 423; Meade, *Life and Letters of Meade*, II, p. 62; 43 *O.R.*, p. 705.

51. Powell, *Fifth Corps*, p. 512; Meade, *Life and Letters of Meade*, I, p. 63; 43 *O.R.*, p. 705.

52. Doubleday, *Chancellorsville and Gettysburg*, p. 155.

CONCLUSION

1. Nicholson (ed.), *Pennsylvania at Gettysburg*, I, p. 36.
2. *S.H.S.P.*, XXVI (1898), p. 121; italics mine in the text.
3. Alexander, *Military Memoirs of a Confederate*, p. 384.
4. Coddington, *The Gettysburg Campaign*, pp. 321–22.

Select Bibliography

PHYSICAL REMAINS

NOT THE LEAST VALUABLE ASSET TO THE HISTORIAN OF THE Battle of Gettysburg is the battlefield itself. In July 1863, shortly after the great combat, Governor Andrew G. Curtin of Pennsylvania, and others, determined to preserve the scene of the action for coming generations to visit and study. As a result, there was created the Gettysburg Battlefield Memorial Association, which purchased lands over which the fighting had taken place, erected markers and tablets, and supervised the placing of organizational monuments. In 1895, the association transferred all of its land and holdings to the War Department of the Federal Government. The field is now administered by the National Park Service, Department of the Interior.

In many respects, the field is essentially as it was during the battle. The lines of battle have been marked accurately by monuments and tablets of a most permanent nature. Macadam roads, totaling over thirty-nine miles, bring the visitor to all portions of the field. Some 440 artillery pieces are in the positions they occupied during the clash. Original trench lines may still be seen in several places. Usually, areas which were wooded at the time of the battle are wooded today; wheatfields and peach orchards which were the scenes of heavy fighting back in 1863 have been maintained in their original ground cover. Even the left and right flanks of most Union regiments are marked. The observer is aided by five steel observation towers, built by the government, and situated at strategic points on the field. Where the musketry was heavy, farmers still plow up bullets, shells, bones, and accouterments.

Every effort is being made by the government, assisted by private organizations, to acquire additional lands over which the combat raged, and to prevent over-commercialization. Gettysburg remains, today, the world's best marked battlefield, and it is a rich storehouse of information to the student who will spend sufficient time reconnoitering it.

MAPS

As to vegetation, ground cover, terrain, and other physical features of the Gettysburg battlefield, the most useful maps are the so-called "Warren Survey Maps" of 1867, prepared under the supervision of Major-General Gouverneur K. Warren, who was chief engineer of the Army of the Potomac during the battle, and the "Hero of Little Round Top."

For troop positions, the three large, detailed maps drawn in 1876 by John B. Bachelder are the most accurate and comprehensive. One map is devoted to each of the three days of battle, and they measure thirty by thirty-six inches. The scale is one inch to every 1,000 feet on the field. Colonel Bachelder, who served for a time as historian of the Gettysburg Battlefield Memorial Association, takes the troop dispositions down to the regimental level. If a unit had more than one position during the battle, each one is indicated on the maps. All fences, stone walls, roads, buildings, etc., are depicted, by the appropriate symbols, as they existed in 1876.

Finally, the Atlas to Accompany the Official Records contains a number of plates pertaining to Gettysburg. This atlas has more recently been republished separately in book form in a slightly inferior printing.

USEFUL PRIMARY SOURCES AND SECONDARY WORKS

Alexander, E. P. *Military Memoirs of a Confederate.* New York: C. Scribner's Sons, 1907.
Anthony, William, ed. *Anthony's*

History of the Battle of Hanover, York County, Pennsylvania, Tuesday, June 30, 1863, Compiled from the Writings of George R.

Prowell and Others. Hanover, Pa.: William Anthony, 1945.

Applegate, John S. *Reminiscences and Letters of George Arrowsmith.* Red Bank, N.J.: J.H. Cook, 1893.

Ashhurst, R. L. *First Day's Battle at Gettysburg.* Philadelphia, 1913.

———— *Remarks on Certain Questions Relating to the First Day's Fight at Gettysburg.* Philadelphia, 1897.

Bache, Richard Meade. *Life of General George Gordon Meade.* Philadelphia: H. T. Coates & Co., 1897.

Banes, Charles H. *History of the Philadelphia Brigade.* Philadelphia: J. B. Lippincott & Co., 1876.

Bates, Samuel P. *The Battle of Gettysburg.* Philadelphia: T. H. Davis & Co., 1875.

Battine, Cecil. *The Crisis of the Confederacy: A History of Gettysburg and the Wilderness.* London: Longmans, Green & Co., 1905.

Beecham, R. K. *Gettysburg, The Pivotal Battle of the Civil War.* Chicago: A.C. McClurg & Co., 1911.

Bellah, James Warner. *Soldiers' Battle: Gettysburg.* New York: David McKay Co., 1952.

Biddle, Chapman. *The First Day of the Battle of Gettysburg.* Philadelphia: J. B. Lippincott & Co., 1880.

Blackford, W. W. *War Years with Jeb Stuart.* New York: C. Scribner's Sons, 1946.

Boudrye, Louis N. *Historic Records of the Fifth New York Cavalry.* Albany: S. R. Gray, 1865.

Bruce, George A. *The Twentieth Regiment of Massachusetts Volunteer Infantry, 1861–1865.* Boston: Houghton, Mifflin & Co., 1906.

Boyle, John Richards. *Soldiers True: The Story of the One Hundred and Eleventh Regiment Pennsylvania Veteran Volunteers and of its Campaigns in the War for the Union, 1861–1865.* New York: Eaton & Mains, 1903.

Carpenter, John A. *Sword and Olive Branch: Oliver Otis Howard.* Pittsburgh: University of Pittsburgh Press, 1964.

Chamberlin, Thomas. *History of the One Hundred and Fiftieth Regiment, Pennsylvania Volunteers, Second Regiment, Bucktail Brigade.* Philadelphia: J. B. Lippincott Co., 1895.

Cheney, Newel. *History of the Ninth Regiment New York Volunteer Cavalry.* Jamestown, N.Y.: Poland Center, 1901.

Clark, Walter. *Histories of the Several Regiments and Battalions from North Carolina in the Great War, 1861–1865.* Raleigh: E. M. Uzzell, 1901.

Cleaves, Freeman. *Meade of Gettysburg.* Norman, Okla.: University of Oklahoma Press, 1959.

Coddington, Edwin B. *The Gettysburg Campaign: A Study in Command.* New York: Charles Scribner's Sons, 1968.

Cook, Benjamin F. *History of the Twelfth Massachusetts Volun-*

teers, *Webster Regiment*. Boston: Twelfth Regiment Assoc., 1882.

Craft, David. *History of the One Hundred and Forty-First Regiment Pennsylvania Volunteers, 1862–1865*. Towanda, Pa.: Reporter-Journal Printing Co., 1885.

Cudworth, Warren H. *History of the First Regiment Massachusetts Infantry*. Boston: Walker, Fuller & Co., 1866.

Cullum, George W. *Biographical Register of the Officers and Graduates of the U.S. Military Academy at West Point, N.Y.* 2 vols.; New York: D. Van Nostrand, 1868.

Culp, Edward C. *The 25th Ohio Veteran Volunteer Infantry in the War for the Union*. Topeka: G. W. Crane & Co., 1885.

Curtis, O. B. *History of the Twenty-Fourth Michigan of the Iron Brigade, Known as the Detroit and Wayne County Regiment*. Detroit: Winn & Hammond, 1891.

Davis, Charles E., Jr. *Three Years in the Army: The Story of the Thirteenth Massachusetts Volunteers from July 16, 1861, to August 1, 1864*. Boston: Estes & Lawnat, 1864.

Dawes, Rufus R. *Service with the Sixth Wisconsin Volunteers*. Marietta, Ohio: E. R. Alderman & Sons, 1890.

Deaderick, Barron. *Strategy in the Civil War*. Harrisburg: Military Service Publishing Co., 1946.

DePeyster, John Watts. *Before, At, and After Gettysburg*. New York: C. H. Ludwig, 1887.

_____ *Decisive Conflicts of the Late Civil War*. New York: Macdonald & Co., 1867.

Doubleday, Abner. *Chancellorsville and Gettysburg*. New York: C. Scribner's Sons, 1882.

Downey, Fairfax. *The Guns at Gettysburg*. New York: David McKay Co., 1958.

Drake, Samuel Adams. *The Battle of Gettysburg, 1863*. Boston: Lee & Shepard, 1892.

Dunaway, Wayland Fuller. *Reminiscences of a Rebel*. New York: Neale Publishing Co., 1913.

Durkin, Joseph T., ed. *John Dooley, Confederate Soldier: His War Journal*. Washington: Georgetown University Press, 1945.

Early, Jubal A. *Autobiographical Sketch and Narrative of the War Between the States*. Philadelphia: J. B. Lippincott Co., 1912.

Eckenrode, H. J. and Conrad, Bryan. *James Longstreet, Lee's War Horse*. Chapel Hill: University of North Carolina Press, 1936.

Eddy, Richard. *History of the Sixtieth Regiment New York State Volunteers*. Philadelphia: Richard Eddy, 1864.

Eggleston, George Cary. *A Rebel's Recollections*. New York: Hurd & Houghton, 1875.

Evans, Clement A., ed. *Confederate Military History*. Atlanta: Confederate Publishing Co., 1899.

Forney, J. W., comp. *Report of the Joint Committee on the Conduct of the War*. Washington: Government Printing Office, 1865.

Fox, William F. *New York at Get-

tysburg. 3 vols.; Albany: J. B. Lyon, Co., 1900.

------ *Regimental Losses in the American Civil War.* Albany: J. B. Lyon Co., 1889.

Freeman, Douglas Southall. *Lee's Lieutenants, A Study in Command.* 3 vols.; New York: Charles Scribner's Sons, 1942.

------ *R.E. Lee, A Biography.* 4 vols.; New York: Charles Scribner's Sons, 1934.

Fremantle, Arthur. *Three Months in the Southern States, April–June, 1863.* New York: J. Bradburn, 1864.

Ganoe, William Addleman. *The History of the United States Army.* New York: D. Appleton-Century Co., 1942.

Gates, Theodore B. *The "Ulster Guard" (20th N.Y. State Militia) and the War of the Rebellion.* New York: B. H. Tyrrel, 1879.

Gordon, John B. *Reminiscences of the Civil War.* New York: C. Scribner's Sons, 1903.

Goss, Warren Lee. *Recollections of a Private: A Story of the Army of the Potomac.* New York: T. Y. Crowell & Co., 1890.

Graham, Ziba B. *On to Gettysburg: Two Days of My Diary of 1863.* Detroit, 1889.

Hall, Hillman, and Besley, W. B. *History of the Sixth New York Cavalry, Second Ira Harris Guard, Second Brigade, First Division, Cavalry Corps, Army of the Potomac, 1861–1865.* Worcester, Mass.: The Blanchard Press, 1908.

Hall, Isaac. *History of the Ninety-*

Seventh Regiment New York Volunteers. Utica: Press of L. C. Childs & Son, 1890.

Hard, Abner. *History of the Eighth Cavalry Regiment Illinois Volunteers During the Great Rebellion.* Aurora, Ill., 1868.

Haskell, Frank A. *The Battle of Gettysburg.* Madison: Wisconsin Historical Assoc., 1908.

Hassler, Warren W., Jr. *Commanders of the Army of the Potomac.* Baton Rouge: Louisiana State University Press, 1962.

------ "The First Day's Battle of Gettysburg," *Civil War History,* VI (Sept. 1960), 259–276.

Haupt, Herman. *Reminiscences of General Herman Haupt.* Milwaukee: Wright & Joys Co., 1901.

Heitman, Francis B. *Historical Register and Dictionary of the United States Army.* 2 vols.; Washington: Government Printing Office, 1903.

Henry, Robert Selph. *The Story of the Confederacy.* Indianapolis: Bobbs-Merrill Co., 1931.

Hitchcock, Ripley, ed. *Decisive Battles of America.* New York: Harper & Bros., 1909.

Hoke, Jacob. *The Great Invasion of 1863, or, General Lee in Pennsylvania.* Dayton: W. J. Shuey, 1887.

Hood, John B. *Advance and Retreat.* New Orleans: Hood Orphan Memorial Fund, 1880.

Howard, Oliver O. *Autobiography of Oliver Otis Howard.* 2 vols.; New York: Baker & Taylor Co., 1908.

------ "The Campaign of Gettysburg," *Atlantic Monthly* (July, 1876).

Hussey, George A. *History of the Ninth Regiment, N.Y.S.M.–N.G.S.N.Y. (Eighty-Third N.Y. Volunteers).* New York: Regimental Veterans Assoc., 1889.

Jacobs, M. *Notes on the Rebel Invasion and the Battle of Gettysburg.* Philadelphia: J. B. Lippincott Co., 1864.

Johnson, Robert U., and Buel, Clarence C., eds. *Battles and Leaders of the Civil War.* 4 vols.; New York: The Century Co., 1887.

Livermore, Thomas L. *Numbers and Losses in the Civil War in America, 1861–1865.* Boston: Houghton, Mifflin Co., 1901.

Livermore, William R. *The Story of the Civil War.* 2 vols.; New York: G. P. Putnam's Sons, 1913.

Locke, William Henry. *The Story of the Regiment* [11th Pa.]. Philadelphia: J. B. Lippincott & Co., 1872.

Long, A. L. *Memoirs of Robert E. Lee; His Military and Personal History, Embracing a Large Amount of Information Hitherto Unpublished.* New York: J. M. Stoddart & Co., 1886.

Longstreet, James. *From Manassas to Appomattox: Memoirs of the Civil War in America.* Philadelphia: J. B. Lippincott Co., 1896.

Macartney, Clarence E. *Highways and Byways of the Civil War.* Pittsburgh: Gibson Press, 1938.

McClure, A. K., ed. *Annals of the War, Written by Leading Partici-*pants, North and South. Philadelphia: Times Publishing Co., 1879.

McKim, Randolph H. *A Soldier's Recollections.* New York: Longmans, Green & Co., 1910.

(Author unknown) *Maine at Gettysburg.* Portland: Lakeside Press, 1898.

Marshal, Francis. *The Battle of Gettysburg, The Crest-Wave of the American Civil War.* New York: The Neale Publishing Co., 1914.

Marshall, Charles. *An Aide-de-Camp of Lee.* Boston: Little, Brown & Co., 1927.

Meade, George. *The Life and Letters of General George Gordon Meade.* 2 vols.; New York: C. Scribner's Sons, 1913.

Miller, Francis T., ed. *The Photographic History of the Civil War.* 10 vols.; New York: Review of Reviews Co., 1911.

Montgomery, James Stuart. *The Shaping of a Battle: Gettysburg.* Philadelphia: Chilton Co., 1959.

Moore, Frank. *The Rebellion Record; A Diary of American Events, with Documents, Narratives, Illustrative Incidents, Poetry, etc.* New York: G. P. Putnam, 1862–1871.

Moore, James, *Kilpatrick and Our Cavalry.* New York: W. J. Widdleton, 1865.

Naisawald, L. Van Loan. *Grape and Canister: The Story of the Field Artillery in the Army of the Potomac.* New York: 1960.

Nevins, Allan, ed. *A Diary of Battle: The Personal Journals of Colonel Charles S. Wainwright, 1861–*

1865. New York: Harcourt, Brace & World, Inc., 1962.

Nichols, Edward. *Toward Gettysburg: A Biography of John F. Reynolds*. University Park, Pa.: Pennsylvania State University Press, 1958.

Nicholson, John P., ed. *Pennsylvania at Gettysburg*. 2 vols.; Harrisburg: William Stanley Ray, 1914.

Nolan, Alan T. *The Iron Brigade: A Military History*. New York: Macmillan Co., 1961.

Norton, Henry. *Deeds of Daring, or, History of the Eighth New York Volunteer Cavalry*. Norwich, N.Y.: Chenango Telegraph Printing House, 1889.

Nye, Wilbur Sturtevant. *Here Come the Rebels!* Baton Rouge: Louisiana State University Press, 1965.

Oates, William C. *The War Between the Union and the Confederacy and its Lost Opportunities*. New York: Neale Publishing Co., 1905.

Owen, William M. *In Camp and Battle With the Washington Artillery of New Orleans*. Boston: Tichnor & Co., 1885.

Paris, Comte de. *History of the Civil War in America*. 4 vols.; Philadelphia: Porter & Coates, 1883.

Park, Robert Emory. *Sketch of the Twelfth Alabama Infantry of Battle's Brigade, Rodes' Division, Early's Corps, of the Army of Northern Virginia*. Richmond: W. E. Jones, 1906.

Pennypacker, Isaac R. *Life of George Gordon Meade*. New York: D. Appleton & Co., 1901.

Phisterer, Frederick. *Statistical Record of the Armies of the United States*. New York: Charles Scribner's Sons, 1883.

Pickerill, W. N. *History of the Third Indiana Cavalry*. Indianapolis: Aetna Printing Co., 1906.

Quaife, Milo M., ed. *From the Cannon's Mouth: The Civil War Letters of General Alpheus S. Williams*. Detroit: Wayne State University Press, 1959.

Powell, William H. *The Fifth Army Corps, Army of the Potomac: A Record of Operations During the Civil War in the United States of America, 1861–1865*. New York: G.P. Putnam's Sons, 1896.

Randall, J. G. *Lincoln the President, Springfield to Gettysburg*. 2 vols.; New York: Dodd, Mead & Co., 1945.

Randall, J. G., and Donald, David. *The Civil War and Reconstruction*. Boston: D. C. Heath & Co., 1961.

Rhodes, James Ford. *History of the United States from the Compromise of 1850*. New York: Harper & Bros., 1899.

Robertson, John. *Michigan in the War*. Lansing: W. S. George & Co., 1882.

Ross, Fitzgerald. *A Visit to the Cities and Camps of the Confederate States*. Edinburgh & London: W. Blackwood & Sons, 1865.

Scott, James K. P. *The Story of the*

Battles at Gettysburg. Harrisburg: Telegraph Press, 1927.

Schurz, Carl. *The Reminiscences of Carl Schurz.* 3 vols.; New York: The McClure Co., 1908.

Shotwell, Randolph. "Virginia and North Carolina in the Battle of Gettysburg," *Our Living and Dead, IV.*

Simons, Ezra D. *A Regimental History: The One Hundred and Twenty-Fifth New York State Volunteers.* New York: E. D. Simons, 1888.

Small, A. R. *The Sixteenth Maine Regiment in the War of the Rebellion, 1861–1865.* Portland, Me.: B. Thurston & Co., 1886.

Smith, A. P. *History of the Seventy-Sixth Regiment New York Volunteers.* Cortland, N.Y.: Truair, Smith, & Miles, 1867.

Southern Historical Society Papers, Richmond: 1876–.

Spaulding, Oliver L. *The United States Army in War and Peace.* New York: G. P. Putnam's Sons, 1937.

Sparks, David S., ed. *Inside Lincoln's Army: The Diary of Marsena Rudolph Patrick, Provost Marshal General, Army of the Potomac.* New York: Thomas Yoseloff, 1964.

Steele, Matthew Forney. *American Campaigns.* Washington: U. S. Infantry Assoc., 1935.

Steinman, David B. *The Builders of the Bridge: The Story of John Roebling and his Son.* New York: Harcourt, Brace and Co., 1945.

Stiles, Robert. *Four Years Under Marse Robert.* New York, Neale Publishing Co., 1904.

Stine, J. H. *History of the Army of the Potomac.* Washington: Gibson Bros., 1903.

Storrick, W. C. *Gettysburg: The Place, The Battles, The Outcome.* Harrisburg: J. Horace McFarland Co., 1932.

Strong, William W. *History of the 121st Regiment Pennsylvania Volunteers.* Philadelphia: Burk & McFetridge Co., 1893.

Swinton, William. *Campaigns of the Army of the Potomac: A Critical History of Operations in Virginia, Maryland and Pennsylvania from the Commencement to the Close of the War, 1861–1865.* New York: Charles B. Richardson, 1866.

Sypher, J. R. *History of the Pennsylvania Reserve Corps.* Lancaster, Pa.: E. Barr & Co., 1865.

Taylor, Walter H. *Four Years with General Lee.* New York: D. Appleton & Co., 1878.

Tevis, C. V. *The History of the Fighting Fourteenth.* [Brooklyn] New York: Brooklyn Eagle Press, 1911.

Thomas, Henry W. *History of the Doles-Cook Brigade, Army of Northern Virginia.* Atlanta: Franklin Publishing Co., 1903.

Thomson, O. R. Howard and Rauch, William H. *History of the "Bucktails," Kane Rifle Regiment of the Pennsylvania Reserve Corps (13th Pennsylvania Reserves, 42nd of the Line).* Philadelphia: Electric Printing Company, 1906.

Tremain, Henry Edwin. *Two Days of War: A Gettysburg Narrative* New York: Bonnell, Silver & Bowers, 1905.

Trescot, William Henry. *Memorial of the Life of J. Johnston Pettigrew*. Charleston: J. Russell, 1870.

Trobriand, Regis de. *Four Years with the Army of the Potomac*. Boston: Ticknor & Co., 1889.

Tucker, Glenn. *High Tide at Gettysburg: The Campaign in Pennsylvania*. Indianapolis: Bobbs-Merrill Co., 1958.

——— *Hancock the Superb*. Indianapolis: Bobbs-Merrill Co., 1960.

Underwood, A. B. *Three Years' Service in the Thirty-Third Massachusetts Infantry Regiment, 1862–1865*. Boston: A. Williams & Co., 1881.

Upton, Emory. *The Military Policy of the United States*. Washington: Government Printing Office, 1912.

Vanderslice, John M. *Gettysburg Then and Now*. New York: G. W. Dillingham Co., 1899.

Vautier, John D. *History of the 88th Pennsylvania Volunteers in the War for the Union, 1861–1865*.

Philadelphia: J. B. Lippincott Co., 1894.

Walker, Francis A. *History of the Second Army Corps*. New York: C. Scribner's Sons, 1886.

War of the Rebellion: A Compilation of the Official Records of the Union and Confederate Armies. 128 vols.; Washington: Government Printing Office, 1880–1901.

Warren, Horatio N. *The 142d Regiment Pennsylvania Volunteers*. Buffalo: The Courier Co., 1890.

Weigley, Russell F. *Quartermaster General of the Union Army: A Biography of M. C. Meigs*. New York: Columbia University Press, 1959.

Weld, Stephen M. *War Diary and Letters of Stephen Minot Weld*. Cambridge, Mass.: Riverside Press, 1912.

Wise, Jennings Cropper. *The Long Arm of Lee*. Lynchburg, Va.: J. P. Bell Co., 1915.

Wood, William. *Captains of the Civil War*. New Haven: Yale University Press, 1921.

Young, Jesse Bowman. *The Battle of Gettysburg: A Comprehensive Narrative*. New York: Harper & Bros., 1913.

MONUMENTS AND TABLETS

According to the Gettysburg National Military Park: "A total of 2,388 monuments, tablets, and markers have been placed along the main battle lines." Most of the monuments are Federal regimental monuments, erected by the survivors of the regiment, often with the aid of the respective states. The inscriptions on most of the monuments include the casualties of the regiment, and a brief description of the fighting in which the unit participated on that ground. The regiment submitted a report of the proposed inscription, usually drawn up by a committee of soldiers who fought with the regiment at Gettysburg, and sent it to either the old Battlefield Memorial Association or, if the monument was erected after 1895, to the Gettysburg National Military Park. In either case, the inscription was carefully validated and corroborated. Most of the inscriptions on these regimental monuments are consequently quite accurate and valuable, since they were usually drawn up by officers and men who had survived the actual fighting on the spot.

The tablets, erected by the federal government, to each Union and Confederate brigade, division, and corps, are also of considerable assistance to the student of the battle. The detailed inscriptions on these tablets were carefully drawn up by the historians of the War Department, often in conference with prominent and minor officers and soldiers of both armies who had actually participated in the operations at the location where the tablet was to be erected. They are, therefore, among the most accurate sources available to the military historian.

Index

132, 154; named to command First Corps, 14; arrives on field at Gettysburg and assumes command, 40–41, 50; doubts wisdom of attack by 149th Pa., 104; importance of stand, 108; finally loses McPherson Ridge, 109–116; appeals vainly to Howard for reinforcements, 111; sends Halstead vainly to Howard for support, 117; skillful withdrawal 116–17; defends Seminary Ridge against Pender, 117–23; loses Seminary Ridge, 123–25; withdraws First Corps through Gettysburg, 123–31; good tactical troop handling, 120, 131; posted by Howard on Cemetery Heights, 134; quoted, 140; evaluated, 153–55

Dow, Charles, 52
Dranesville, Va., 5
Dudley, W. W.: wounded, 120
Dunaway, W. F., 16
Duncan's battery, 33
Dwight, Walton, 59, 103, 106

Early, Jubal A., 3–5, 11, 12, 26–27, 33, 62, 71, 73, 108, 109, 127, 137, 151, 155; arrives on battlefield, 74–75; division of, deploys, 75–78; fight with Schurz, 78–84; assessed, 154
Edward's Ferry, Md., 4
Eggleston, Cpl. (of 6th Wisc.), 48
Einsiedel, Detleo von, 70
Ellsworth, T. E., 46
Emmitsburg, Md., 12, 13, 20
Evans, Clement A., 76
Evans, Sgt. (of 88th Pa.), 92–93
Ewell, Richard S., 3–5, 11, 12, 17–19, 26, 29, 33, 56, 62, 75, 139; receives discretionary order from

Lee, 130; divisions of, exhausted, 137; hit in wooden leg, 137; assessed, 155

Fahnestock building; used by Howard, 65
Fairchild, Lucius, 40, 51
Fairfield, Pa., 13
Falmouth, Va., 6
Faribault, G. H., 111
Faucette, W. F., 122
Fayetteville, Pa., 4, 11, 15, 19, 29
Forney, J.: buildings of, 31
Fountaindale, Pa., 13
Foust, Benzet F., 89
Fowler, Douglas, 71
Fowler, Edward B., 39, 40, 46, 47
Fox, William F.: quoted, 142
Frederick, Md., 8, 11, 12
Fredericksburg, Va.: battle of, 6
Frueauff, John F., 70
Fry, B. D., 51, 53
Fry, W. C., battery of: arrives on field at Oak Hill, 63; deployment, 87; engages Federals, 87, 110

Gamble, William, 13, 20, 57, 58; brigade of: deployed, 28, 30; engages Heth's advance, 30–35, 110; relieved by Doubleday's troops, 51; thwarts Pender briefly on Seminary Ridge, 118, 122, 123
Garber, A. W.: artillery battery of, 77, 78
Gates, Lt. (of 157th N.Y.), 83
Gates, Theodore B., 57, 58, 115, 122
Geary, John W.: division of, nears Gettysburg, 138
Gettys, James, 3
Gettysburg, Pa.: significance of battle at, vii–viii; armies converge on, 3–20; described, 3; battlefield de-

scribed, 21–25; Federal retreat through, 126–31

Gibbon, John, Meade visits, 139

Gibson, J. Catlett, 77

Gilligan, Sgt. (of Robinson's division), 93

Gilsa, Leopold von, brigade of: deployed north of town, 69–73; attacked and driven back by Gordon, 78–84

Glenn, James, 106

Glen Rock, Pa., 12

Godwin, A. C., 77

Goodgame, John C., 89

Gordon, G. T., 121

Gordon, John B., 11, 123; defeats Gettysburg militia, 4; deployment,, 76; drives Barlow off knoll, 78–81; pursues retreating Federals, 82–84; quoted, 129

Green, C. A.: artillery battery of, 77, 78, 79

Greencastle, Pa., 4

Greenwood, Pa., 29

Greer, George, 129

Gregg, David M., 5, 12, 20

Grimes, Bryan, 89, 96

Grover, Andrew J., 39, 42

Gutelius, Frank, 128

Hadden, William M., 118

Hagerstown, Md., 13

Haines, Benjamin F., 95

Hall, James A.: battery of, 38, 39, 44, 46, 49, 50, 58, 106

Hall, J. M., 89

Halleck, Henry W.: and Hooker, 7; Meade sends reports to, 8, 17, 27, 134–35; sends views to Meade, 13, 139

Halsey, D. P., 93

Halstead (Doubleday's adj. gen.): vainly seeks reinforcements from Howard, 117

Hancock, Winfield S., 4, 19, 131, 138; quote of, on Buford, 134; ordered by Meade to assume command at Gettysburg, 135; proceeds to Gettysburg, 135–36; challenged by Howard as to right to command, 136; rallies troops, 136; reports to Meade on terrain suitability, 137, 138–39; reports in person to Meade at Taneytown, 139; evaluated, 155

Hanley, Capt. (of 9th N.Y. Cav.), 31

Hanlon, Joseph, 77

Hanover, Pa., 15, 20

Harman buildings, 110

Harney, George, 46

Harper's Ferry, Va., garrison of, 7

Harris, Andrew L., 71

Harrisburg Pa., 3, 5, 7, 10–12, 15

Harrison (Confederate scout), 10

Hart, Alexander, 76

Hartung, Adolph von, 67, 71

Harvey, Lt. (of 14th N.C.), 128

Hays, Harry T., brigade of: deploys on field, 76–77; attacks and flanks Barlow, 78–83; pursues Federals through Gettysburg, 83, 127

Heckman, Lewis, battery of: arrives at Gettysburg, 69; goes into action near college, 81; loses guns and is driven back, 79, 82

Heidlersburg, Pa., 12, 15, 18, 19, 33, 34, 62, 68

Herr Ridge: described, 23

Heth, Henry, 4, 13, 16, 18, 19, 29, 38, 49, 55, 75, 87, 150, 151; battle with Buford, 30–35; commits Pettigrew and Brockenbrough, 88,

109; wounded, 117; relieved by Pender's division, 117–18; appraised, 153

Hill, A. P., 4, 11, 12, 14, 15, 19, 34, 62, 76, 117, 139, 151; allows Heth to advance on Gettysburg, 18, 29; voices regret at Crippen's death, 116; divisions of, exhausted, 130–31, 137; appraised, 152

Hills, in vicinity of Gettysburg, 22–24

Hodges, Alpheus, 31

Hoffman, John S., 77

Hoffman, N.: buildings of, 31

Hoke, Robert F.: brigade of, 77–83

Hoke, W. J., 118

Hood, John B., 4, 14, 19

Hooker, Joseph, 4, 7, 9, 75

Hormann, J. W., 42

Howard, Oliver Otis, 5, 14, 28, 55, 56, 64, 68, 72–73, 75, 135, 140, 150; ordered to Gettysburg, 30, 37; arrives on battlefield, 64–65; assumes command of field, 65; orders to Doubleday, 65; determines to follow course of Buford and Reynolds, 66; orders two corps to fall back to Cemetery Hill, 107, 123; refuses Doubleday reinforcements, 111; urges Slocum to come up and command, 132; posts his own and Doubleday's troops, 134; challenges Hancock's authority, 136; evaluated, 65, 153–55

Howell, Chaplain: slain, 128

Huidekoper, Henry S., 105, 106, 113

Hurt, W. B.: battery of, 33, 53, 101

Hyattstown, Md., 12

Hyman, J. H., 118

Imboden, John D., 14

"Iron Brigade." *See* Meredith, Solomon

Irvin, Capt. (of 149th Pa.), 106

Iverson Alfred, 62, 106; evaluated, 99, 154; brigade of: arrives at Oak Hill, 62, 74; deployment, 87–90; attack repulsed, 67, 91–98

Jackson, Allen H., 82

Jackson, Thomas J. ("Stonewall"), 75, 155

James, Cyrus W., 32

Jefferson, Pa., 4, 19

Jenkins, A. G., 4

Jennings, W. W., 3

Johnson, Edward, 4, 11, 12, 17, 19, 29, 35

Johnson, M.: battery of, 33, 101

Jones, H. P., 129; artillery battalion of: deployed, 77; engages Schurz, 78, 81; assessed, 154

Jones, Lt. (of 8th Ill.), 31

Jones, W. B., 76, 101

Jones, William E., 11

Kellogg, Josiah H., 30

Kelly, Daniel F., 81

Kelly, William, 114

Kenan, T. S., 98

Kilpatrick, Judson, 12, 15, 20

Kirkland, W. W., 77

Kovacs, Stephen, 70

Krzyzanowski, Wladimir, brigade of: deploys north of town, 70–73; attacked and driven back, 78–84

Lamar, John H., 76

Lane, James H., 58, 142, 150; brigade of: deploys on field, 118; role in final movement against Doubleday, 118–125

Law, Evander, 14

Pierce, Volney J., 47
Pipe Creek, Md., 9, 13, 14, 20, 27, 134
Pleasonton, Alfred, 5
Plum Run, 24
Point of Rocks, Md., 5
Poolsville, Md., 4, 20
Potomac, Army of the, 3–20
Prey, Gilbert G., 94–96
Price, Confederate Sgt., 105
Pye, Edward, 48
Pyrrhus: quoted, 134

Raison, Henry, 32
Ramseur, Stephen D., 62, 123; assessed, 154; brigade of: arrives at Oak Hill, 62, 74; deployment, 87–90; attack, 91–98; success of attack, 98–99; pursues Federals through Gettysburg, 127
Reese, W. J., artillery battery of arrives on Oak Hill, 63; deployment of, 69, 87; engages Federals, 69, 73, 87
Reynolds, Gilbert H.: battery of, 91, 124; arrives on field, 56; wounded, 58–59; position on Seminary Ridge, 120
Reynolds, John F., 4 13, 29, 34, 111, 135; Meade confers with, 8; in movement toward Gettysburg, 8–14, 17, 20, 28; named to command Left Wing, 14; advances and engages Confederates west of Gettysburg, 36–41; death of, 40, 64; appraised, 38, 41, 153
Rice, R. S.: battery of, 33, 101
Riddle, William, 64, 135
Ridges, in vicinity of Gettysburg, 22–24
Ridgeville, 12
Riley, Sylvester, 93

Roads, in vicinity of Gettysburg, 21–22
Robertson, Beverly, 11
Robinson, James S., 70
Robinson, John C., 59, 67, 70, 71, 76, 84, 109, 142, 154; division of: arrives at Seminary, 56, 61; deploys on Oak Ridge, 86–89; engages Rodes, 90; initially repulses Rodes, 90–98; is finally driven back, 98–99; defense of Railroad Cut, 101–108
Robinson, William W., 40, 51
Rock Creek, 24
Roder, John William, 33
Rodes, Robert E., 4, 5, 11, 19, 26, 29, 38, 63, 67, 75, 108, 109, 124, 150, 151; division of: arrives at Oak Hill, 62, 74; deployment, 87–90; attacks Robinson, 90–91; is initially repelled, 91–98; drives Robinson back, 98–99; attack on Railroad Cut, 101–108; appraised, 99, 154
Root, Adrian, 62, 94, 95
Rosengarten, Joseph G., quoted, 150–52
Round Tops, the, 24
Rowley, Thomas, 101, 104, 109, 111; division of, 30; arrives on field at Seminary, 56, 57; evaluated, 58, 153
Ruger, Thomas, division of, nears Gettysburg, 138

Sackett, William E., 30
Salmon, Edward, 71
Scales, Alfred M., 142, 150; wounded, 119; brigade of: deployment, 118–19; advances against Doubleday on Seminary Ridge, 119–20; shattered by Stewart's battery, 121

Schimmelfennig, Alexander, 65; evades capture in town, 128; brigade of: deploys north of town, 68, 69–73; attacked by Confederates and driven back, 78–84

Schurz, Carl, 65, 95, 132; moves toward Gettysburg, 64; corps of, arrives and deploys north of town, 66–73; reports problem confronting him, 73; is attacked and defeated, 75–84; appraised, 154–55

Schwarz (Union soldier), 130

Scotland, Pa., 12, 19

Scott, Winfield, 61

Sedgwick, John, 5, 12, 20

Seminary Building, Buford and Reynolds at, 37

Seminary Ridge: temporarily occupied on June 30 by Pettigrew, 16; described, 22–23

Shepard, S. G., 40, 51

Shippensburg, Pa., 29

Sickles, Daniel E., 5, 14, 19, 135, 140; informs Meade and Howard of his advance toward Gettysburg, 107; corps of arrives on field, 138

Skinner, James H., 77

Slagle, Lt. (Doubleday's aide): sent to Howard for reinforcements, 111

Slocum, Henry W., 5, 20, 135, 140; named to command Right Wing, 14; declines at first to assume command of first, 132; sends report to Meade, 136–37; informs Howard of his advance toward Gettysburg, 107; arrives on field and assumes command, 138

Slough, Nelson, 91

Smith, James M., 76

Smith, Orland, 130, 132; brigade of posted on Cemetery Hill, 68

Smith, William ("Extra Billy"): brigade of, deploys on field, 77; reports approach of Federal reinforcements, 137–38

Smith, William F., 115

South Mountains, 10–13, 18

Spangler's Spring, 24

Spofford, Lt. Col. (of 97th N.Y.), 98

Stafford, Leroy A., 77

Stannard, George J.: brigade of, arrives on field, 138

Steinwehr, Adolph von, division of: 111, 130, 132; moves toward Gettysburg, 64; posted in reserve on Cemetery Hill, 68

Stevens, Greenleaf T., battery of: arrives on field, 56, 59; position on Seminary Ridge, 120

Stone, J. M., 43

Stone, L. W., 118

Stone, Roy, 92, 98, 150; wounded, 104; quoted, 155; brigade of: deployed on McPherson Ridge, 56, 59–60; resists Daniel's attacks at Railroad Cut, 101–108; finally loses McPherson Ridge, 109–116; position and fight on Seminary Ridge, 115, 121–23

Stuart, J. E. B., 4, 5, 10, 11, 15, 18, 19, 26; appraised, 153

Susquehanna River, 8, 15

Sykes, George, 7, 14, 19

Taneytown, Md., 19, 20, 54, 135, 139

Tanner, W. A.: battery of, 77, 78

Tate, S. M., 77

Thomas, Edward L.: position of, 118, 119

Thomson, Lt. (of 16th Me.), 97

Tidball's battery, 29

Tilden, Charles W., 94
Trimble, Isaac: quoted, 6
Two Taverns, Pa., 20
Tucker, Glenn: quoted, vii, 131
Turney, J. McLeod, 118

Union Mills, Pa., 19–20
Uniontown, Pa. 19

Vance, Zebulon, 128
Van de Graaff, A. S., 51
Vanderslice, John M.: quoted, 142, 151
Veil, Charles H., 40
Virginia, 5

Wade, Jennie: killed, 128
Wadsworth, James A., 38, 50, 55, 109, 120, 136, 154; division of: ordered to Gettysburg, 30; fight with Heth, 39–49; placed on Culp's Hill, 137
Wainwright, Charles S.: artillery brigade of, arrives on field, 56, 59; posts batteries on Seminary Ridge, 120
Walker, R. Lindsay: artillery reserve of, 32
Wallace, Moses, 98
Wallace, Samuel: battery of, 33, 101
Waller, Francis A., 48
Warren, Gouverneur K., 140; helps prepare defensive positions on Cemetery Hill, 136
Washington, D.C., 5–8, 135
Weather, on July 1, 1863, 26
Weidensaul, 1st Sgt. (of 150th Pa.), 119

Weld, Stephen: sent by Reynolds to Meade, 37
West, Speight B., 91
Westminster, Md., 9, 12, 13, 134
Wheatfield, 24
Wheeler, William: battery of, 66, 69, 84, 87
Wheelock, Charles, 86, 89; captured and escapes, 98, 130
Widdis, Cornelius C., 106
Wiedrich, Michael: battery of, 68, 69, 132
Wilkeson, Bayard: battery of, arrives at Gettysburg, 69; battery of, goes into action at Barlow's Knoll, 69, 72; mortally wounded, 78, 80
Williams, Alpheus S.: named to command Twelfth Corps, 14; corps of, arrives at Gettysburg, 138
Williams, Jeremiah, 71
Williams, Samuel J., 51
Willis, Edward, 72
Willoughby Run, 34; described, 23
Winn, D. R. E., 72
Wister, Langhorne, 56, 59, 60, 105, 106, 115
Witmoyer, John, 92–93
Wolf Run Shoals, 4
Woodsborough, Md., 12
Wrightsville, Pa.: bridge at, 5, 11
Wyburn, William A., 47

York, Pa., 11, 15
Young, Jesse Bowman: quoted, vii

Ziegler's Grove, 24
Zimmerman, William E.: battery of, 32

214